THE DEATH OF DEATH

For Mike from with good wishes [signature]

THE
DEATH
OF
DEATH

Resurrection and Immortality
in Jewish Thought

NEIL GILLMAN

Jewish Lights Publishing
Woodstock, Vermont

Library of Congress Cataloging-in-Publication Data

Gillman, Neil.
The death of death : resurrection and immortality in Jewish thought /
by Neil Gillman.
p.   cm.
Includes bibliographical references and index.
1. Death—Religious aspects—Judaism—History of doctrines.
2. Future life—Judaism—History of doctrines.
3. Judaism—Doctrines. I. Title.
BM635.4.G55   1997
296.3'3—dc21   96-30048

First edition

10 9 8 7 6 5 4 3 2

Manufactured in the United States of America
Book and jacket designed by Glenn Suokko

For People of All Faiths, All Backgrounds

Published by Jewish Lights Publishing
A Division of LongHill Partners Inc.
P.O. Box 237
Sunset Farm Offices, Route 4
Woodstock, Vermont 05091
Tel: (802) 457-4000   Fax (802) 457-4004

In Memory of
Ernest and Rebecca Gillman
and
Harry Fisher

and in Tribute to
Rose Fisher

Then came the Blessed Holy One
And slaughtered the angel of death....

—HAD GADYA
(from the Passover Haggadah)

Contents

FOREWORD

SURELY, I AM not the only writer to realize that issues I dealt with decades ago and believed were safely buried forever have an uncanny power to return and engage my interest once again.

While recently cleaning out some papers, I came upon the essays that I submitted in 1954 as part of my application to the Rabbinical School of The Jewish Theological Seminary of America. To my amazement, those essays, written under the impulse of my first serious involvement with Judaism as an undergraduate at McGill University in Montreal, were permeated with the theme of messianism. It was clear that I believed, even then, that the messianic hope was central to Jewish religion.

Some years later, I wrote a doctoral dissertation for Columbia University on the thought of the French, Christian existentialist, Gabriel Marcel. It was in Marcel's writings that I first came across the issue of my relationship with my body, with the notion that "I am my body," with the notion of secondary reflection (the latter, in the work of Marcel's students, came to be called "second naiveté"), and with the claim that our philosophy should take seriously our intuitive inclination to hope for some form of individual destiny beyond our death.

Like most doctoral students, I was so relieved to have completed my thesis that I was determined never to look at it again, and went on to other concerns. Ironically, all these issues are central to my thinking in the pages of this book.

My initial plan was to write a book on Jewish eschatology as a whole. My original interest in this subject was revived by my many conversations with the late Professor Gerson Cohen, Chancellor of The Jewish Theological Seminary from 1972 to 1985, who insisted that no significant movement in the course of Jewish history had lacked an eschatology. My brief treatment of the subject, in the concluding chapter of my previously published *Sacred Fragments,* had attracted a good deal of attention, and I felt that the topic demanded a more extensive treatment. I quickly realized, however, that this broad topic was overwhelmingly complex and considerably beyond the scope of one book. I then determined to study only one dimension of that broader subject, the one that intrigued me the most, the eschatology of the individual human being.

Much of the thinking that went into this book was first aired in courses that I have taught at the Seminary. I am convinced that most scholarly research takes place precisely in the classroom, and I am indebted to my students for helping me refine my ideas, forcing me to confront new issues, and, gently but firmly, pointing out the discrepancies and contradictions in my conclusions. Every page of this book reflects their impact on my thinking. I am also grateful to my former students, now colleagues in the rabbinate, who have invited me to share my conclusions with their congregants.

The present Chancellor of the Seminary, Professor Ismar Schorsch, has always been unstinting in his support for my work. Seminary Provost, Professor Menahem Schmelzer, was a constant source of encouragement throughout the period of research and writing.

I am particularly grateful to them for their concern.

My friend and colleague Rabbi Ira Stone was the first to review the preliminary draft of some of my chapters, and to reassure me that my work was worth pursuing. His excitement, at that early stage of writing, meant more to me than I can possibly express. My colleague on the Seminary faculty, Professor David Kraemer, saved me from a number of serious errors in my interpretation of biblical and rabbinic texts, and urged me to do the work of constructive theology reflected in my concluding chapter. Professor Shaul Magid helped me immeasurably by clarifying the elusive teachings of Jewish mysticism, Rabbi Alfredo Borodowski did the same with medieval Jewish philosophy, and Professor Tikva Frymer-Kensky shared with me her understanding of the mysterious events that took place in the Garden of Eden. Professor Robert Pollack of Columbia University introduced me to the mysteries of modern microbiology, and its implications for notions of human immortality. It was reassuring to know that I could always call on Professors Stephen Garfinkle and Burton Visotzky, for help on specific questions as they arose. The Seminary is my Jewish community and I shall be eternally grateful for the opportunity to study and teach within its walls.

A former student of mine, Erwin Cherovsky, kept reminding me that the issue of death and immortality was important to many lay people in the community at large, and helped me focus on the audience that might read a book of this kind. Ms. Annette Muffs Botnick, Seminary Research Librarian, was always available to assist me on bibliographical questions, and Ms. Sharon Liberman Mintz, Assistant Curator of Jewish Art at the Seminary, helped me track down graphic representations of the issues discussed here.

I need not add that whatever errors or inadequacies this book may reflect are my responsibility alone.

Over the years in which the book was being researched and written, a number of my students graciously served as my research assistants. They traced bibliographical references, checked my translations, helped me with the basic research, and saved me from the pitfalls of word-processing. For all of this, I am grateful to Ben Begleiter, Dana Bogatz, Ellen Cahn, Cory Lebson, Amy Levin, Sara O'Donnell and Anna Weisberg for their assistance. Lea Gavrieli and Kelly Washburn, in particular, devoted countless hours to the final stages of bringing the manuscript into print.

Some two years ago, during a long stroll on the grounds of the Concord Hotel in the Catskills, I aired the possibility of writing a book on resurrection with Stuart Matlins, founder and publisher of Jewish Lights. Stuart responded generously, as he always does, and added, "When you're into it, call me if you wish." I did, he read an early draft, and quickly called to assure me that Jewish Lights would be happy to publish the book. I owe Stuart, his staff, and in particular, my editor, Arthur Magida, a debt of immense gratitude for their patience and support. Arthur was simply a joy to work with and his detailed comments, almost line by line, have made this book much stronger than it would otherwise have been.

One note on translations. Unless explicitly specified, all translations of biblical texts are those of the 1985 edition of *Tanakh*, published by The Jewish Publication Society of America.

To my family, my wife Sarah, my daughters Abby and Debby, my son-in-law Michael, and my grandson Jacob, I offer my undying affection and gratitude for their constant encouragement and devotion.

Finally, I am grateful that God has blessed me with the health and vigor which have enabled me to bring this project to completion. The creative surge that I experience daily as I pursue my studies and my writing can only be God's gracious gift to me. I pray that I may continue to enjoy God's manifold blessings as I now move on to other work.

Hoshana Rabbah 5757
October 1996

THE DEATH OF DEATH

"And death? Where is it?"

He searched for his accustomed fear of death and could not find it. Where was death? What death? There was no fear because there was no death.

Instead of death there was light.

"So that's it!" he exclaimed. "What bliss."

All this happened in a single moment, but the significance of that moment was lasting. For those present, his agony continued for another two hours. Something rattled in his chest; his emaciated body twitched. Then the rattling and wheezing gradually diminished.

"It is all over," said someone standing beside him.

He heard these words and repeated them in his soul.

"Death is over," he said to himself. "There is no more death."

He drew in a breath, broke off in the middle of it, stretched himself out, and died.[1]

LEO TOLSTOY, *The Death of Ivan Ilyich*

A realistic expectation...demands our acceptance that one's allotted time on earth must be limited to an allowance consistent with the continuity of the existence of our species. Mankind...is just as much a part of the ecosystem as is any other zoological or botanical form, and nature does not distinguish. We die so that the world may continue to live. We have been given the miracle of life because trillions upon trillions of living things have prepared the way for us and then have died—in a sense for us. We die, in turn, so that others may live. The tragedy of a single individual becomes, in the balance of natural things, the triumph of ongoing life.[2]

SHERWIN B. NULAND, *How We Die*

I

THE ESCHATOLOGICAL IMPULSE

THIS IS NOT a book about death. If anything, it is a book about life. It is not about how to live, but about the meaning of a human life.

In our day, the term "meaning of life" has become trivialized. That trivialization is a defense against the urgency of the issue. Most of us are caught up in the routine of our daily existence, in each day that slips by all too quickly. It takes a special effort to step back, to look at our life experience as a whole, to seek some integrating factor, a principle of coherence which might bring together the fragmented elements of our personal experience here on earth—and to make them whole. But to speak of "the meaning" of human life is to speak also of death, for the fact that we all die is an inescapable part of our lives. The question then becomes: What is the place of death in our experience of life? How do we integrate the reality of death into our understanding of life?

One conventional answer to that question is that death marks the end of life. That is the message of Dr. Sherwin Nuland, a surgeon and teacher of medicine at Yale University,[3] quoted above, and it is also the answer of a classical passage from the Book of Ecclesiastes:

A season is set for everything, a time for every
   experience under heaven:
A time for being born and a time for dying... (3:1–2)

We are born. And we die. Birth and death represent the twin terminals of life. That death represents the *terminus ad quem,* or end-point, of human life is, in fact, the view of much of biblical religion. It is also the conventional opinion of most moderns, not only the secularists among us but also many believing Jews and Christians.

In time, in the second century BCE, Judaism came to assert that death may represent one event within the framework of human life, but not the final event. This later Jewish tradition broadens the time-frame of human destiny; it asserts that, at some time in the indefinite future, all of the dead will be brought to life once again. Or to make the point more emphatically, and to use Tolstoy's words, this later tradition asserts that we can anticipate an age in which "there is no death," that death itself will die. On the details of this ultimate event, opinions vary. But the certainty that there will be such an event has been a central Jewish belief for two millennia.

When this final event will take place is less important than affirming *that* it will take place. The issue is: What is the broad frame within which we locate a human life-experience? The notion of "frame" here is crucial. It is the reigning metaphor for the function of religion. Religion is a matter of establishing frames or frameworks, structures or parameters for the human experience. When we speak of giving meaning to human life, much of our task is to understand how different religious traditions structure the human experience.

WHAT *DO* RELIGIONS DO?

The late anthropologist Clifford Geertz defines religion as

> a system of symbols which acts to establish powerful, pervasive, and long-lasting moods and motivations in men by formulating conceptions of a general order of existence and clothing these conceptions with such an aura of factuality that the moods and motivations seem uniquely realistic.[4]

This understanding of religion can be called "anthropological" because it views religion from the perspective of human beings, and not, as most traditionalist approaches to religion have proposed, from the perspective of God. Geertz is exclusively concerned with how religion evolves from and how it works in the lives of people. His definition stems from his observation and study of human beings and their communities. Whatever God (or a god) may have to do with the emergence of religion is, at least for the purposes of his inquiry, set aside.

The core of Geertz's definition is the phrase "formulating conceptions of a general order of existence." In elaborating what he means by this notion, Geertz quotes from two other authors. First, he quotes the Spanish philosopher Salvador de Madariaga who gives religion a minimalist definition: Religion is "the relatively modest dogma that God is not mad."

More extensively, he quotes from the American philosopher, Susanne K. Langer:

> [Man] can adapt himself somehow to anything his imagination can cope with, but he cannot deal with Chaos. Because his characteristic function and highest asset is conception, his greatest fright is to meet what he

cannot construe.... It need not be a new object; we do
meet new things, and 'understand' them promptly...;
but under mental stress even perfectly familiar things may
become suddenly disorganized and give us the horrors.
Therefore our most important assets are always the symbols of our general *orientation* in nature, on the earth,
in society, and in what we are doing: The symbols of our
Weltanschauung ("world-outlook") and *Lebensanschauung* ("life-outlook").[5]

In this view, religion is the attempt to wrest cosmos out of
chaos, order out of the apparently anarchic character of our lives
and of the world in which we live, sense out of senselessness.

To order human experience so as to make sense of it is to
structure it, to stipulate where something begins and where it ends,
primarily, though not exclusively, in space and in time. The first
chapter of Genesis describes God's creation of the world as an act
of establishing boundaries—between light and darkness, heaven and
earth, waters above the heavens and waters below, between vegetation, animals, fish, birds and human beings. Jewish religion is
permeated with distinctions: Foods that we may eat and those we
must avoid; Jews and non-Jews; people we can marry or have sexual
relations with and those we cannot. Boundaries are omnipresent.

In this view, undifferentiation or homogeneity are chaotic.
That's why all religions structure space by locating some geographic
point as the heart of the world, as the point of orientation for the
rest of the universe. For three millennia, in Judaism, that focal point
has been the Temple in Jerusalem, or more narrowly, following
Exodus 25:22, the point between the upswept wings of the cheru-
bim on the cover of the sacred ark in the Holy of Holies which
contained (in the desert Sanctuary and in the Temple of Solomon,
at least) the twin tablets of the covenant. It is from this narrow point
that God will address the community. The rest of the world is then

structured in a descending hierarchy of sanctity around that point: The Temple, the Temple grounds, Jerusalem, the Holy Land and then the rest of the world.

In a similar way, Judaism structures time. It orders not only the liturgical cycle of days, weeks, months and seasons and the human life cycle, but more important for our purposes, the broadest possible canvas, the beginning and the end of all things. The beginning is the creation of the world; the end is defined by biblical and later Jewish eschatology.

MAKING SENSE OF THE WORLD

Eschatology (from the Greek words *eschatos*, "end," "final" or "last"); and *logos* ("discussion of..." or "reasoning about...") is that branch of theology which discusses the events that lie at the very end of history and of time as we know and experience it.

Every culture has an eschatology; it is part of our inescapable human attempt to make sense of the world. But Jewish eschatology is particularly rich and has decisively shaped its two daughter religions, Christianity and Islam. In a more secularized form, it can be discerned in the utopian visions that pervade Western culture and it is even at the heart of Marxism which is precisely structured on the biblical model. Like the Bible, Marxism structures history around three periods: A primal state of innocence, followed by a period of social tension, which is, in turn, supplanted by a new era of harmony, the communist society of the future.[6]

In very broad strokes, and setting aside for the moment the gradual evolution of Jewish eschatology over centuries, Jews came to believe that, at the end of days, the dead will be resurrected and come before God to account for their lives on earth, that the righteous will be rewarded and the evil punished; that Jews, free from the yoke of the exile, will return to their homeland, rebuild it, and become masters of their own destiny; that they will rebuild the Temple and reinstitute the Temple cult; that the nations of the world will flock to study Torah with the Jewish people; that peace and justice will rule; that the tensions that now pervade the world of nature will disappear, that "the wolf shall dwell with the lamb" (Isaiah 11:6); and that all people will come to know and worship the God of Israel. Finally, this entire scenario will be brought to pass through the initiative of a charismatic or quasi-divine figure called the Messiah (literally, "the anointed one").

The details of this complex scenario evolved slowly over the course of more than a millennium, roughly from the time of the classical Prophets (ca. eighth century BCE) to the close of the Talmud (ca. 500 CE). Its more universalist themes—the end of warfare, for example—are explicit in the prophecies of Isaiah. On the other hand, the idea that human beings will live again after death cannot be found in Jewish writings much before the second century BCE, and the idea that we possesses a soul which never dies is not found until roughly a century later. But the scenario as a whole pervades post-talmudic Judaism until Jews encounter modernity at the dawn of the nineteenth century when significant portions of it are discarded or reformulated. There are also many differences among Jewish thinkers on precisely how this final drama would unfold. But the above represents a fair summary of the doctrine as a whole in its classic form.

But as important as the details of this scenario may be, it is equally important that Jews evolved this kind of vision in the first place. As one part of Judaism's attempt to set the broad frame for human history, it represents the final parenthesis that closes the age of history, for which the story of Creation in the early chapters of Genesis forms the opening parenthesis. We now live in the "in-between," in the age of history, but we live with the awareness that there was a beginning and that there will be an end. In this way, human existence acquires its temporal frame.

THE IMPORTANCE OF THE "MIDDLE"

Without this frame, without boundaries, a portrait has no integrity, no coherence. Without a beginning and an end, there is no middle. And without that, we would never know precisely where we are and where we stand against the backdrop of human experience as a whole. We would have no way of orienting ourselves in time; to use a spatial metaphor, we would have no "home." To paraphrase Genesis, we would be exiled, and to be in exile is to tumble into chaos.

That is the import of the early Genesis stories. In Genesis, God creates a fully ordered world in which everything is structured and has its proper place. As the story unfolds, the original human beings also have their place in Creation and their home: The Garden of Eden. That pristine order was disrupted by paradigmatic sins, first of Adam and Eve, then of Cain. These sins are affronts to the cosmos that God created and disrupt God's ordered world. Both are sins of displacement: Adam and Eve want to be like God, and Cain wants to supplant his brother's place in God's favor. Both introduce chaos into God's creation.

In response, God punishes chaos with chaos, disruption with disruption, displacement with displacement. Adam and Eve are expelled from the Garden of Eden and Cain is condemned to a life of wandering. All three are exiled, and Cain captures the full import of that punishment: "Anyone who meets me may kill me" (Genesis 4:14). To be in exile is to be condemned to a life of wandering, to have no "place," no "home." It is also, as Cain understood, to be vulnerable. To grasp that sense of vulnerability, all we need do is contemplate the fate of the many homeless people on our cities' streets.

In the biblical world-view, this expulsion from Eden begins the age of history in which humanity is condemned to a state of intrinsic, almost metaphysical homelessness and vulnerability. That condition captures a central dimension of human life as we all

23

experience it to this day. We live in a world that manifests a generalized order. We speak, somewhat longingly, of "the order of nature."
The sun rises every morning and sets every night and the seasons
change on schedule. But hovering around the fringes of human
existence is a barely suppressed sense of impending doom: Illness,
natural disasters, economic distress, warfare and an acute sense of
alienation and vulnerability.

That would be the end of the story were it not for the vision
that this age of history between Eden and the eschatological end of
days represents an "in-between," that it will come to an end, and
that this end will banish the tensions inherent in history and nature
and restore the totally ordered world that God created at the beginning.

The rich complexity of this world-view is best captured by
the institution of the Sabbath. The Sabbath is a memorial to the six
days of creation (Ex. 31:17) and also, in the talmudic tradition, a
foretaste of the age to come. In its insistence on rest and avoiding
work, on not disrupting the natural order, the Sabbath recalls the
cosmos that was and anticipates the cosmos that will be. It is a classic "in-between" institution.

All eschatologies are impelled by a sense that the inherent
condition of human life is profoundly flawed. That is why they are
all visions of perfection, of a time when human existence will no
longer be flawed. Eschatologies are resolutions; they bring closure
to the in-between-ness of our lives.

The richness of Jewish eschatology lies in the fact that it deals
with the three dimensions of our identity in which these flaws are
apparent. We are simultaneously individual human beings, members
of the Jewish people, and part of humanity. Jewish eschatology imag-
ines an age when the flaws that pervade all these dimensions of our
being will be banished. The details of this tripartite cosmos-to-come
may have evolved in the course of Jewish history, but there was never
a time when Judaism did not have some vision of an ideal end for

24

humanity as a whole, for the Jewish people, and for each individual human.[7]

MYTH VS. NONSENSE

All eschatologies are imaginative constructs. They must be imaginative not only because they deal with events that no human has ever beheld, but even more because these events will inaugurate an age which is properly timeless. The very phrase, "end of days," captures the frustrating ambiguity of the notion of eschatology for neither our language nor our conceptual skills can deal with an "end" to time. There is no "after" to time, for "after" is itself a temporal notion. There is only an "after" within time. But eschatology takes us out of time, as does any talk of creation. As with eschatology, creation-talk—even the "big bang" of modern astronomy—is an imaginative construct.

Another way of making this point is to speak of the stories of creation and the end of days as myths. Of definitions of myth, there is no end, but here are three.

The psychologist Rollo May writes:

A myth is a way of making sense in a senseless world. Myths are narrative patterns that give significance to our existence. Whether the meaning of existence is only what we put into our life by our own individual fortitude..., or whether there is a meaning we need to discover..., the result is the same; myths are our way of finding this meaning and significance. Myths are the beams in a house; not exposed to outside view, they are the structure which holds the house together so people can live in it.[8]

The physicist-theologian Ian Barbour says that

In broad terms, a myth is a story which is taken to manifest some aspect of the cosmic order.[9]

And the philosopher John Hick calls myths

responses to the mystery of human existence. Ancient
tradition has further specified this mystery in the three
questions: Where do we come from? Why are we here?
and Where are we going?[10]

These definitions overlap. They tell us that myths are stories,
that these stories are responses to the most intuitive questions posed
by the very nature of human existence, that the function of these
stories is to make sense out of the apparent senselessness of human
life, and that they do this by showing how the world came to manifest a fundamental order.

Rollo May, in particular, illuminates a particular dimension
of myths. They are, he suggests, "like the beams of the house; not
exposed to outside view, they are the structure which holds the house
together." Myths are almost invisible, so deeply buried in our consciousness that we are barely conscious of their presence. They are
spectacles which we wear without being aware of their presence, but
without which we could not see. The beams of the house may not
be easily perceived, but they are there. And without them, the house
would not stand.

Note that we have now moved from defining myth as the story
of how the cosmic order came to be, to defining myth as a description of that very order itself. But that distinction is less important
than the assumption that myths are the devices which lend order to
our otherwise fragmented experience of the world.

It is the invisibility of myths that leads us to identify them as legends, fictions, or illusions. That identification leads to the common tendency to distinguish between myths and "reality," or myths and "facts." But that distinction is misleading, for without myths, there would be no "facts" in the first place. We would not know which of all of the possible facts around about us are worth noting, let alone how they cohere. It is the myth as the "beam" of our individual and collective "houses" that determines which facts must be accounted for and how they are held together.

But like the beams of the house, myths are not totally invisible. They are canonized in such sacred texts as Scripture and liturgy, for example, and re-enacted in ritual behavior. The grand pageants of Jewish life—the High Holidays, the Sabbath, the Passover seder, and the rites surrounding such life passages as birth, marriage and death—express in dramatically vivid words and actions the enduring message of the Jewish religious myth.

As a structuring or ordering device, the myth captures the integrating pattern that pulls together various dimensions of our experience. But patterns are notoriously difficult to see; we see the individual details, but it is more difficult to see how the details fit together. To use a different metaphor, the myth is how we connect the dots of our experience, except that in contrast to the "connect-the-dots" books of our childhood, the dots here are not numbered, or multiple numbers are assigned to the same dot, or there is no pre-arranged way to determine which dots are needed to form the picture we want to form.

Myths, then, are not illusions or fictions. Nor are they scientifically, objectively "true." They cannot be true in this sense because there is no reality "out there" with which we can compare our myths, as we compare our hypothesis with the results of a scientific experiment. More precisely, there is no "out there" because we cannot even begin to see the "out there" without the spectacles provided by the myth. To put it another way, we cannot escape our humanness. We must carry a myth—*some* myth—with us, if not one myth than another. Without the ordering work of myths, we cannot begin to make sense of our world. The issue is never myth or no myth, but rather *which* myth, *which* organizing or structuring device we want to use.

This implies that there are multitudes of myths, manifold ways of making sense of our world, many ways of connecting the dots of experience. How then do we decide which myth to use? If myths are never *objectively* true, then in what sense *are* they true? Or false? And how do we choose one over another?

The answer to these questions is fourfold: First, we are all raised and educated within a specific mythic structure which, if our upbringing and education are effective, becomes an almost unconscious dimension of our world-outlook. The ultimate purpose of education is to teach children the myth which cements the identity of a particular culture or civilization.

Second, myths are "true" in a "soft" sense of that term. That is, they roughly correspond to what life and the world "looks like" to us. Myths are not formed out of the blue; they originate out of a human community's experience of the world and of life, and can be expected, again in this rough kind of way, to mirror that experience. To put this another way, if the purpose of the myth is to uncover a pattern in life and the world, then this pattern is "there" to be uncovered. It may not be the only such pattern, but it still has an "out there" which makes it discoverable.

Third, myths are existentially true. That is, they are true because they invoke within us responses to life which we intuitively feel to be appropriate. This last is most important. Myths "are" not true or false, but rather "become" true or false, if and when we conduct our collective or communal lives in accord with their message.

Finally, to use a more pragmatic criterion, myths are true to the extent that they work, to the extent that they make it possible for us to live a meaningful and integrated life as members of a community.

Eschatological myths are true in all these ways. They describe one dimension of the underlying order of the world and relate how it came to be. They answer one of Hick's three questions about human existence: "Where are we going?" By responding to this question, they help make sense of what otherwise appears to be a senseless world. They are one of the beams which support the house of our daily existence.[11]

THE VARIETIES OF MYTHIC EXPRESSION

A "living" myth works effectively on behalf of the members of a community. It gives meaning to their individual and corporate lives. The clearest evidence that a myth is alive for a member of a religious community is his or her ability to worship and participate in the ritual life of that community. A myth is "dead" when it no longer works in this fashion.

A "broken" myth is one that has been exposed; it is acknowledged to be a myth, no longer considered to be an objective, true photograph of the ultimate nature of reality, nor an objective account of how that order came to be. Instead, it is now included among several possible equally subjective, impressionistic, imaginative constructions, all created by a community from its initial almost inchoate experiences of the world. In effect, once the essential teachings of Judaism are characterized and accepted as mythic, we have "broken" its myth.

The precarious nature of that moment in our religious development cannot be underestimated. There are three possible responses to having one's myth broken. One is to completely reject the notion of myth, to revert to a literalist understanding of religion, to insist that its teachings are objectively true, to close one's eyes and ears and deny what one has learned and return to the safe haven of literalism.

29

The second is to proclaim that the broken myth is "dead," to effectively dismiss it as "just" a myth, as patently illusory, a deliberate fiction. A typical expression of that stance is to claim that if Judaism is "just" a myth, then why be Jewish?

The third possibility is to embrace the myth as "broken"—*and* as "living." The best characterization of that subtle embrace is to call it an experience of "second naiveté" or "willed naiveté." It is "naive" because through it we recapture the primitive, almost childlike stage of our awareness about how the world works. But it is a "second" naiveté because it follows a stage in our development in which our critical faculties tell us that this picture is not objectively true, that God did not literally create the world in the way that Genesis 1 relates, or that God did not literally descend on a mountaintop to reveal the Torah to our ancestors as Exodus 19–23 relates. Those stories need no longer be viewed as literally or objectively true—or, for that matter, as literally or objectively false. And it is "willed" because it is embraced through a conscious, deliberate act of the will.[12]

The French philosopher Paul Ricoeur captures the fragile and almost painful weight of that moment:

> Does that mean that we could go back to a primitive naiveté? Not at all. In every way, something has been lost, irremediably lost: immediacy of belief. But if we can no longer live the great symbolisms of the sacred in accordance with the original belief in them, we can, we modern men, aim at a second naiveté in and through criticism. In short, it is by *interpreting* that we can *hear* again.[13]

Indeed something *has* been irremediably lost: The comforting sense that the world is the way we believed it was. But the loss is not fatal. And much is gained, notably intellectual integrity.

Again, the best indication of our success in moving from the critical phase of our thinking to a second naiveté is our ability to continue to worship within the believing community and to live its ritual patterns. We walk back into the myth, revel in its imaginative playfulness, allow our consciousness to absorb its magic and live it. Jewish eschatology as a whole and the doctrine of resurrection in particular is both a broken and living myth.

DO WE "INVENT" GOD?

The theological assumptions that underlie this approach which views the classic teachings of Jewish religion as mythical cannot be avoided. They merit being explicitly articulated at the outset.

The approach should be labeled "naturalist" to contrast it to the "supernaturalism" of traditionalist understandings of religion in general and of Judaism in particular. Religious supernaturalism teaches that religion originates through the initiative of a God Who is beyond the natural order, and Who intervenes in history to reveal a teaching to a specific community.

In contrast, religious naturalism views religion as a thoroughly "natural" expression of the life of a community. To quote a student of mine, communities produce religions as apple trees produce apples. Religion is the intuitive way in which communities make sense of the world and of the human experience. As it is the thoroughly natural function of apple trees to produce apples, so it is the equally natural function of communities to develop religions.

Jewish traditionalism believes that a supernatural God revealed the tenets and practices of Jewish religion to our ancestors, most eminently at Sinai. It understands the narrative of that revelatory event in Exodus 19–23 as historically accurate and literally true.

In contrast, Jewish naturalism understands the Sinai narrative as part of or "within" the classic Jewish religious myth. It rejects the traditional understanding of that event which portrays God as "descending" to a mountaintop and "speaking" to human beings. If God is really God, neither natural nor human, then God does not literally descend or speak. These terms are metaphors, human attempts to grapple with and comprehend what is intrinsically beyond human characterization. But if God does not literally "speak," then the words of Torah and by extension the tenets and beliefs of Judaism are not explicitly God's words or will. The only alternative is to understand them as human words, our ancestors' perception of what God wanted from them.

The most striking attempt to capture that view of revelation is Abraham Joshua Heschel's claim that "as a report about revelation, the Bible itself is a *midrash*."[14] A *midrash* is an interpretation, an admittedly human interpretation, usually of a biblical passage, verse or word. To characterize the entire Torah as a midrash is to say, in effect, that it is, in its entirety, a human understanding of a "text" which, in its pristine, original form, is beyond human awareness. It is to say that what we have is not God's will in its purity, but our very human understanding of that will. Only God knows what God wants this community to believe and how it should live; what *we* have is our human perception of that will. Torah then becomes both a cultural document that reflects the age and the conditions in which it was first composed, and also divine. It is a "cultural" document because it preserves a human community's understanding of God's presence and will for that community, and that perception inevitably reflects the cultural conditions in which it was originally formulated. But it remains "divine" because it is *God's* presence and will that the community insists it is perceiving.

Heschel's view that Torah is a midrash is designed not to demean Torah, but to preserve God's transcendence. What *is* demeaning is to portray God as literally doing the things that human beings do. That is idolatry, the cardinal sin in Judaism.

Instead, God must be portrayed through metaphors which

stem from genuine human experiences of God's work in nature and history and in the personal experience of individuals and communities. A metaphor is never literally true: The lion is not literally "king" of the beasts nor does one want to weigh a "heavy" heart or measure the "cruelty" of the month of April. But metaphors are also more than useful fictions. They vividly and dramatically capture analogies between the more elusive dimensions of our experience and the aspects of that experience that can be expressed in human language. They are revelatory. They let us see what would otherwise escape us.

To say that the way we characterize God is metaphorical is to say that our images of God are also "within" the myth, for a myth is a way to organize an ensemble of metaphors. Thus the question: Do we invent God? Or do we discover God? The only answer is that we discover God—and we invent the metaphors. Which comes first? It depends. Sometimes the metaphor enables us to experience God. "God is my shepherd..." helps me identify a certain quality of my experience of God, God's nurturing. But someone, somewhere had an experience of nurturing that came from a reality outside and beyond him or her and that person coined the metaphor of God as shepherd. The same with the metaphors of God as "rock of Israel," as person, as lover, parent, or judge; the same with the darker metaphors of God as abusive, unfair, abandoning and punitive.

It bears repeating, if only because it is so often misunderstood, that this theological approach does not eliminate God from the picture. God still remains, but humans cannot perceive God's presence and activity in their purity since there is no objective demonstration that God *is* or of what God *does*. There are only human perceptions of these realities. It is with these that we must work.

The impact of this understanding of religion cannot be denied. It makes all religious or theological claims relative to the individual or the community that pronounces them. No more is there

33

a single religious "Truth," one authentic, objective or literally true account of God and God's workings among humans. Rather, there are multiple visions, multiple myths, multiple perceptions of how the world is ordered. The authority behind any one such vision is no longer a transcendent God, but a human community which reads God's will in one particular way.

Why then be Jewish? Not because it is "the" Truth, not because it originated in the explicit word and will of God, but rather because of its intrinsic richness, its ability to help us cope with life, to make sense of our world.[15]

AN AFTERLIFE FOR EACH JEW

Eschatology is central to the Jewish religious myth. And central to Jewish eschatology is the doctrine of an afterlife for each Jew. That doctrine, as it developed over time, taught that our death is not final, that at the end of days God will raise our bodies from the grave, reunite them with our souls, and reconstituted as we were during our lifespan on earth, that we will be brought before God to account for our lives and receive the appropriate reward or punishment. At that time, as implied by the passage from Tolstoy's *The Death of Ivan Ilyich* which opened this chapter, death itself will die. God will banish death forever.

All this is classic myth, part of the way Jewish religion imposes a framework on human existence. It is not the only such possible framework. The Yale University surgeon Sherwin Nuland, author of the National Book Award–winning *How We Die*, has a framework of his own. Nuland's framework is dictated by a botanical/zoological myth, the product of contemporary science. For Nuland, death is the thoroughly natural and desirable end of human life. We must die to maintain the balance of the ecosystem.

Nuland even proposes his own version of an afterlife: We die so that others may live. For "plants and animals," he writes, "renewal requires that death precede it so that the weary may be replaced by the vigorous. This is what we mean by the cycles of nature."[16] Nuland views humans as part of the plant/animal world, as part of nature, and he contends that our ultimate destiny is to be understood in terms of the inevitable cycle of the natural world.

Nuland's myth is more popular today than its Jewish counterpart, if only because it carries the aura of science. But it is equally mythic, one of the many possible ways we have of introducing order into our life experience. It is no more objectively "true" than any other since there is no clear, irrefutable, scientific evidence available to Nuland about what happens to us after we die or what will happen to us when history comes to a close. On this issue, neither Nuland nor Tolstoy has "the" Truth. On this issue, there is no "the" Truth. Instead, there are many truths, many different ways of defining the parameters of human life, all equally imaginative, subjective and speculative. All are myths, and the issue is never myth or no myth, but *which* myth.

But there is a strong, compelling case to be made for the Jewish myth of the afterlife, one that argues that human beings are more than plants and animals, that human needs cannot be adequately addressed by a framework that rests on botany and zoology alone. We are animals but we also feel, deliberate and think. We have the ability to inquire into the meaning of our lives. And we have self-awareness; We are conscious of our "inner" life. This self-consciousness distinguishes us from plants and animals.

This case for the Jewish myth of the afterlife further argues that the classic Jewish teaching that we will be reconstituted, at the end of days, as we were during our lifetime here on earth, body and soul together, is eminently, if mythically, true.

To appreciate the full power of the Jewish view of the afterlife, we have to inquire first into how this doctrine originally entered Jewish consciousness, what it says, what intrinsically human questions it came to answer, and how it evolved through the course of Jewish history. To this we now turn.

II

THE ORIGINS OF DEATH

WHEN THE GALLA tribe of East Africa sought to explain why death entered the world, they told how God sent a bird to human beings with a message that their lives could be renewed by changing their skins. En route, the bird came across a snake feeding on some meat. The bird told the snake he would tell him God's message if he shared his meat. God, angered that the secret of immortality was revealed, punished the bird and the message was never delivered. Therefore, all people die.

This theme of a message that goes astray, or is garbled, or more generally of some primordial capricious mistake is one of the classical ways that the ancients explained the origins of death in the world.

Another explanation understands death as punishment for the foolish action of some primordial human being, usually a woman. The aborigines of New South Wales tell how in the beginning, God forbade people to go near a certain hollow tree in which bees had nested. Men obeyed but women wanted the honey. Finally, one woman hit the tree with an axe—and out flew death in the form of a bat, the death which now claims all humans.

Finally, some cultures portray death as the outcome of a primordial debate. The Blackfoot, a North American Indian tribe, relate how the first old man and the first old woman debated the value of immortality. The man wanted it, but the woman claimed it would lead to too many people on earth. They agreed to leave the matter to a sign: If a buffalo bone they threw into a river floated, they would opt for immortality; if it sank, they would opt for death. The woman changed the fragment into a stone and it sank. Hence, we all die.[1]

We are so familiar with death as the inevitable end-point of human life that it rarely occurs to us to ask: Why is there death in the first place? We accept death's reality as a given. We live, and then we die. But a mythic consciousness, a consciousness that seeks to understand the structures of meaning, the connections that weave the discrete data of human experience into a pattern, would not conclude "...and *then* we die." Rather, it would conclude "...and *therefore* we die." So to pose our question in religious terms: Why does God create or permit human beings to die? Or why does God decree that they *must* die?

That question may seem incongruous, but hardly a single culture in the course of human civilization did not speculate on the origins of death and weave myths to account for it. Biblical Israel is no exception to this rule. Echoes of these themes appear in the Bible itself. The problem is that the biblical texts are enigmatic and their intent is not always clear.

ADAM'S RETURN TO DUST

What the Bible tells us about death's origins depends on how we interpret four early Genesis texts, 2:16–17, 3:4–5, 3:17–19 and 3:22. All these relate to the story of Adam and Eve in the Garden of Eden.

Specifically, they tell of God's command that Adam not eat from "the tree of knowledge of good and bad" (or as more commonly translated, "of good and evil");[2] of the serpent's reassurances that God's command need not be understood literally; of Adam and Eve's flouting of God's command; and of God's reactions to their disobedience. In scholarly language, these myths are etiological: They describe how certain things came to be. They teach us that death—and such common phenomena of human existence as why women suffer in childbirth and why we must toil for our food—are explained by events that occurred in primordial time.

The first text is God's original command:

> And the Lord God commanded the man, saying, "Of every tree of the garden you are free to eat; but as for the tree of knowledge of good and bad, you must not eat of it; for as soon as you eat of it, you shall die." (2:16–17)

But the serpent reassures the woman:

> [T]he serpent said to the woman, "You are not going to die, but God knows that as soon as you eat of it your eyes will be opened and you will be like divine beings who know good and bad." (3:4–5)

So Adam and Eve eat of the tree. God then addresses first the serpent, then the woman, and finally Adam:

> "Cursed be the ground because of you;
> By toil shall you eat of it
> All the days of your life:
> Thorns and thistles shall it sprout for you.
> But your food shall be the grasses of the field;
> By the sweat of your brow

39

Shall you get bread to eat,
Until you return to the ground—
For from it you were taken.
For dust you are,
And to dust you shall return." (3:17–19)

Finally, comes God's decision that Adam be banished from Eden:

And the Lord God said, "Now that the man has become
like one of us, knowing good and bad, what if he should
stretch out his hand and take also from the tree of life
and eat, and live forever!" So the Lord God banished
him from the garden of Eden.... (3:22–23)

One familiar way of understanding this story is to see Adam
as rebelling against God's command, being punished for that disobedience, and that his punishment is twofold: He is condemned
to toil for his food, and he is to "return to the ground." That is, he
is to die. In this view, God did not originally create human beings
to die. Rather, death enters the world as punishment for sin. That
Adam is dust who must now return to dust echoes the earlier narrative of Adam's creation in Genesis 2:7: "The Lord God formed
man from the dust of the earth."

But God's address to Adam (3:17–22) is sufficiently ambiguous to suggest a different meaning, namely that Adam's punishment
ends with the fact that he will have to eat bread by the sweat of his
brow. How long will this punishment last? Until he "returns to the
dust." That is, until he dies. But *that* he has to die is assumed by
the text. In this view, death is part of the picture for human beings
from the very outset, part of God's original creation. God created
human beings to die. God's original command to Adam in 2:16–17
does not threaten him with death. What it does specify is *when* Adam

40

will die. Note the emphasis: "*As soon as you eat of it,* you shall die."

There are two problems with this reading: First, nowhere in these Genesis texts are we told that God created human beings to die. Genesis does not mention death until God's command to Adam in 2:16–17. And second, Adam does not die "as soon as" he eats of the tree. The sequence of events in this narrative may not be precise, but Genesis 4:25 informs us that Eve gave birth to a (third) son named Seth, after Cain killed Abel, which, according to the biblical narrative, took place after Adam's expulsion from the garden.

The problem with the notion that death is punishment for sin is that it fails to relate the origins of death to Adam's specific disobedience, to his eating of the tree of knowledge of good and bad. The punishment explanation deals with disobedience as a generic act. Any act of disobedience could have served the purposes of the story. But all these texts suggest that death has something to do with knowledge, specifically with "knowledge of good and bad." And three of the texts associate the knowledge gained from eating of this tree with becoming like God and, hence, immortal. Somehow, then, we must try to understand how this kind of knowledge would make human beings God-like, why God did not want this to happen, hence why we must die, and hence why, in the last of the texts, Adam and Eve had to be expelled from Eden, lest they eat of the tree of life and live forever.

The key to untangling this puzzle rests on understanding the enigmatic phrase, "knowledge of good and bad." Not surprisingly, the literature on the possible meanings of this phrase could fill a library.[3] But the most felicitous interpretation is suggested by James Barr, Professor of Hebrew Bible at Vanderbilt Divinity School. Barr suggests that the phrase "knowledge of good and bad" means "the power of rational and especially ethical discrimination."[4]

"Discrimination" is the crucial word here. What Adam and Eve learned from eating of the tree of knowledge is, in Barr's words, the power of "knowing the difference," specifically knowing the difference between "good and bad." It was

> a coming of consciousness of lines that must not be crossed, of rules that must be obeyed, and in this sense a discernment of "good and evil." It was also a coming of self-consciousness: as God pointed out, how else did Adam and Eve know that they were naked?[5]

This power of discernment, this new self-consciousness, elevates Adam and Eve above the limitations of their purely physical existence. "The eyes of both of them were opened," we are told in Genesis 3:7, and they now perceive that they are naked. This self-awareness, this power to know the difference, to discriminate, is what makes them "like God."

Barr fixes on the notion of "discernment" or "discrimination" as the key to interpreting this phrase because of the specific kind of knowledge yielded by this tree. It is the tree of knowledge of "good and bad." "Good and bad" are polar notions; they are opposites, antitheses, reversals of each other. What Adam and Eve gained from this eating, then, is the ability to appreciate the difference between the two, or more precisely, to appreciate the very fact of differentiation.

Barr's understanding of the phrase is confirmed by the rest of the narrative. Again and again, it underlines the notion of differentiation. First, immediately upon eating, Adam and Eve perceive that they are naked (3:7) and now, in contrast to their original state (2:25), they feel shame and cover themselves. What they perceive now is that they are different from each other. Second, all the participants in the drama are subjected to a reversal of their original conditions: The serpent, who originally walked upright, now must crawl on his belly. That is, he must walk differently than human beings do. Eve, who was commanded to procreate, now must suffer in childbirth. Adam, whose original task was to till and tend the garden (2:15), now must earn his bread by the sweat of his brow. And finally, the ultimate reversal: Immortality ends and death becomes a fact of life.

Underlying all these distinctions is the distinction between God and human beings. In a garden filled with trees, only two are singled out: The tree of knowledge of good and bad and the tree of life. The twin powers of discrimination and immortality are prerogatives of God alone. Both were originally denied to human beings for human beings were not to become "like one of us" (3:22), like God. Now that Adam and Eve had achieved the first, they must be denied the second. In Barr's words, this was the ultimate line "that must not be crossed." Now that they are somewhat like God, God must act to deprive Adam and Eve of immortality. God then banishes them from Eden, lest they "take also from the tree of life and eat, and live forever."

DEATH MAKES US FULLY HUMAN

In contrast to our initial interpretation of the story of Eden, death is now not understood as punishment. The distinction is subtle, but significant. Death is not punishment for disobedience, but rather the inevitable result of the full flowering of our humanity. The story of Eden now acquires a tragic dimension. God, Who is fully aware of the seductive quality of the tree of knowledge, knows that Adam and Eve will partake of its fruit. On some level, God wants them to eat of it, because only then will they become fully human. But with this flowering of their humanity comes death. Thus is launched the biblical saga of humanity and its history.

In fact, Martin Buber's interpretation of this narrative, which is essentially similar to Barr's, stresses that God's decree of death was an act of compassion. Now that human beings have discovered

43

the tensions inherent in human life, God acts to prevent "the aeons of suffering" that would result from eating of the tree of life. Hence, death.[6]

The strength of Barr's explanation is that in contrast to the punishment explanation, it relates God's response to the specific act of eating of the fruit of this particular tree of knowledge of good and bad. We are no longer dealing with a generic act of rebellion, but rather with this specific act. Death is the result not of rebellion *per se,* but rather of this newly acquired awareness or knowledge.

Barr argues vigorously that from the outset, God did create human beings to die, that human mortality was part of God's original creation. What Adam and Eve lost in the garden was what they might have gained from eating of the tree of life: The hope for immortality. That was the trade-off for their newly found powers of discernment, for becoming God-like.[7]

To put this another way, Barr does not read the larger story as explaining the origins of death. What it does explain is its very opposite: Why God denies human immortality.

Barr's arguments for this reading of the broader story are not convincing.[8] More important, they do not affect his interpretation of the phrase "knowledge of good and bad." That interpretation stands on its own.

To summarize then, God created human beings to be immortal, immortal but innocent, child-like, limited to their physical capacities. The tree of knowledge of good and bad offered them the opportunity to transcend their limitations, to achieve self-awareness and the powers of discernment. But with this newfound awareness comes death.

We are now left with three possible explanations for the origins of death: Death is either punishment for the sin of disobedience. Or it is part of God's original creation. Or finally, it is the inevitable trade-off for the emergence of human self-awareness.

THE BATTLE BETWEEN GOD AND CHAOS

In the story of the creation of man recorded in Genesis 1:24–28, there is no mention of death. Genesis 1–2:4a is commonly understood to represent an independent creation narrative, separate and distinct from that recorded in Genesis 2:4b–3 which includes the story of the garden of Eden. (The Bible frequently preserves two or more versions of the same story, presumably because each had become accepted as canonical and could not be discarded.)[9] This narrative's silence on the origins of death should not be overlooked.

This first creation story is commonly understood to teach that God created something out of nothing, but that interpretation is not accurate.[10] Rather, it teaches that creation involved God's forming cosmos out of primitive chaos (i.e. darkness, the deep and the "unformed and void" as described in 1:2), that God brought order out of anarchy. The leading motif of this story is that God introduced structures, boundaries or parameters—between light and darkness, day and night, heaven and earth, waters above and waters below, the sun for day and the moon and stars for night; then vegetation, living things and finally human beings. This ordering work shaped the primitive, anarchic conditions that prevailed at the outset of creation.

It is noteworthy that a God who was concerned with establishing parameters did not establish parameters for human life. It may be argued that this theme simply was not part of the agenda of the author of Genesis 1. In support of this view, note that the second creation story puts the creation of a human being at the very heart of its narrative. Indeed, it precedes the creation of the rest of the world which is allotted just three verses (Genesis 2:4–6). This author's version of creation stresses the creation of a human being and promptly begins describing this man's experiences in Eden.

In contrast, the author of Genesis 1 is very much concerned with how the *entire* world came into being; the creation of the human person remains just one part of this broader perspective. It might be the climax of creation, but it is still just one part of the whole story. The concerns in Genesis 1 are cosmic, then, while the concerns of Genesis 2–3 are more anthropological. How man came to die is much more important to the author of Genesis 2–3 than to the author of Genesis 1.

But if, in the spirit of Genesis 1, creation is how God wrests cosmos out of chaos, we may catch a glimpse of an even more elusive explanation of why death is part of God's creation, for the Bible preserves hints of other creation narratives which depart from those recorded in Genesis. Genesis 1 suggests that God's creation was without challenge or opposition: God speaks and the world immediately comes into being. In Genesis 2–3, the challenge to God comes not *during* creation but *after*, through the disobedience of Adam and Eve.

In contrast, these two passages from Psalms:

O God, my king from old,
>who brings deliverance throughout the land;
>it was You who drove back the sea with Your might,
>who smashed the heads of the monsters in the waters;
>it was You who crushed the heads of Leviathan,
>who left him as food for the denizens of the desert;
>it was You who released springs and torrents,
>who made mighty rivers run dry;
>the day is Yours, the night also;
>it was You who set in place the orb of the sun;
>You fixed all the boundaries of the earth;
>summer and winter—You made them. (74:12-17)

And:

You made the deep cover it [the earth] as a garment;

the waters stood above the mountains.
They fled at Your blast,
    rushed away at the sound of Your thunder,
    —mountains rising, valleys sinking—
    to the place You established for them.
You set bounds they must not pass
    so that they never again cover the earth. (104:6-9)

Or this passage from Job:

Who closed the sea behind the doors
When it gushed forth out of the womb?...
When I made breakers My limit for it,
And set up its bar and doors,
And said, "You may come so far and no farther;
Here your surging waves will stop"? (38:8–11)

These passages paint a very different picture of creation. They portray a primordial combat between God and the forces of chaos. Here, God's act of creation is not unopposed. God subdues and confines the forces of darkness and the waters, but does not destroy their power. That power hovers on the periphery of God's creation, threatening always to erupt once again, but kept in check only through God's eternal vigilance.

Other biblical passages portray God crushing the primitive monsters Leviathan (as in Psalm 74 above) and Rahab. Both symbolize primitive chaos:

You rule the swelling of the sea...
You crushed Rahab; he was like a corpse...
    (Psalm 89:10–11)

47

And:

> It was you that hacked Rahab in pieces,
> That pierced the Dragon. (Isaiah 51:9)

The verbs in these passages—"crushed," "hacked," "pierced"—suggest a full-fledged battle between God and the anarchic forces in nature which strenuously resist God's cosmos-making power. These forces had to be crushed and smashed, yet they threaten to engulf us. Again, only God's eternal vigilance prevents chaos from erupting again. And sometimes, as in the flood story that follows, a punishing God destroys the structures separating the waters above from the waters below (Genesis 7:11) and the flood covers the earth. At the end of that story, God promises Noah that the original structures of Genesis 1 will be re-established forever:

> So long as the earth endures,
> Seedtime and harvest,
> Cold and heat,
> Summer and winter,
> Day and night
> Shall not cease. (Genesis 8:22)

But Psalm 74 suggests that however successful God may have been in confining the adversarial forces of nature, God has not been as successful in confining the chaotic forces of history. Note the context of the passage from Psalm 74:

> Till when, O God, will the foes blaspheme,
>   will the enemy forever revile Your name?
> Why do You hold back Your hand, Your right hand?
> Draw it out of Your bosom!... (10–11)
> Be mindful of how the enemy blasphemes the Lord,

how base people revile Your name.
Do not deliver Your dove to the wild beast;
  do not ignore forever the band of Your lowly ones.
Look to the covenant!
For the dark places of the land are full of the haunts of
  lawlessness. (18-20)

To the Harvard University biblical theologian Jon D.
Levenson, this complex theological claim draws attention to "the
painful and yawning gap between the liturgical affirmation of God's
absolute sovereignty and the empirical reality of evil triumphant and
unchecked."[11]

But if God's creation demanded a primordial combat with
chaos, and if those chaotic forces are still very much alive, both in
nature (for it is clear to us, if not to the psalmist, that natural chaos
remains part of our human experience) and in history (as testified
to by the triumph of biblical Israel's enemies), then it is only a short
step to the further claim that death may also be part of that primitive chaos that God never totally conquered at the outset.

In this view, death is independent of God, a force that God
has not yet been able to subdue. Scholars have also called attention
to the Ras Shamra tablets which preserve a Ugaritic myth in which
the god of the underworld is called *Mwt,* the cognate for the Hebrew term for death, *mavet.*[12] In this myth, Mwt triumphed against
Baal, the god of fertility, and forced Baal to descend to the underworld. But Anath, Baal's sister, then killed Mwt. Both Anath and
Baal returned to life, but at different times. Scholars interpret this
myth as referring to the change of the seasons: Baal rules when the
rainy season begins, and dies when the rain ceases, which is when
Mwt begins to rule.[13]

A trace of this personification of death is found, for example,
in this lamentation in Jeremiah 9:19–20:

Hear, O women, the word of the Lord,
Let your ears receive the word of His mouth,
And teach your daughters wailing,
And one another lamentation.
For death [in Hebrew, *mavet*] has climbed through our
    windows,
Has entered our fortresses,
To cut off babes from the streets,
Young men from the squares.

Or in this passage from David's prayer of gratitude to God
for having been saved from the hands of his enemies and from Saul:

For the breakers of Death encompassed me,
The torrents of Belial terrified me;
The snares of Sheol encircled me,
The toils of Death [*mavet*] engulfed me.
    (II Samuel 22:5–6)

Or in God's promise in Hosea:

From Sheol itself I will save them
Redeem them from very Death [*mavet*].
Where, O Death, are your plagues?
Your pestilence, where, O Sheol? (Hosea 13:14)

In these passages death becomes personified. Death climbs
through windows; its snares, engulfs and encircles humans. These
texts convey a sense of death as a power that seems to be able to
challenge God. Modern biblical scholarship views this independent
power as a relic of paganism—presented here as an ancient pagan
divinity—which the Bible's monotheistic framework has not
obliterated.[14]

But the most fascinating allusion to this notion of death as an independent power emerges in Isaiah 25:8, an eschatological apocalypse which describes God's eventual triumph over all of God's and Israel's enemies:

> He will destroy death [*hamavet*] forever.
> My Lord God will wipe the tears away
> From all faces
> And will put an end to the reproach of His people
> Over all the earth....

This is one of three biblical texts which contradict the overwhelming biblical view that the death of a human being is final, that there is nothing for us to anticipate after death. But this text, alone among the three, goes further than promising the simple resurrection of the dead. It announces the death of death, here personified as a pagan god. It forecasts an age in which people will no longer die. But in the meantime, death is still very much "alive," and it continues to exist as a power over which God has no control.

Tentatively, then, we conclude that the Bible has preserved shards of an ancient notion in which a personified "death" co-exists with the monotheistic God; that it represents part of the primitive chaos which, together with the anarchic forces in nature and history, God has not yet abolished. Later, this figure is demoted and becomes the Angel of Death, one of God's messengers but totally under God's control. A still later tradition then portrays God as slaughtering the angel of death, thus banishing death forever.

In this view, death is neither punishment for human sin nor a function of our having to return to the dust of the earth from which we were originally created. Nor is it a trade-off for the flowering of human potential. Here, death was not created by God, but co-exists with God whose power is still limited. Only toward the end of the biblical period is God portrayed as sufficiently powerful to vanquish death forever, not in historical time, but at the end of days. This vision represents the final stage in the triumph of monotheism and becomes a central theme in later Jewish eschatology, which celebrates the eventual emergence of an age of uninterrupted cosmos under the sovereignty of an all-powerful God.

HOW DEATH ENTERED THE WORLD

We are left then with four possible biblical accounts of the origins of death in the world: Death is punishment for sin; it is part of God's original creation of man; it is the inevitable result of humanity achieving self-awareness and the power of discrimination; or it is an independent power over which God does not yet exercise full control. The first three explanations are based on interpretations of the early Genesis texts which, in varying ways, view death as a conscious divine decree. The last, which stems from an alternative creation tradition that is preserved in other biblical texts, views death as a force which, within history, remains independent of God's will.

Each of these explanations has serious theological implications, and each implies a distinctive image of God. In each, eschatology is tied to theodicy, to the need to make sense of the presence of evil and suffering in a world created and ruled by God. Two assume divine omnipotence: God creates us immortal, but for some reason, later decrees our death. The explanation that views death as part of God's original creation of human beings leaves us with the question: But *why* did God create us to die? So we should return to the earth from where we were created? But why did God create us from the dust of the earth in the first place? The last explanation, that death is a force that lies beyond God's sovereignty, requires us to accept the notion of an inherently limited God, a God Whose power is not yet complete and manifest in the world.

That image of a limited God may shock some contemporary

readers, but it is amply documented by numerous biblical passages. The reality is that however omnipotent God seems to be, God's omnipotence is more *de jure* than *de facto*: In the biblical narrative, God rarely achieves what God hopes to achieve, partly because God's power is limited by divinely endowed human freedom which can be used to rebel against God. But even beyond this, passages such as Psalm 44 or Psalm 74 recognize that in some mysterious way, God's power does not always manifest itself in historical events on behalf of causes which God is supposed to champion, such as the security of Israel.

Our own modern sensibility has extended that recognition to natural events as well. To us, the persistence of chaos in both nature and history seems to defy God's vaunted omnipotence. But there is no questioning that this fourth explanation of death requires a significantly greater theological leap than the first two, if only because it challenges our commonly accepted view of God's omnipotence.

The later rabbinic tradition picks up two of these explanations: Death is either punishment for Adam's sin, or part of God's original creation. Rabbi Judah interprets Deuteronomy 32:32—"The grapes for them are poison...."—as meaning:

> You are the descendants of primeval Adam, for whom I decreed death, both for him and for his descendants who follow him, until the end of all generations.[15]

On the other hand, Rabbi Meir interprets God's statement after the world was created, "And, behold, it was very good" (Genesis 1:31) to refer to death: "And, behold, death was good" (Genesis Rabbah 9:5).[16] And the mishnah in *Avot* (4:22) stresses:

> Those who are born will of necessity die...for perforce were you created, perforce were you born, perforce do

you live, perforce will you die.

Christianity enshrined the punishment theme by placing it at the heart of its doctrine of original sin which is transmitted through procreation and from which all faithful Christians are vicariously redeemed by Jesus' death on the cross. The 1994 edition of the Catechism of the Catholic Church, the repository of authoritative Roman Catholic teachings, reads

> All men are implicated in Adam's sin, as St. Paul affirms: "By one man's disobedience many [that is, all men] were made sinners" (Romans 5:12,19): "sin came into the world through one man and death through sin, and so death spread to all men because all men sinned...." The Apostle [Paul] contrasts the universality of sin and death with the universality of salvation in Christ. "Then as one man's trespass led to condemnation for all men, so one man's act of righteousness leads to acquittal and life for all men." (Romans 5:18)[17]

This Christian reading of Genesis may have served as the incentive for some rabbinic traditions to distance themselves from the punishment explanation.

But I prefer either the punishment theme or James Barr's reading which views death as the inevitable trade-off for the flowering of humanity's self-awareness. Both of these readings account for the introduction of death precisely at the climax of the Garden of Eden narrative, not in the varying accounts of the creation of the human being, not even explicitly in the notion that God formed the human being from the dust of the earth (Genesis 2:7). The fact that death is introduced precisely at this point in the narrative is surely telling.

In further support of this claim, note our two alternative

interpretations of Genesis 2:16–17. We claimed above that this text is ambiguous: It could mean either that death comes as the result of eating of the tree of the knowledge of good and bad, or that the result of the eating would be *instant* death, "...*as soon as* you eat of it, you shall die." But this latter warning did not come to pass; Adam and Eve did not die on the day they ate of the fruit. The verse then strengthens the claim that death was not part of God's original plan, but rather the result of eating the forbidden fruit.

Finally, the fourth explanation—that death is an independent power which resisted God's ordering work of creation—is not sufficiently supported by explicit biblical texts. It may be alluded to in a few texts, but its pagan overtones are so subversive of biblical monotheism that they remain ambiguous. It is clearly not the central biblical statement on this issue.

So we are left with two clear biblical accounts of the origins of death: Death is either punishment for the sin of disobedience or it is the inevitable trade-off for the emergence of our distinctive humanity. I prefer the latter because it ties the emergence of death, not to some indeterminate act of rebellion, but to the specific act of eating of the tree of knowledge of good and bad; the punishment account fails to do this. It also lends a tragic, existential dimension to this primordial myth. Death is the result of our becoming fully human and it takes place within the context of God's full and somewhat saddened awareness of its inevitability.

DEATH DOES NOT HAVE THE LAST WORD

There is a certain symmetrical elegance in the notion that death was not part of God's original plan for humanity. The structure of the classical Jewish religious myth deals with the tension between chaos and cosmos. In a rough, preliminary way, the Bible relates that out of primitive chaos, God created a perfectly ordered world. That order

55

was destroyed by the primordial human beings whose disobedience returned chaos to the world. By punishing chaos with chaos, i.e. with expulsion from the Garden and with death, the age of history in which we now live, and in which cosmos and chaos are intermingled, was inaugurated. In its later development, the myth envisions an eschatological age in which cosmos alone will rule.

Eschatologies are frequently restorative: They envision an ideal end as a recapitulation of an ideal beginning. To preserve this symmetry, the eschatological age in which death will die can be viewed as a return to an earlier age in which death was unknown.

From this perspective, death enters the world not because that is how we were created nor because God's power is limited. But rather because of some event that occurred after the creation of human beings. This would locate the Jewish myth squarely within the broader context of other ancient mythologies, all of which explain death as originating from some event that occurred after creation. It does not have to fit into this context, but we can understand *why* it could.

There is no reason why we must choose between these varying explanations of the etiology of death. The Bible is not one internally coherent book. Rather, it is a library, a collection of documents composed at various times by various communities. Until it was canonized, each document went through an extensive process of composition. It is not uncommon, then, for the Bible to preserve multiple and even contrary explanations of historical events and natural phenomena.

If there is a difference between the four accounts of the origins of death, it rests in how we understand the Jewish claim that death will ultimately be forever abolished. Our two favored interpretations see this state as restorative, a return to a primitive ideal state of affairs. Their alternatives view eschatology as vectoral, that is as moving from an imperfect state at the outset to an ideal state at the end.

But in each case, the doctrine of the resurrection of the dead will mark a significant step in the evolution of the doctrine of a monotheistic God. It insists that the death of a human being is only temporary, that God's power will ultimately destroy death. In the punishment explanation, God's destruction of death is an act of grace which remands the punishment originally vested on human beings. In Barr's explanation, the inevitability of death is overwhelmed by the later biblical tradition's need to vindicate God's justice. In the other explanations, the death of death affirms that one of the transformations that will characterize the end of days will be the emergence of God's absolute power. That promise will become central to the later stages of this book.

III

DEATH IN THE BIBLE

FROM THE AGE of the Talmud to our own day, Judaism has taught that human beings can anticipate some form of life after death. But very few allusions to this doctrine can be found in the Bible. In fact, were we to rely solely on the Bible, we would conclude the very opposite. Almost throughout, the Bible views death as absolutely final. Only three biblical passages unambiguously affirm that at least some individuals will live again after their death. And the only one of these texts that can be dated with some precision is from the mid-second century BCE, a very late date for a biblical text. Apart from these texts, the Bible is quite clear that all human beings die and that their death is final. In fact, we are informed of the death of just about all of the personalities in the biblical narrative: Adam, Noah, the three patriarchs die, as do the matriarchs Sarah and Rachel, Joseph, Moses, Miriam and Aaron.

There are only two enigmatic exceptions to this rule. Genesis 5:21–24 recalls Enoch, one of the ten generations from Adam to Noah. We are told that nine of these men lived a number of years, then they had children, then they lived a certain number of additional years until they died. Of Enoch, however, we are told, "Enoch walked with God; then he was no more, for God took him" (Genesis 5:24). This enigmatic statement may be a way of telling us that Enoch too died, but here, the text is not explicit.

The second exception is Elijah. II Kings 2:11 informs us that "a fiery chariot with fiery horses suddenly appeared and separated one from the other, and Elijah went up to heaven in a whirlwind." It is worth noting that eventually, both Enoch and Elijah—particularly the latter—would play a significant role in the Jewish imagination, probably because neither was explicitly reported to have died.

THE FINALITY OF DEATH

But apart from these two men, all biblical personalities die and the Bible repeatedly emphasizes that death is the ultimate fate of all human beings. See, for example, Psalm 49:6–13:

> In time of trouble, why should I fear
>   the encompassing evil of those who would supplant
>   me—
>   men who trust in their riches,
>   who glory in their great wealth?
> Ah, it cannot redeem a man,
>   or pay his ransom to God;
>   the price of life is too high;
>   and so one ceases to be, forever.
> Shall he live eternally,
>   and never see the grave?
> For one sees that the wise die,
>   that the foolish and ignorant both perish,

leaving their wealth to others.
Their grave is their eternal home,
    the dwelling-place for all generations
    of those once famous on earth.
Man does not abide in honor;
    he is like the beasts that perish.

Or Psalm 146:2–4:

I will praise the Lord all my life,
    sing hymns to my God while I exist.
Put not your trust in the great,
    in mortal man who cannot save.
His breath departs;
    he returns to the dust;
    on that day his plans come to nothing.

Death marks the end of all human activity. It also marks the end of our ability to relate to God.

The heavens belong to the Lord,
    but the earth he gave over to man.
The dead cannot praise the Lord,
    nor any who go down into silence.
But we will bless the Lord
    now and forever.
Hallelujah. (Psalm 115:16–18; see also Psalm 6:6,
    30:9–10; Isaiah 38:18–19)

The psalmist contrasts the living and the dead. "We"—the living—can praise God, but the dead cannot. Neither will God be able to reach us after our death.

Hear my prayer, O Lord;
  give ear to my cry;
  do not disregard my tears;
  for like all my forebears
  I am an alien, resident with You.
Look away from me, that I may recover,
  before I pass away and am gone. (Psalm 39:13–14)

God, the psalmist claims, must deliver me while I am alive. After my death, it will be too late. God's power over my destiny ends with my death.

If there is any place in the Bible where the doctrine of an afterlife might have been introduced had Israelite religion provided for its possibility, it is in the Book of Job. Job is the story of a righteous man who suffers terribly because God has wagered with Satan that, despite his suffering, Job would remain faithful to God. The bulk of the book consists of attempts by Job's friends to explain and vindicate God's judgement, and thereby to console him for his woes. But nowhere does the book even suggest that Job should accept the sufferings of this world in exchange for the well-being that will follow after his death. In fact, the very opposite is the case.

Man born of woman is short-lived and sated with trouble.
He blossoms like a flower and withers;
He vanishes like a shadow and does not endure....
His days are determined;
You know the number of his months;
You have set him limits that he cannot pass....
There is hope for a tree;
If it is cut down it will renew itself;
Its shoots will not cease.
If its roots are old in the earth,
And its stump dies in the ground,

At the scent of water it will bud
And produce branches like a sapling.
But mortals languish and die;
Man expires, where is he? (14:1–10)

Two themes in this passage, one of Job's responses to his consolers, are noteworthy. First, that God has set immutable boundaries for a human life recalls the language of Psalm 104:9 where God is described as having done the same thing with the waters at creation. In both instances, creation is understood as an act of structuring, defining, limiting or setting boundaries, both with the primeval waters and with human life. It is God, then, who has defined the limits of human life. Second, note the comparison with natural phenomena, especially the tree. The tree can enjoy what seems to be perpetual rejuvenation, for even forests that are devastated by fire have the ability to bloom once again. Not so the human being; his death is final.

So, too, in this passage:

My days are few, so desist!
Leave me alone, let me be diverted a while
Before I depart—never to return—
For the land of deepest gloom;
A land whose light is darkness,
All gloom and disarray,
Whose light is like darkness. (10:20-22)

The Bible does dwell on the rewards due to those loyal to God, but these will be attained in one's lifetime. In Deuteronomy 11:13–15 and 28:1–14, obedience to God will be rewarded with material prosperity, rainfall, crops, food, children, military victory, national security, health, length of days (specifically as a reward for honoring parents as in Exodus 20:12 and Deuteronomy 5:16), and all manner of blessing. And disobedience will be punished with the very opposite: Famine, poverty, illness, military defeat, exile, curses and early death (Deuteronomy 11:16–17 and 28:15–68). Nowhere is any form of reward or punishment after death mentioned. In prophetic literature, though the framework is national rather than individual, the emphasis is the same: Righteousness will be rewarded with military victory and national security. Disobedience will be punished with military defeat and exile. Both for the individual and for Israel, the rewards for obedience and the punishment for disobedience remain thoroughly this-worldly, within history and within the normal span of human life.

In this same spirit, look at two of the Bible's death scenes. Both are recorded in the last chapter of Genesis, and describe the last moments of Jacob and Joseph. What concerns them here? Jacob asks his sons to bury him with his immediate forebears in the cave of Machpelah; Joseph instructs his sons to take his bones with them when God delivers them from Egypt. In neither case is there any reference to their fate after death, only with the final resting place for their remains.

The same with Moses. The final lines of Deuteronomy report his death "at the command of the Lord" (34:5), his burial "in the valley of the land of Moab, near Beth-peor" (34:6), that he was "a hundred and twenty years old when he died; his eyes were undimmed and his vigor unabated" (34:7), and that the Israelites mourned him for thirty days (34:8).

There is nothing in this report of Moses' death to suggest an afterlife. In fact, the editorial comment in 34:6 that "no one knows his burial place to this day," seems to emphasize the very finality of the death of this man, clearly the single most significant personality in Israel's early history. Even more, no other biblical personality, with the possible exception of Job, deserved some form of eternal reward for his devotion to God than Moses. Yet Moses was even denied entry to the Promised Land because he failed to sanctify God's name at the Waters of Meribah (Numbers 20:1–13; Deuteronomy 32:50–52, 34:4).[1] The finality of Moses' death—even more, its apparent injustice—is striking testimony that at this stage, biblical religion knew of no afterlife.

WHERE DO THE DEAD GO?

The most common biblical name for the "land of deepest gloom" where Job anticipates going upon his death is *Sheol*. This term and its synonyms, *Shahat, Bor* and *Abbadon,* appear throughout the Bible. *Sheol* is the place where the dead "go." Its location as the opposite pole to heaven is specified in several texts where the term appears without being linked to death. It is the netherworld, the bowels of the earth, the pit. The limit of possible human awareness, it is a metaphor for God's ultimate mystery, as in Job 11:7–8:

> Would you discover the mystery of God?
> Would you discover the limit of the Almighty?
> Higher than heaven—what can you do?
> Deeper than Sheol—what can you know?

The Bible abounds with vivid descriptions of *Sheol.* Its gates and bars make escape impossible (Isaiah 38:1–10). It is a monster with gaping jaws that aggressively devours all men and is never sated (Isaiah 5:14; Proverbs 27:20). It is a place of maggots and decay (Job 17:13–16).

To claim that the dead "go down" to *Sheol* is to say that they descend to the bowels of the earth, beyond the bounds of human awareness. They lose any possible relationship with God, with the living, even with the other inhabitants of the netherworld, and with what transpires on earth. Of the inhabitants of *Sheol,* Job 14:21–22 claims:

His sons attain honor and he does not know it;
They are humbled and he is not aware of it.
He feels only the pain of his flesh,
And his spirit mourns in him.

They also lose their relationship with God. Psalm 88:11–13
asks rhetorically:

Do you work wonders for the dead?
　Do the shades rise to praise You?
Is your faithful care recounted in the grave?
　Your constancy in the place of perdition?
Are your wonders made known in the netherworld,
　Your beneficent deeds in the land of oblivion?

This psalmist, at the point of death, is painfully conscious of
what he is about to lose:

For I am sated with misfortune;
　I am at the brink of Sheol.
I am numbered with those who go down to the Pit;
　I am a helpless man
　abandoned among the dead,
　like bodies lying in the grave
　of whom You are mindful no more,
　and who are cut off from Your care. (88:4–5)

The contrast between the inhabitants of *Sheol* and the living
is illuminated in this passage from the prayer of King Hezekiah "when
he recovered from the illness he had suffered":

For it is not Sheol that praises You,
Not [the Land of] Death that extols You;

Nor do they who descend into the Pit
Hope for Your grace.
The living, only the living
Can give thanks to You
As I do this day... (Isaiah 38:18–19)

Why then, the psalmist cries, would God desire my death?

I called to You, O Lord;
   to my Lord I made appeal,
  "What is to be gained from my death,
   from my descent into the Pit?
Can dust praise You?
Can it declare Your faithfulness?..." (Psalm 30:9–10)

Job knows full well that there is no returning from *Sheol*:

My days are few, so desist!
Leave me alone, let me be diverted a while
Before I depart—never to return—
For the land of deepest gloom... (Job 10:20-21)

Or again:

As a cloud fades away,
So whoever goes down to Sheol does not come up;
He returns no more to his home;
His place does not know him. (7:9–10)

In the Joseph narrative, upon hearing that Joseph has been killed, Jacob refuses to be comforted: "No, I will go down mourning to my son in Sheol" (Genesis 37:35). Jacob knows that he will never see Joseph again. Nor will he have any further contact with his son in *Sheol*, for later in the narrative, in contemplating the possibility that Benjamin may also have to travel to Egypt, he exclaims:

> "My son must not go down with you, for his brother is dead and he alone is left. If he meets with disaster on the journey you are taking, you will send my white head down to Sheol in grief." (Genesis 42:38)

When Jacob dies, he will never know Benjamin again for there is no relationship among the inhabitants of *Sheol*. *Sheol* does not discriminate between the righteous and the evil; all human beings, even Jacob, end up there, and that certainly does not represent the Bible's verdict on Jacob's righteousness.

Not unexpectedly, the biblical portrayal of *Sheol* is not as coherent as we have described it thus far. First, the Bible could not abide the notion that there are territorial boundaries to God's rule:

> If I ascend to heaven, You are there!
> if I descend to Sheol, You are there too. (Psalm 139:8)

However metaphorical this description of God's range of influence may be, the use of this particular metaphor is suggestive.

More important, despite our insistence that *Sheol* marks the absolute end of human destiny, the fact remains that there is some form of human continuance there, that people are not totally extinguished at death. If Jacob claims that he will mourn his son in *Sheol*, it means that his son is there for him to go to. This in no way ameliorates or dilutes the reality of his son's death, but it does suggest that in some way, his son continues to "be" even after death.[2]

The problem here is the difficulty of conceiving just what happens to a person after death, or more crudely, just where that person "goes." Today, we speak of our departed as if they are still in some way "with us." Many of us speak this way even if we do not believe in any form of substantive life after death.

The ancients clearly shared that sense. That the body is buried in the earth probably led them to locate *Sheol* in the bowels of the earth. They also knew that the body disintegrates in the earth. Yet the dead person, in some way, continues to "be" after burial. This should in no way be interpreted to refer to the continued existence, after death, of a human "soul"; there is no notion of this kind of entity, independent of the body, in the Bible. But it does suggest that the human being is in some way more than merely a body and that this extra dimension of the personality continues after death. Finally, there is no questioning the overwhelming testimony of the Bible that any form of continued existence in *Sheol* is singularly compromised.

THE "GOOD" DEATH

In all the texts quoted above, biblical personalities contemplate death with terror. But in other contexts, the Bible's depiction of death avoids the tragic and painful descriptions associated with going down to *Sheol*. Abraham, for example, is portrayed as dying "at a good ripe age, old and contented" (Genesis 25:8). When Moses died, "his eyes were undimmed and his vigor unabated" (Deuteronomy 34:7). The Bible knows of a peaceful death that follows upon a rich and accomplished lifetime, though this in no way dilutes the reality or the finality of death. In all these cases, however, the rewards of a good life are experienced here on earth, not in some afterlife.

Instead of going down to *Sheol*, Isaac and Jacob are each portrayed as being "gathered to his kin" (Genesis 35:29 and 49:33), and David "slept with his fathers" (I Kings 2:10). There are no references to *Sheol* here, though presumably, that's where the "kin" and the "fathers" are to be found. In general, then, the term *Sheol* is used to characterize a particularly tragic or premature death, one that follows a painful life experience or event.

Psalm 88:4–5 noted above is representative of a number of texts which reflect the experience of one who is near death. Here, the psalmist characterizes himself as being "at the brink of Sheol" (v. 4). Some of these texts seem to imply that God can actually deliver the dead from *Sheol* itself. Typical of these is Psalm 30:2–4:

> I extol You, O Lord,
>> for You have lifted me up,
>> and not let my enemies rejoice over me.
> O Lord, my God,
>> I cried out to You,
>> and You healed me.
> O Lord, You brought me up from Sheol,
>> preserved me from going down to the Pit.

Or in Jonah's prayer from the belly of the fish:

> The waters closed in over me,
> The deep engulfed me.
> Weeds twined around my head.
> I sank to the base of the mountains;
> The bars of the earth closed upon me forever.
> Yet You brought my life up from the pit… (2:6–7)

What these passages celebrate is God's power to frustrate death, to rescue the individual from the clutches of *Sheol,* to *prevent* him even from going down to *Sheol* in the first place, that is, from dying. They have nothing to do with God's power to raise the dead from *Sheol.* In effect, then, what is being praised is God's power to cure or to heal, as opposed to letting death have its way.

This illuminates two biblical passages commonly cited as proving that the Bible does portray God as having the power to resurrect the dead. Deuteronomy 32:39 reads:

> See, then, that I, I am He;
> There is no god beside Me.
> I deal death and give life;
> I wounded and I will heal:
> None can deliver from My hand.

The Hebrew phrase for "I deal death and give life"—*Ani memit u'mehaye*—was eventually incorporated into the daily rabbinic liturgy, where it is clearly understood to mean that God has the power to bring death and to resurrect the dead after their death. But that meaning reflects post-biblical thinking. In the Bible itself, the phrase means that God has the power both to allow people to die or to heal them, to prevent them from dying, or simply to keep them alive. That this is in fact the meaning of *mehaye* in the Bible is obvious from Nehemiah 9:6 where it appears without *memit*, and where it clearly means "You keep them alive." This illuminates the almost parallel text in Hannah's prayer in I Samuel 2:6–7:

> The Lord deals death and gives life [again *memit u'mehaye*],
> Casts down into Sheol and raises up.
> The Lord makes poor and makes rich;
> He casts down, He also lifts high.

There is no hint of resurrection here. What is being acclaimed is God's ultimate power to do whatever God wills to do (apart, of course, from raising the dead). To express this, the author employs the rhetorical device of listing a series of polar opposites—death and life, poor and rich, casting down and lifting high—and insisting that God can do both of these and, by implication, everything in between. The ultimate thrust of these passages, then, is to celebrate

God's unlimited power, although at this stage, God's power does not extend to raising the dead from *Sheol*. Death is final.

On the other hand, the almost parallel use of the phrase in Isaiah 26:19, *yihyu metecha* ("Let your dead revive!"), clearly does refer to resurrection as the context implies. It is one of the three biblical texts that do, as we shall see below.

CONSORTING WITH SPIRITS

But there is one biblical narrative in which someone *does* return from *Sheol*. This is the fascinating story, related in I Samuel 28, of Saul's encounter with the woman from En-dor who was reputed to be able to consult ghosts.

Although Samuel crowned Saul as the king of Israel, their relationship quickly deteriorated after that point. Samuel eventually tore the kingship away from Saul for not obeying God's command to exterminate Amalek, and anointed David to be Saul's successor. As David's popularity among the people increased, Saul sank deeper into depression. After Samuel's death, Saul prepared to confront the Philistine army, and tried to consult with God, but received no answer. He then asked his courtiers to find a woman who consults ghosts. They brought him, stealthily and in disguise (for Saul had outlawed recourse to ghosts and spirits), to the woman from En-dor whom he asks to produce Samuel from *Sheol*.

In an enigmatic encounter, the woman sees Samuel, though Saul does not, and Saul hears Samuel's voice, though she does not. The ensuing conversation is singularly unhelpful to Saul for Samuel simply reiterates that God has abandoned him and that he will die in the forthcoming battle.

Not only is this the one biblical reference to anyone returning from death, but Samuel is clearly unhappy that he has been brought up from the grave. "Why have you disturbed me and brought me up?" he asks. But, if anything, the absolutely singular quality of this episode is the exception that proves the rule. Nothing here suggests the possibility of a generalized or permanent resurrection of the dead, for Samuel quickly returns to *Sheol* forever. The story is simply one further testimony to the deteriorating state of Saul's mental health.

This mysterious story assumes even more significance against the background of the oft-repeated warning in the Bible against consulting with dead spirits (Leviticus 19:31, 20:6,27; Deuteronomy 18:11). Psalm 106:28 explicitly associates this practice with the pagan cult of Baal Peor. In fact, we are told in I Samuel 28:3 that Saul had himself forbidden any recourse to ghosts and spirits precisely because of its pagan, idolatrous connotations. Necromancy was considered idolatrous because it blurred the boundary between God and human beings and could lead to the deification of the dead. Only God lives eternally; human beings die and their death is final.[3]

The dead remain dead. They are buried and mourned: Abraham buries Sarah—and mourns her. Isaac and Ishmael bury Abraham—and mourn him. Esau and Jacob bury Isaac—and mourn him. Jacob buries Rachel—and mourns her. Jacob's sons bury their father—and mourn him. The Israelites bury Aaron and Moses—and mourn them. The survivors then go on with their lives without recourse to the dead. There is not the slightest hint that anyone turned for guidance to the dead Moses.

In fact, the Bible goes out of its way to distance the religious life of the community from the dead. Death is the ultimate source of ritual impurity. Any contact with death, whether with the carcass of an animal or the corpse of a human being, even being under the same roof with a corpse, renders one ritually impure (Leviticus 11:24–31, 39; Numbers 19:11). This applies even more stringently to *kohanim,* the biblical clergy, who, when in a state of impurity, were forbidden to have any role in the Temple ritual (Leviticus 21:1–4). These stipulations accentuate the notion that death and the dead

73

can play no role whatsoever in the ritual life of the community, lest the community be contaminated by pagan practices.

THE VISION OF THE DRY BONES

One further text is typically cited as supporting the claim that resurrection entered into biblical literature at an early date. That text is Ezekiel 37, the prophet's vision of the dry bones that are clothed with flesh, infused with breath, and brought back to life.

But the key to understanding this passage lies in God's own interpretation of the prophet's vision:

> "...O mortal, these bones are the whole House of Israel. They say, 'Our bones are dried up, our hope is gone; we are doomed.' Prophesy, therefore, and say to them: Thus said the Lord God: I am going to open your graves and lift you out of the graves, O My people, and bring you to the land of Israel." (Ezekiel 37:11–12)

It is clear, then, that this vision of bones that assume flesh and live again is a metaphor for the national regeneration of Israel, for God's power to bring this people out of the Babylonian exile (following the destruction of the first Temple in 587 BCE; Ezekiel prophesied during the first part of the sixth century BCE), and return them to their homeland. It is, then, a political statement, not a prophecy of bodily resurrection.

What remains suggestive about this text, however, is the very use of the metaphor of bodily resurrection for national regeneration. Whence and why this metaphor? Where did the prophet learn of that very possibility? Further, a God who has the power to restore to flourishing life a people whose national life has expired could conceivably also raise people from the grave. In this specific case,

74

absent any further substantive biblical evidence that the possibility of bodily resurrection was known and accepted in mid–sixth century BCE Israel, and in the light of the manifold textual evidence to the contrary, we can only conclude that the prophet's vision was limited to Israel's national regeneration, not to the later doctrine of bodily resurrection.

This text remains significant, however, for it marks one of the steps which, in time, leads the later tradition to go beyond the metaphorical use of this theme and to understand it in a much more concrete way, as an even further extension of God's unlimited power.

WHAT HAPPENS UPON DEATH?

For much of the past two millennia, the Western world, Jews included, has characterized death as the soul's separation from the body. This view stems originally from Greek philosophy, certainly from Plato and possibly from the earlier mid-sixth century Orphic religion.[4] In Plato's dialogue, *Phaedo,* set in the hours before Socrates' suicide, Socrates characterizes death as "the separation of soul and body," and continues

> And to be dead is the completion of this [separation]; when the soul exists in herself, and is released from the body and the body is released from the soul, what is this but death?[5]

However much this notion of separation of soul from body became part of Judaism's understanding of the afterlife, it is not at all the biblical view.

Biblical anthropology knows nothing of this dualistic picture of the human person which claims that the human person is a composite of two entities, a material body and a spiritual or non-material

75

soul. In Greek thought, the soul is a distinctive entity which pre-exists the life of the person, enters the body at birth, separates from the body at death and continues to exist in some supernal realm.[6]

The Bible, in contrast, portrays each human as a single entity, clothed in clay-like flesh which is animated or vivified by a life-giving spark or impulse variously called *ruah, nefesh, neshamah,* or *nishmat hayyim.*

In the later tradition, these terms came to be understood as synonymous with the Greek "soul." But this identification is not in the Bible. The term *"nefesh"* signifies the neck or the throat (as in Psalm 69:2), or the breath (that passes through the throat, as in Job 41:13), or the life-blood (as in Leviticus 17:10–11). By extension, it signifies a living human being since it refers to the two characteristics that make a person alive: Breath and blood. When Exodus 1:5 numbers Jacob's progeny as "seventy *nefesh,*" it means simply seventy persons, not seventy disembodied "souls."

In the Bible, the term *neshamah* also means breath (as in I Kings 17:17) and, again by extension, a living person. The last verse of Psalm 150 does not mean that all disembodied souls will praise the Lord, but rather that "all that breathes"—all living beings—will do so. Job 34:14–15 further identifies *neshamah* with *ruah. Ruah* can mean "wind" or "breath."

> His breath [*ruah*] departs;
>> he returns to the dust;
>> on that day his plans come to nothing. (Psalm 146:4)

Death is understood as the "going out" of the *ruah,* or of the similar "going out" of the *nefesh* (as in Genesis 35:18), or of God's "taking away" the *nefesh* (as in I Kings 19:4) or the *neshamah* (as in Job 34:14).

It is precisely this notion that something "goes out" of the body at death that enabled the later tradition to identify this "something" with Plato's soul. But in the biblical context, what leaves the person is not a distinct entity but rather that vivifying spark which had initially given life to the clay-like flesh in the first place. Key to understanding all these passages is the Genesis 2:7 account of the creation of the human person:

> [T]he Lord God formed man from the dust of the earth. He blew into his nostrils the breath of life [*nishmat hayyim*], and man became a living being [*nefesh hayyah*].

If at creation, the clod of dust became a living being when God breathed the breath of life "into" his nostrils, then death occurs when that same breath of life "goes out" of the body. Identifying this breath of life with what was later called a "soul" would attribute to it a distinct identity which would include self-consciousness. But it simply does not have any of this in these biblical texts. Here, the reference is rather to an impersonal spark that, eventually, simply dissipates.

The only significant biblical anticipation of that later doctrine may be found in Ecclesiastes, which is commonly understood to reflect a Hellenistic world view. In 12:7, the typical "going out" of the *ruah* becomes a "return to God":

> And the dust returns to the ground
> As it was,
> And the lifebreath [*ruah*] returns to God
> Who bestowed it.

This text is clearly an extension of Genesis 2:7. It distinguishes between the dust of the ground and the lifebreath. Each returns to where it came from: The dust (or body) to the ground and the lifebreath to God. This reference, unusual in the Bible, to the *ruah*'s "return to God" may echo the Greek notion that the *ruah* is an entity which comes from God and at death "returns" to some "place." If this interpretation is accurate, Ecclesiastes represents a way-station between the characteristic biblical view and the more dualistic anthropology of the later tradition. But it is equally likely that the text simply recapitulates the view in Genesis that the lifebreath was breathed into the dust by God, and that at death, it simply returns to God.[7]

In the Bible, then, death occurs when the lifebreath that originally made the person alive, leaves the body and dissipates. It has no distinct identity, nor does it go nor return to any specific place.

ONLY GOD IS IMMORTAL

If one were to speculate on why biblical religion insists upon the finality of death for human beings, two answers are possible. The first is part of the Bible's generalized injunction against imitating the idolatrous practices of the surrounding pagan religions. Worship of the dead was prevalent in all the surrounding cultures and biblical religion feared any pagan contamination. That is why consulting dead spirits is frequently on a list of other forbidden pagan practices, as in Leviticus 20:2–6 where an injunction against turning to spirits follows an injunction against giving one's offspring to Moloch. This is a reference to the pagan cult which, it was believed, practiced the ritual burning of children.[8]

Another answer might lie in the biblical insistence on preserving a sharp demarcation between God and human beings: Only God is immortal; humans die. That is precisely the difference between the two. Only much later, when the community faced new religious challenges, was it possible to look at this doctrine anew and revise it. But that stage was centuries away. For the present, we are left with the stark message of Ecclesiastes 3:1–2:

78

A season is set for everything, a time for every
   experience under heaven:
A time for being born and a time for dying.

And from Psalm 90:

The span of our life is seventy years
   or, given the strength, eighty years;
      but the best of them are trouble and sorrow,

Therefore:

Teach us to count our days rightly,
   that we may obtain a wise heart. (vv. 10, 12)

Since we cannot anticipate any destiny beyond death, our only hope is to treasure our lifespan on earth and to live wisely.

DEATH IS REAL AND TRAGIC

Despite the later development of a rich doctrine of the afterlife, Judaism never abandoned its original sense of the reality of death. There is no echo in Judaism of the triumphalism of Paul's claim: "Death, where is your victory? Death, where is your sting?" (I Corinthians 15:55), or of Socrates' anticipation of death as the ultimate and longed-for liberation of the soul from its bodily prison. Contemplating his imminent death, Socrates exclaims:

There is great reason to hope that, going whither I go, when I have come to the end of my journey, I shall attain that which has been the pursuit of my life. And therefore I go on my way rejoicing, and not I only, but

79

every other man who believes that his mind has been made ready....[9]

None of this temper is in Judaism. That death is not ultimately victorious is compatible with the later tradition, but neither Paul's nor Socrates' triumphalism is to be found in these later sources. Even Maimonides, the Jewish thinker who most clearly reflects the impact of Greek philosophical thinking on this issue, never claims that we should long for our death or rejoice at its immanence.

To this day, Jews are commanded never to hasten the process of dying. When death occurs, Jews bury the corpse as soon as possible. It is neither embalmed nor beautified. The body is washed, its hair is combed, and its nails are trimmed. It is "purified" by pouring water over it, reciting passages from Song of Songs.[10] It is clothed in shrouds and buried in a plain wood coffin so it may return to the dust in a thoroughly natural way. In the house of mourning, twice daily, Jews recite Psalm 49: "Man does not abide in honor; he is like the beasts that perish." That the later tradition insists that Jews recite this psalm, precisely in the house of mourning, even despite that tradition's claims about the afterlife, is stark testimony to the realistic nature of its view of death.

Nor is Jews' mourning attenuated. For seven days, they remain in their homes. They do not bathe, change their clothing, wear leather, or engage in sexual relations. Men do not shave. The mourners sit on the floor or on lowered chairs as the community comes to console them and join them in worship. For thirty days, or, for a parent, eleven months, they avoid public entertainment.[11]

Nor is the reality of death diminished even as one glimpses the afterlife to come. Precisely at the graveside, when the coffin has been lowered and covered with earth, Jews recite a form of the prayer known as the *kaddish* which vividly paints the totality of the eschatological scenario:

May God's great name be exalted and sanctified in the world which will be renewed, and where God will revive the dead and raise them to eternal life, and rebuild the city of Jerusalem and rebuild the Temple within it, and uproot alien worship from the earth, and return the worship of Heaven to its place, and where the Holy One will reign in sovereignty and splendor....[12]

This form of the *kaddish* is called the *kaddish d'itchadeta,* literally "the renewal *kaddish,*" because it speaks of God's forthcoming "renewal" of the world. It is one of the most powerful traditional texts on the age to come. The Jew is commanded to recite it precisely at the moment when he or she is most inclined to despair of any future beyond the grave.[13] The grave is covered and one returns home to mourning which is as real and as concrete as the death just encountered.

Judaism views every death as tragic. That remains part of the Jewish tradition even after Judaism came to affirm that it does not mark the end of our relationship to God, or of God's power to affect our ultimate destiny. It is only toward the very end of the biblical period that this overwhelming affirmation of the finality of death begins to be challenged, and at the outset, only in a very partial and elusive way. That the later tradition could literally stand these biblical sources on their head is striking testimony to Judaism's power to unearth new and strikingly original layers of meaning in ancient texts—that is, to the power of midrash.[14]

IV

JUDAISM ON THE AFTERLIFE:
THE EARLY SOURCES

That the death of each human being is final, that God has no power over our destiny after death, is the overwhelming testimony of the Bible. But as the biblical age drew to a close, two doctrines entered into Jewish writings which overturned that belief. One of these—that at some point in the future, God will raise at least some human bodies from their graves—is enunciated in three brief but striking biblical passages. The second—that the human body is mortal, but that every human possesses a soul which separates from the body at death and enjoys a continued existence with God—is not in the Bible. But it is explicit in a number of books written by Jews roughly between the second century BCE and the second century CE, commonly referred to as the intertestamental period.

These two doctrines eventually merge and form the core of a Jewish doctrine of the afterlife which becomes canonical in Judaism from the age of the Talmud to the dawn of modernity.

Only three biblical passages explicitly affirm that God will return at least some dead to life. Two of these are in Isaiah and the third is in Daniel. We begin with the Daniel passage because it is easier to date.

"THOSE THAT SLEEP IN THE DUST WILL AWAKE"

Daniel 12 is the climax of a unit (chapters 10–12) which includes a vision (10) and an oracle (11–12:4). The opening verse of chapter 10 dates what follows "in the third year of King Cyrus of Persia" (who reigned ca. 550-530 BCE). The author describes a vision of a celestial being who announces that he has come "to make you understand what will befall your people in the days to come" (10:14) and "what is recorded in the book of truth" (10:21).

The oracle which follows is an overview of the history of the Jews in the four centuries from Cyrus to the reign of Antiochus IV (175–164 BCE): The reign of four Persian kings will be followed by that of Alexander the Great whose kingdom will be divided after his death. All this is covered concisely in 11:2–4. A description of the conflicts between Alexander's successors, the "kings of the south" (the dynasty of the Egyptian Ptolemies) and the "kings of the north" (the dynasty of the Syrian Seleucids), is the prelude to a more detailed review of the reign of Antiochus IV, who is known to Jews as the villain of the Hanukkah story. The account of his rule occupies the remainder of the chapter (vv. 21ff), which concludes with an account of his death (v. 45).

Then follow the opening verses of chapter 12, arguably one of the most discussed passages in all Scripture:

> At that time, the great prince, Michael who stands beside the sons of your people, will appear. It will be a time of trouble, the like of which has never been since the nation came into being. At that time, your people will be rescued, all who are found inscribed in the book.

84

Many of those that sleep in the dust of the earth will awake, some to eternal life, others to reproaches, to everlasting abhorrence. And the knowledgeable will be radiant like the bright expanse of sky, and those who lead the many to righteousness will be like the stars forever. (12:1–3)

When Daniel asks for the meaning of these events, he is told enigmatically that "these words are secret and sealed to the time of the end" (v. 9). Nevertheless, he is reassured:

But you, go on to the end; you shall rest, and arise to your destiny at the end of the days.

This is the last verse of the book as a whole.

JOB'S EXPERIENCE WRIT LARGE

Dating this material is a relatively simple task. The text (10:1) informs us that the vision described in chapters 10–12 took place in the third year of the reign of Cyrus, that is, in the middle of the sixth century BCE. That is clearly a fictitious date, for it assumes that the entire oracle predicts events that will take place in the course of the four centuries that follow. The detailed review of the history of that interval, particularly of the reign of Antiochus IV, makes such an assumption highly unlikely.

Instead, we must conclude that this material was written by someone familiar with the history of that entire period. More important, that it was written by someone intimately familiar with the events of Antiochus IV's reign, for the detailed account of those events coincides neatly with our other sources on this period.[1] It coincides, that is, until we reach the very end of the chapter, 11:45, which describes Antiochus' death. Here, a discrepancy arises between this account and what we know of his death from our other sources. Antiochus died, not "between the sea and the beautiful holy mountain" (that is, between the Mediterranean Sea and Jerusalem), but rather in Persia, and his death took place in late 164 BCE. The author is apparently unaware of the precise site or date of his death, just as he is unaware of other events that took place in the last months of Antiochus IV's reign, the most dramatic of which was the rededication of the Temple under the Maccabees in late 164. Had the author known of this event, he would hardly have kept silent about it and the entire chapter would have ended on a much more triumphal note than it does.[2]

These final moments of Antiochus' reign are not recorded here because they had not yet occurred at the time of writing. We must conclude, then, that Daniel 10–12 was written in late 165 or early 164 BCE, and by someone who witnessed and probably participated in the tumultuous events of the day.

Jewish memory recalls Antiochus IV (who adopted the surname Epiphanes, "The God Made Manifest") as one of the great enemies of the Jews, and his reign as an unmitigated disaster for the Jewish people. The "persecutions of Epiphanes"—the desecration of the Temple, the prohibition of Mosaic law, and the coercion of Jews to perform pagan religious practices or be killed—have been indelibly etched into the consciousness of generations of Jews by the liturgy, which is recited countless times during Hanukkah:

> In the days of Mattathias son of Yohanan, the Hasmonean *kohen gadol* [High Priest] and his sons, a cruel power rose against Israel, demanding that they abandon Your Torah and violate Your commands. You, in Your great mercy, stood by Your people in time of trouble....[3]

The author of Daniel refers to this period as "a time of trouble, the like of which has never been since the nation came into being" (12:1). Indeed, these persecutions were unprecedented in the Jewish experience. Never before had pious Jews been martyred precisely because they were loyal to God and Torah. We know that the destruction of the Kingdom of Israel by Assyria and the events surrounding the destruction of Jerusalem and the Temple by Babylonia (586 BCE) must have cost countless Jewish lives, but the prophetic reading of those events understood them as punishment for Israel's sin. Hence they were justified and did not call God's justice into question. Now, however, pious Jews were being persecuted, precisely because of their piety.

So unprecedented were these events that Jewish historians have struggled to understand what impelled Antiochus to launch these persecutions. The Greeks were religious relativists, and were perfectly comfortable with the fact that every people worshipped its own god in its own way. Why then abolish Torah? To account for this departure from Hellenistic policy, the historian of antiquity Elias Bickerman suggests that, in fact, Antiochus merely complied with decrees that had been initiated by Jewish hellenizers who were determined to coerce the entire Jewish community to adopt Greek culture.[4]

Victor Tcherikover, another historian of the period, disagrees with Bickerman. His thesis, which is even more subversive of the Hanukkah story as it has been recited by Jews for generations, claims that the persecutions did not precede, but rather followed the Maccabean revolt. They constituted the king's punishment of the pious Jews who had rebelled against his rule in the name of Torah. If the Jews rebelled under the flag of Torah, then Torah must be abolished.[5]

Whichever one of these is true, it is clear that the Jewish experience at this time constituted a severe test of faith for the pious Jew. It was, in fact, the experience of Job, writ large. Job is the story of a man who suffered precisely because he was pious. Now, the land

87

was filled with countless Jobs whose suffering and martyrdom challenged God's justice, power and compassion. More important, the final words of the Book of Job provided little comfort. True, Job's fortunes were restored, but the theological message of the book, conveyed in God's addresses to Job out of the tempest at the end of the book, was that there was no explanation for the suffering of the pious, that God could not be held morally accountable for human suffering, precisely because God *was* God and totally beyond human moral reckoning.[6]

Nor was the classic theodicy of the Torah (as expounded, for example, in Deuteronomy 28:15–64) of any help, for it taught that suffering was invariably retribution for sin. But in this case, where was the sin? And to compound the problem, not only were the pious suffering, but the evildoers were thriving!

Theology does not exist in a vacuum. It always emerges from and always responds to the experiences of real human beings. Pious Jews, nurtured on the conviction that God is omnipotent, compassionate and just, and that God loves Israel and will never abandon it, could only despair about their fate. Why then be faithful to God? Why observe the commands of Torah? Why suffer martyrdom? Why indeed, if, as the overwhelming message of the Torah at that time taught, death marked the ultimate end of the human experience, of God's power over human destiny, and of the ability of human beings to reach God? Out of this historical matrix the doctrine of resurrection first emerges in Jewish consciousness.

DANIEL'S MESSAGE

The author of Daniel 10–12 was writing precisely for these pious Jews. In fact, he was also, as most theologians do, writing for himself. And he was writing at a time when the persecutions had not abated, when the revolt of the Maccabees had not as yet reached its

88

successful conclusion. That is why the pre-164 BCE dating of the chapter is important.

It is to these Jews that the author promises: "Many of those that sleep in the dust of the earth will awake, some to eternal life, others to reproaches, to everlasting abhorrence."

This passage is not concerned with the resurrection of masses of Jews, nor with the resurrection of all the dead, nor the dead of prior generations. Nor is the author concerned with the mechanics of resurrection. He is concerned only with those who died in the persecutions of his day. And he is concerned only and specifically with two groups of Jews, the "some" and the "others." These two groups are clearly the pious Jews who died as martyrs, and the evil-doers who died triumphant in their program of hellenization and persecution. This author is not even concerned with the middle group of Jews who stood by passively and did not engage in the struggle. It is only the Jewish activists and their evil opponents who now, or soon, will lie "in the dust of the earth." These two groups will arise from their graves. The first will be destined to eternal life, and the second, to eternal reproach and abhorrence.[7]

Here, the motive for resurrection is retribution; only incidentally is it a matter of God's power. At issue is God's justice. For some reason, God's justice has not manifested itself during the lifetime of these participants. But now, in sharp contrast to the overwhelming message of the biblical tradition, their life on earth is no longer the whole story. The frame which marks the parameters of a human life extends beyond death; God's justice will ultimately assert itself beyond the grave. This requires that the dead awaken and live again so that each group can receive its proper retribution: Eternal life or eternal reproach. Resurrection becomes the means whereby God's justice will ultimately triumph. A new revisionist, individualized eschatology is introduced to resolve the challenge of theodicy, the attempt to vindicate God's justice.[8] The new doctrine of resurrection vindicates God.

By using the word "awake" (in Hebrew, *yakitzu*) as a metaphor for resurrection, the author of Daniel explicitly repudiates other biblical texts which claim that the dead will never "awake." He repudiates, for example, Job 14:12:

> So man lies down never to rise;
> He will awake [*yakitzu*] only when the heavens are no more;
> Only then be aroused from his sleep.

Given the broader theological message of the Book of Job, the phrase "when the heavens are no more," is a poetic way of saying "never." He also repudiates Jeremiah 51:39 who insists that the evildoers will "sleep an endless sleep, never to awake [*yakitzu*]." This deliberate reference to earlier contradictory texts is a striking measure of the author's awareness that his vision constitutes a significant revolution in Jewish thought.

WHO WERE DANIEL'S TEACHERS?

The only other biblical texts that affirm the resurrection of the dead are two verses from Isaiah 25 and 26, part of a unit of the Book of Isaiah (chapters 24–27) called the Isaiah Apocalypse. This unit as a whole vividly describes the imminent judgement which God will visit upon the earth as a whole, the host of heaven, and the kings of the earth. God, Who will then be enthroned as God of all peoples, will vindicate Israel and destroy its enemies. Interspersed throughout this Apocalypse are songs celebrating God's victory. It concludes with a promise that Jews will be summoned with the sound of a ram's horn from the lands of their dispersion in Egypt and Assyria and gather to worship God in Jerusalem.

The references to resurrection in Isaiah occur as part of the prophet's description of God's last judgement. Within their immediate context, the passages are:

> ...He [God] will destroy on this mount the shroud
> That is drawn over the faces of all the peoples
> And the covering that is spread
> Over all the nations:
> He will destroy death [*mavet*] forever.
> My Lord God will wipe the tears away
> From all faces
> And will put an end to the reproach of His people
> Over all the earth... (25:7–8)

And:

> We were with child, we writhed—
> It is as though we had given birth to wind;
> We have won no victory on earth;
> The inhabitants of the world have not come to life!
> Oh, let Your dead revive!
> Let corpses arise!
> Awake and shout for joy,
> You who dwell in the dust!—
> For Your dew is like the dew on fresh growth;
> You make the land of the shades come to life. (26:18–19)

In contrast to the Daniel text, scholars are seriously divided on the dating of Isaiah 24–27, with speculation ranging from the seventh to the late second century BCE.[9] The issue of dating the Isaiah texts is important because it helps us understand which of our texts came first, which influenced the other, and more narrowly, just when the doctrine of resurrection first appears in Jewish writings. Dating these passages from the late second century would, of course, preclude their having influenced the author of Daniel.

The parallels between Daniel and Isaiah are clear. To take the most vivid example, Daniel's "many of those that sleep in the dust of the earth will awake" echoes Isaiah's "let corpses arise! Awake and shout for joy, you who dwell in the dust...." More generally, both passages deal with God's judgement of Israel's enemies, with the restoration of Israel's fortunes, the vindication of pious Jews and the punishment of Israel's oppressors. Both passages provide a setting and a justification for the theme of resurrection.

But a closer look at these texts reveals significant differences between the visions of resurrection in Daniel and Isaiah, and suggests that the author of Daniel 10–12 post-dates Isaiah and, further, that he knew and expanded the Isaiah material.

Daniel goes beyond Isaiah 26 in two specific ways. First, for Isaiah, resurrection is itself the vindication of God's justice and of the pious. For Daniel, resurrection is the means by which the righteous will gain their reward of eternal life, and evildoers, their punishment, everlasting abhorrence. Second, Isaiah promises only the resurrection of the righteous; Daniel envisions a resurrection of both the pious and their oppressors. Both of these details suggest that Daniel post-dates Isaiah.[10]

The word "abhorrence" (in Hebrew, *dera'on*) suggests yet another source for the author of Daniel, namely Isaiah 66:24, the only other occurrence of this word in Hebrew Scriptures:

> For as the new heaven and the new earth
> Which I will make
> Shall endure by My will...
> So shall your seed and your name endure.
> And new moon after new moon,
> And sabbath after sabbath,
> All flesh shall come to worship Me....
> They shall go out and gaze
> On the corpses of the men who rebelled against Me:

Their worms shall not die,
Nor their fire be quenched;
They shall be a horror [dera'on]
To all flesh. (Isaiah 66:22–24)

Scholars agree that the prophecies in Isaiah 40–66 are not
the work of the eighth century prophet called Isaiah. Some scholars further subdivide this unit, claiming that Isaiah 56–66 is the work
of yet a third author, the so-called Third Isaiah, distinguished from
the author of 40–55, who is usually called Second or Deutero-Isaiah.
Second Isaiah is consensually dated from the end of the Babylonian
and the beginning of the Persian period (the mid-sixth century BCE).
Whether or not Third Isaiah constitutes a unit distinct from 40–
55, whether it is even a distinct unit in the first place, and
consequently its precise date are still unresolved, though there is
somewhat of a consensus that much of Third Isaiah is somewhat
later than Second Isaiah, and dates from the end of the sixth to the
beginning of the fifth centuries BCE.[11]

Again, the theme of Isaiah 66 is God's vindication and restoration of Israel as part of a broader judgement which God will
bring upon the world as a whole (the "new heaven and the new
earth"). Again, all flesh will come to worship the God of Israel, and
again, God will judge the rebels and the oppressors of Israel. But
here there is no mention of resurrection. Instead, the punishment
will be that their corpses will not be buried, will rot in the sun, and
thus become an "abhorrence to all flesh."

THE DEATH OF DEATH?

For the author of Daniel, however, this punishment is not sufficient.
He has the persecutors resurrected as well so that God's punishment may be meted out to them while they are alive, even after they

93

had died. This notion of the resurrection of the evildoers is an indication that this author is familiar with Isaiah 66—and goes beyond it.[12]

Isaiah's evildoers are not Daniel's; the historical settings are clearly different. But Isaiah 66 provides Daniel with the notion that rebels against God will be ultimately punished and will become an "abhorrence to all flesh."

If Isaiah 25:8, "He will destroy death [*mavet*] forever," is taken literally, the claim would be a stunning anticipation of the final stage in the development of the doctrine of resurrection: God will not only resurrect the dead, but will also destroy the fact of death itself. Only much later in Jewish history was this further claim explicitly articulated. But what does the author mean by this reference to "death"? To understand it as an abstraction, as we moderns would, is quite contrary to biblical thought and language which never deals with abstractions of this kind. There are, for example, no biblical terms for "birth" or "creation."

For this reason, some scholars suggest that for this author, what will be destroyed is not death itself, but rather the kind of mass dying caused by warfare.[13] If so, it would be an extension of (First) Isaiah's eschatological vision (2:4) which describes how people will beat their swords into plowshares and spears into pruning hooks, and "never again know war."

Yet a third possible interpretation of this elusive verse suggests that in this passage, the Hebrew term *mavet,* "death," is neither an abstraction nor a reference to mass dying. Rather, it is a relic of the pagan god of the underworld, Mwt, who triumphed against Baal, the god of fertility, was later killed by Baal's sister and still later returned to life together with Baal.

Previously, we used this interpretation as one possible biblical explanation for the etiology of death, in which a personalized death appears as a vestige of an ancient pagan power, independent of God. In this context, then, our verse from Isaiah prophesies God's

94

ultimate triumph even over this independent power. Understanding the text in this way conveys essentially the same message as our first interpretation above: At some time in the future, God will destroy the very fact of death.

Another explicit reference to Deutero-Isaiah is preserved in Daniel 12:3. "And the knowledgeable will be radiant like the bright expanse of sky, and those who lead the many to righteousness will be like stars forever and ever." The "knowledgeable" (in Hebrew, *maskilim*) and "those who lead the many to righteousness" (in Hebrew, *matzdike ha-rabbim*) are obvious references to God's "servant" as described in the "Servant Songs" of Isaiah 49–53; the first term appears in 52:13, and the second in 53:11.

Precisely who is God's servant has been hotly debated by Bible scholars: Is the reference to an individual, or to a collective?[14] But the author's description of the career of the servant—that he is innocent, but suffers, is condemned and killed, yet will be ultimately vindicated—provided rich source material for the author of Daniel 10–12. He read these passages as applying to the events of his own day, and he understood Isaiah's "servant" to be the leaders of the pietistic movement who challenged Antiochus IV and the Jewish hellenizers. They will receive a distinctive reward, even more than that allotted to the "some" who will be resurrected for eternal life. That they will be "like stars" probably means that they will become angels.[15]

That the knowledgeable will be "radiant like the bright expanse of sky" has been preserved in the Jewish consciousness through its use in the *El Maleh Rahamim* ("Lord, All-Compassionate...") prayer that is recited at every Jewish funeral and at *Yizkor* (Memorial) services to this day. It now applies to all Jews.[16]

The author of Daniel 10–12, then, created an intricate midrash that incorporates familiar themes from earlier biblical texts and goes significantly beyond them.

95

CULTURAL BORROWING
OR INTERNAL DEVELOPMENT

But inquiring into the sources from which the author of Daniel drew must involve going beyond discovering earlier or contemporaneous biblical texts which he might have read. It is to ask an even more basic question: Where did the *idea* of resurrection come from? How did it get into the heads of these authors in the first place? What is its provenance?

An almost intuitive approach to these questions is to look at the literature of the cultures surrounding biblical Israel for some hint of the presence of this notion, and then to assume that it was later transmitted to Israel. On the afterlife, two ancient near-eastern cultures might qualify as the source for biblical thinking: Egypt and Persia. Ancient Egypt, which believed that the dead live on in the realm of Osiris, developed elaborate funerary rites to prepare the dead for the voyage to this realm. The problem here is that these Egyptian texts are significantly older (dating from the third millennium BCE) than the biblical material, that none of their details corresponds to the biblical account, and that there is no clear way to trace the process of transmission. Finally, and most important, these texts do not speak of a resurrection: They simply claim that the dead continue to enjoy a form of existence in the netherworld.

A Persian influence is more likely. Zoroastrian texts are closer in time to the Bible (from the ninth to the second century BCE), they speak of resurrection and, as in the Bible, their broader setting is one of judgement. Further, from the middle of the fifth century BCE on, Jews lived among Persians. If this is a case of cultural borrowing, the likely candidate would be Zoroastrianism.[17]

But it is equally conceivable that there was no cultural borrowing here at all, that the idea of resurrection evolved within Israel as a thoroughly natural development of ideas deeply planted in biblical religion from the outset. If, in fact, God created the world and humanity in the first place, if God is the ultimate force Whose power extends over all of nature and history, if God can send Israel into exile and then redeem it once again (from Egyptian slavery and in the time of Cyrus), if God can renew the natural cycle each year, if God can, as Isaiah 66 promises, create "a new heaven and a new earth," then why cannot God raise human beings from the grave? Why cannot God, in the words of Isaiah 25:8, "destroy death forever"? Why should God's power over one's fate end with death? Why is death more powerful than God?

The earlier strata of biblical religion could not contemplate human immortality, probably because that would muddy the distinction between God and human beings. But with the authors of Daniel and the Isaiah Apocalypse, the need for an alternative theodicy to those proposed in the Torah and in Job, the need to reconcile God's justice with God's power, served as the existential impetus for overturning the classical biblical message. No longer does death mark the end of the individual's destiny. God's power now extends beyond the grave.

Finally, one further note on just when the notion of an afterlife entered into Jewish consciousness. We claimed, above, that Daniel 12 must be dated to 165 BCE, its latest possible date. But could it have been significantly earlier? If we posit a Zoroastrian influence, that borrowing could have taken place as early as the late sixth century BCE. And if the notion represents a natural evolution within biblical religion, then what better setting for the emergence of a doctrine of an afterlife for the individual than one that has witnessed the national restoration of a supposedly dead people from their exile? The emergence of the doctrine would then coincide roughly with the prophecies of restoration in Second Isaiah (as in Isaiah 40) and in Third Isaiah as well (chapters 60–62). If this is the case, then Ezekiel 37's vision of the dry bones that come to life again can be understood as more than a metaphor for national regeneration. It could also mark the transition from concern for the destiny of the people to that of the individual.

There is no clear resolution of this issue, for it is also possible that a number of factors—the historical setting, theological impulses inherent in Jewish religion, and the need to resolve pressing existential issues relating to God's power and justice—all combined to extend the scope of Jewish thinking in this new and significant way.[18]

THE NEW INDIVIDUALISM

This breakthrough in understanding the ultimate destiny of the individual could never have taken place without another major revision within biblical religion: The full recognition that each human is recognized as an individual in the economy of God's salvation.

Again, the overwhelming testimony of much of biblical religion is that God's central concern relates to the destiny of the collective, to the Israelite community as a whole. The Pentateuch concentrates on the struggle between God and the community over God's wishes as articulated in the Sinai covenant. That same emphasis is implicit in prophetic historiography and in the historical books of the Bible (Joshua, Judges, and the two Books of Samuel, Kings, and Chronicles). Throughout this material, the focus is on the Israelite people as a whole and its relationship to God. The twists and turns of that relationship determine the course of Israelite history: Obedience is rewarded by material sustenance, peace, tranquility, and military victory; disobedience is punished with plague, famine and military defeat. The Bible rarely describes how Israel's fate as a people affects the lives of individual Israelites, for neither wholesale blessings nor plagues discriminate among individuals. They affect only the community as a whole.

The Bible does refer to certain individuals, but these are invariably the elite—kings, judges and prophets. They are rarely ordinary human beings and their equally ordinary personal life-experiences. There are two significant exceptions to this rule: A number of psalms clearly reflect the personal trials and triumphs of their largely anonymous authors; and of course, the Book of Job tells of one individual's tragic personal experience of apparently unjustified suffering. But these are exceptions to the broader biblical concerns.

One way to trace the emergence of God's new concern for the fate of the individual emerges in the evolution of the doctrine that punishment for the sins of parents will be visited upon their progeny. An explicit statement of that doctrine is in Exodus 34:6-7, in God's self-revelation to Moses following the sin of the golden calf. In response to Moses' request that God reveal God's ways to him, Moses is commanded to fashion new tablets to replace the ones that he had broken, and to await God's revelation. God then appears and proclaims:

> The Lord! the Lord! a God compassionate and gracious, slow to anger, abounding in kindness and faithfulness, extending kindness to the thousandth generation, tolerating iniquity, transgression, and sin;[19] yet He does not remit all punishment, but visits the iniquity of parents upon children and children's children, upon the third and fourth generations.

That God punishes children for the sins of parents is echoed in Exodus 20:5 and in Deuteronomy 5:9—the two versions of the Ten Commandments—with one significant change. In both of these texts, God punishes the third and fourth generation "of those who reject Me." The implication is that the transmission of punishment to children is not an absolute rule, but is rather conditional upon the behavior of those children.

That small change reflects a major revision in the doctrine as expressed in Exodus 34:6–7, for now God recognizes that the children of sinners are individuals in their own right whose fate is to be determined by their own behavior. But three later biblical texts proclaim the explicit overthrow of that earlier doctrine in its totality:

> Parents shall not be put to death for children, nor children for parents: a person shall be put to death only for his own crime. (Deuteronomy 24:16)

Jeremiah 31:29–30 echoes this revision, substituting "sin" for "crime":

> In those days, they shall no longer say, "Parents have eaten sour grapes and children's teeth are blunted." But every one shall die for his own sins: whosoever eats sour grapes, his teeth shall be blunted.

This view, proverb and all, is echoed almost *verbatim* in Ezekiel 18:2–4:

> What do you mean by quoting this proverb upon the soil of Israel, "Parents eat sour grapes and their children's teeth are blunted"? As I live—declares the Lord God— this proverb shall no longer be current among you in Israel. Consider, all lives are Mine; the life of the parent and the life of the child are both Mine. The person who sins, only he shall die.

God is now portrayed as relating to each human in terms of his or her own individual destiny. The stage is now set for the still later proclamation that God's power to shape that destiny extends beyond the death of the individual.

EXTRA-BIBLICAL PARALLELS

There are significant references to resurrection in the apocryphal and pseudepigraphal literature. These books date from roughly the second century BCE to the second century CE, and are not incorporated into the Jewish biblical canon, probably because of their late date, though many are included in some versions of the Christian canon.[20]

Some of these books testify that the notion of resurrection, which had been introduced by Daniel, had penetrated Jewish consciousness. They provide a bridge for the eventual emergence of a far more fully-developed theology of the afterlife in the literature of the talmudic rabbis from the first century CE and thereafter.

Though the precise dating of these texts is open to debate, some of these references could be roughly contemporaneous with Daniel.[21] Enoch 91:10 reads:

> Then the righteous one shall arise from his sleep, and the wise one shall arise; and he shall be given unto them (the people) and through him the roots of oppression shall be cut off. Sinners shall be cut off...

And Enoch 92:2 reads:

> The Righteous One shall awaken from his sleep; he shall arise and walk in the ways of righteousness...

Both texts use the metaphor of resurrection as awakening from sleep, familiar to us from Daniel 12:2, and both are set in the context of God's ultimate judgement of evildoers.

Much more vivid is the story of a mother and her seven sons recounted in II Maccabees 7. This book is dated about a century following Daniel 10–12.[22]

This story tells of the torture of seven brothers who, together with their mother, had refused to accept Antiochus' edicts against observing the Torah. Each brother speaks before he dies. Interspersed are two speeches by the mother. Four of these speeches, one of the mother's and three of the sons', deal with the subject's readiness to accept death because of God's promise of resurrection.

Thus the second son exclaims:

> "You, you fiend are making us depart from present life, but the King of the universe will resurrect us, who die for the sake of His laws, to a new eternal life." (7:9)

The third willingly puts forth his tongue and hands to be cut off because "I received these from Heaven, and...from Him I hope to receive them back." (7:11) The fourth son adds, in contrast to Daniel's belief that the evildoers too will be resurrected for eternal punishment, that though he will be resurrected, "you [the tyrant] shall have no resurrection unto life." (7:14)

Finally, the mother exclaims:

> "I do not know how you came to be in my womb. It was not I who gave you spirit and life.... Surely, then, the Creator of the universe, Who shaped man's coming into being....with mercy will restore spirit and life to you..." (7:22–23)

The mother here seems to be resorting to a logical argument: If God had the power to create human beings from the outset, presumably out of nothing, then God surely has the power to bring human beings who have once lived back to life again. The setting then is as in Daniel, one of retribution, but almost imperceptibly, the argument has moved beyond Daniel's concern for retribution to seeing resurrection as a manifestation of God's power.

II Maccabees departs from Daniel in one further respect. In Daniel, resurrection is the means for the ultimate vindication of the righteous. In II Maccabees, resurrection itself is the vindication; its views are then more closely aligned with those of the Isaiah 25-26 passages noted above.

Finally, several texts dating at least from the late first century CE go well beyond the Daniel text by anticipating a universal resurrection.

Fourth Ezra 7:32 echoes Daniel's metaphor of resurrection as awakening:

> The earth shall give up those who are asleep in it, and the dust those who dwell silently in it.

The Sibyline Oracles IV:180 echoes the fourth son's speech from II Maccabees:

> God himself will again form the bones and ashes of men, and he will raise up mortals again, as they were before. And then judgement will take place....

Finally, The Testament of Benjamin 10:6–8 goes still beyond all previous texts:

> Then you will see Enoch, Noah and Shem, and Abraham, Isaac, and Jacob rising on the right hand in gladness. Then we also shall rise, each over our tribe, worshipping the king of heaven.... Then all will rise, some to glory and some to dishonor....

The "some to glory and some to dishonor" is Daniel 12:2 again, but here resurrection is not limited to the victims and perpetrators of the persecutions of Antiochus. It extends at least to the elite of previous generations, and it will soon become completely universalized.

These are just a sampling of some of the references to resurrection in this body of literature.[23] They are, however, sufficient to indicate that at least from the middle of the second century BCE on, the doctrine of resurrection is in the air. And also that in significant ways, the scope of the doctrine has been expanded beyond the relatively narrow focus it receives in Daniel. We are well on our way to its far richer formulation in Talmudic literature.

RESURRECTION BECOMES UNIVERSALIZED

One further body of Jewish literature from this period might also reflect the spread of the doctrine of resurrection, the Dead Sea Scrolls. But there are few references to this doctrine in this material and most of these are ambiguous.[24] One text however, "The Messiah Apocalypse," dated between 100 and 80 BCE, includes a description of God's works which not only echoes a biblical description (Psalm 146:5–9) but also, by adding resurrection to the list, anticipates a parallel recitation that will appear in the rabbinic liturgy:

> He [God] frees the captives, makes the blind to see, and
> makes the bent over stand straight....
> For He will heal the sick, revive the dead, and give good
> news to the humble
> And the poor He will satisfy, the abandoned He will lead,
> and the hungry He will make rich....[25]

Resurrection is no longer reserved only for the pious and the evildoers alone, nor even for figures of the Jewish past. Now it is one of God's powers, extended in principle to everyone. So within two centuries, a revolutionary doctrine has become familiar and democratic. The rather limited resurrection envisioned by the author of Daniel 12, has been broadened even further to include all people.

Finally, though resurrection as retribution remains central to the theme, these texts clearly anticipate a significant theological shift which will become central in rabbinic literature. What is now being celebrated is not only the justice of God, but God's power, the final stage in the development of the monotheistic idea. Now, God is more powerful even than death.

THE IMMORTALITY OF THE SOUL

A second theory of the afterlife of the individual enters Judaism during the period that bridges the end of the biblical age and the emergence of rabbinic Judaism. This is the notion that every human being is composed of a material body and a non-material "soul"; that the soul, precisely because it is a spiritual substance, is indestructible; and that, at death, it leaves the body and enjoys eternal life in some supernal beyond.

This dualistic view of the human is not to be found in the Bible. We have seen that three Hebrew terms later came to be used to designate the human soul: *Nefesh, neshamah,* and *ruah.* But in the Bible, the first of these primarily means "neck" or "throat," then "blood" or "breath" (which passes through the neck or throat), and finally, by extension, an entity that has blood and breath, a "living being" (Exodus 1:5), even one who was previously living (Numbers 6:6). The second again typically designates "breath," or "one that breathes" (Psalm 150:6), and again by extension, a living being. The third usually means "wind" or "breath" and, in Job 34:14–15, is synonymous with *neshamah.* None of these signifies an entity such as the "soul" of the later tradition which is distinct from the body, and can then enjoy an existence independent of the body after death.

In the Bible itself, the human is not a composite of two distinct entities, but rather a single entity, a breathing, "living" clod of earth. And death is understood as the "going out" or dissipation from the body of the life-breath which originally, according to Genesis 2:7, God breathed into the clod of earth thus vivifying it. This life-breath has none of the qualities which later came to be identified with the soul: Awareness, a sense of self-identity and memory.

PLATO ON BODY AND SOUL

In contrast to the uncertainty regarding the provenance of the idea of bodily resurrection, the notion of the immortality of the soul clearly has its source in Greek philosophy and religion from as early as the sixth century BCE, and is even more fully developed in the writings of Plato in the late fifth to early fourth centuries BCE.

Plato's sharp body/soul distinction is but one of a number of dualisms that are identified with his thought. He distinguishes between the "really real" Forms or Ideas, and the concrete "particulars" that populate our everyday world; between sensation (which yields imperfect knowledge) and reason (which alone is the source of truth), hence between "belief" or "opinion" and true "knowledge"; and between the authentic life of the philosopher and the trivial life of most people. The philosopher seeks knowledge, while the common folk are satisfied with opinion.

For Plato, the soul is intrinsically immortal: It pre-exists the body in which it is later incarnated as if in a prison. If, during the life of the individual, the soul is nourished by philosophical activity, then it will anticipate death as its ultimate liberation and will enjoy an uninterrupted existence among the world of Forms.[26]

Plato's views on death and immortality are most sharply presented in his dialogue, *Phaedo*. The dialogue takes place just moments

106

before Socrates will die by drinking poison. When asked how he contemplates his imminent death, Socrates replies that the true philosopher has been pursuing death throughout his life; that the very act of philosophy is a dying; and that far from fearing death, he welcomes it as his ultimate reward.

That philosophy *is* dying refers to Plato's view that we attain truth only when our soul separates from our body and from our bodily senses, and enters into relation with the spiritual substances, the Platonic world of Forms, themselves immortal. In this view, the body is a source of pain, pleasure and desire which impede the search for truth, and our bodily senses are the source of error and misconception. To attain true knowledge, we must leave our body behind and let our soul enter the world of the true and ultimate realities, the world of Forms. This ultimate philosophical act is what philosophers are supposed to do all the time. In our lifetime, we achieve this only partially and fleetingly. After death, we may attain this goal forever. Hence:

> ...if this be true, there is great reason to hope that, going whither I go, when I have come to the end of my journey, I shall attain that which has been the pursuit of my life. And therefore I go on my way rejoicing, and not I only, but every other man who believes that his mind has been made ready and that he is in a manner purified.[27]

Philosophy, then, is more than an intellectual exercise. It is redemptive, the gateway to authentic existence and the source of ultimate and eternal reward.

This view—that humans are a composite of two entities, body and soul; the disparagement of bodily existence; the notion of death as welcome liberation; the promise that the soul is intrinsically immortal—has had an incalculable impact on the course of Western thought to our very own day, largely because it was later appropriated by Christianity.

By and large, Judaism never embraced this fully-developed dualism, though it did appropriate portions of it. It never embraced Plato's disparagement of the body or of bodily existence nor did it ever teach that the soul is intrinsically immortal. It never taught that death should be welcomed as liberation from the tensions of bodily existence. But eventually, in the talmudic tradition, it did teach that the human soul is a distinct entity, that it separates at death from the body and that it continues to enjoy an existence with God until the moment of resurrection when it rejoins the body and comes before God for judgement. Plato never embraced a doctrine that foretold the eventual return of the soul to the body. That would have been totally antithetical to his beliefs.

In Judaism, the one figure who did embrace a sharp anthropological dualism together with its implications for the doctrine of the afterlife was Maimonides. Maimonides concluded that though bodies will be resurrected, the ultimate destiny of the individual is for the soul alone. Maimonides was able to draw upon talmudic texts to authenticate his own views which were highly controversial in Jewish circles both in his own day and thereafter. However, the doctrine of spiritual immortality and of the soul's "journey" after death became central in Jewish mysticism, and was embraced in the modern age by liberal thinking Jews who found it infinitely more palatable than the doctrine of bodily resurrection.

THE WISDOM OF SOLOMON ON THE IMMORTALITY OF THE SOUL

One apocryphal book reflects this hellenistic dualism: The Wisdom of Solomon, commonly believed to have been written in Alexandria toward the middle of the first century CE by a thoroughly hellenized Jew. It is composed as a discourse condemning the godless for their hedonism and their persecution of the righteous, and spurring the righteous on to godly behavior.[28]

Of the evildoers' attack on the righteous, the author states,

> They were ignorant of God's mysteries;
> they entertained no hope that holiness would have its
>   reward,
> and passed up the prize of unblemished souls.
> But God created man for immortality,
> and made him an image of his own proper being;
> it was through the devil's envy that Death entered into
>   the cosmic order,
> and they who are his own experience him. (2:22–24)

Note that the author's claim that "God created man for immortality" is a clear departure from Plato for whom the soul is intrinsically immortal. Note also that the soul is an "image" of God's own being, a reference to the "image of God" in which, according to Genesis 1:27, God created man. Maimonides will later echo this interpretation of the Genesis verse. Finally, note that for this author, God did not create death. Death is the work of Satan who, out of envy, induced Adam to disobey God and be punished by death.

But for the author of The Wisdom of Solomon, the righteous are immune from death:

> But the souls of the just are in God's hand,
> and torment shall in no way touch them.
> In the eyes of the foolish they seemed to be dead;
> their end was reckoned as suffering
> and their journey utter ruin.

But they are at peace.
For even if in the sight of men they shall have been
    punished,
their hope is full of immortality. (3:1–4)

For this author, rewarding the righteous does not require
resurrection. In fact, the doctrine of bodily resurrection is nowhere
in this book. Instead, the souls of the righteous are in God's hands
in their lifetimes because of their deeds. After their death, they may
seem to be dead, but only their bodies have died. Their souls are
immortal and "are at peace." God does not have to do anything
now as would have been the case were there to be a resurrection
because the soul is intrinsically immortal unless it associates with
Satan and death. God did everything that needed to be done at the
outset by creating the immortal human soul. Immortality is a present
acquisition for the righteous.

The righteous may suffer in their lifetimes, but this is simply
God's way of purifying them while preparing them for their ultimate vindication:

In the moment of God's gracious dispensation they will
    blaze forth,
and like sparks in the stubble they will fly in all
    directions,
They will judge nations and hold sway over peoples,
and the Lord shall be their sovereign for all eternity.
    (3:7–8)

What we have here is an intricate blending of Platonic and
more classically biblical doctrines. From Plato, the author of The
Wisdom of Solomon takes his body/soul dualism and a mild disparagement of the physical body: "for a perishable body weighs down
the soul and this tent of clay encumbers a mind full of cares" (9:15).

From Plato also comes the notion that the soul is the "real" person; that only the body dies and the soul is the source of human immortality.

But there is no hint here that death is to be welcomed. For this author, the gateway to immortality is not philosophy, but righteous living—a concept that is clearly biblical in its origin. What is redemptive is not acquiring authentic knowledge as in Plato, but rather obeying God's will. There is also no echo of Plato's notion that the soul is immortal because of its very nature; rather, it is immortal because that is the way God created it. Finally, the grand eschatological event in which God and the immortal righteous will be vindicated and judge the nations echoes similar eschatological judgement scenes in Daniel 12 and Isaiah 66. The details are much more vague than in the biblical texts and the author's existential situation is never as sharply delineated as it is in Daniel. Nor is there any hint as to when and how this grand event will take place. Despite the absence of any notion of bodily resurrection, this author's biblical roots are obvious.[29]

Coupling a dualistic notion of the human together with the doctrine of spiritual immortality is found elsewhere in these early sources, such as in the writings of a contemporary of the author of The Wisdom of Solomon, Philo of Alexandria, whose work foreshadowed Maimonides' later attempt to harmonize Torah and Greek philosophy. Though Philo's writings were highly influential in non-Jewish circles, he was totally unknown to Jews until the Renaissance.[30] Dualism and spiritual immortality are also reflected in other texts from this period[31] and in Josephus' (somewhat later) version of the beliefs of the Essenes, a second- to first-century BCE Jewish school that may have produced the Dead Sea Scrolls.[32] In time, in the writings of Maimonides for example, and much later with the dawn of Jewish modernity in the eighteenth century, the doctrine of spiritual immortality will overshadow that of bodily resurrection and become the heart of Jewish thinking on the afterlife.

These two doctrines—bodily resurrection and spiritual immortality—seem to have entered Judaism independently. There is no evidence that the author of Daniel knew of spiritual immortality, nor that the author of The Wisdom of Solomon knew of bodily resurrection. In fact, the two doctrines could be viewed as contradictory: The first attributes afterlife to the body; the second, to the soul. The first says nothing about the soul; the second ignores the destiny of the body. In the later tradition, however, the two doctrines merge, and in this form, remain a centerpiece of Jewish eschatology into the modern age.

V

THE CANONIZATION OF A DOCTRINE

THREE CENTURIES AFTER Daniel, the doctrine of resurrection has become authoritative Jewish teaching. The Mishnah—compiled about 200 CE—reads:

> All Israelites have a share in the age to come [not, as commonly translated, "world to come"][1] as it is said, "Your people also shall be all righteous, they shall inherit the land forever; the branch of my planting, the work of my hands, that I may be glorified." (Isaiah 60:21)[2]

> And these are the ones who have no portion in the age to come: He who says, the resurrection of the dead is a teaching that does not derive from the Torah, and the Torah does not come from heaven, and an Epicurean.[3] (*Mishnah Sanhedrin* 10:1)

With the exception of tractate *Avot* (which is commonly called

"Ethics of the Fathers"), the Mishnah rarely deals with matters of belief. It is a compendium of laws stemming both from Scripture and the oral tradition, the most comprehensive and the most authoritative such code to be compiled after the Bible. It deals with behaviors, not beliefs. The doctrines listed in the mishnah cited above are not dogmas in the strict sense of the term: Binding beliefs that must be embraced for one to become a member of a religious community. No one suggests that a Jew who does not accept these notions is not a Jew.[4] Nevertheless, they represent one of very few instances (Maimonides' Thirteen Principles is another) where a Jewish text or author comes close to prescribing such a set of beliefs.

But even if we read this text more narrowly, as simply indicating that one who does not believe that the doctrine of resurrection derives from the Torah will not enjoy its rewards, the fact that the Mishnah gives this notion such unusual and significant standing testifies to its impact.

Our commonly used text of the Mishnah stipulates that the required belief is not simply resurrection itself—that seems to be beyond question—but rather that resurrection is derived "from the Torah." But, as we have seen, resurrection is not derived from the Torah, at least not explicitly. However, some manuscripts of the Mishnah omit this latter phrase, and read simply: "He who says there is no resurrection of the dead, and [he who says that] the Torah is not from heaven, and an Epicurean."[5] This latter reading may reflect an older tradition that questioned the doctrine of resurrection itself and may have caused the Mishnah to emphasize its centrality. If this is so, then our text may reflect a later stage when what was questioned was not the doctrine itself, but its textual basis in the Bible.

By the end of the second century CE, the doctrine of resurrection has achieved a singular significance within the ensemble of rabbinic beliefs. This evolution is especially striking since it has only the flimsiest of textual support in the Bible and is, in fact, explicitly denied by multiple passages in the Bible itself. How did this occur?

We have traced the first stages of this evolution in various texts composed in the period following the composition of Daniel. Another strand lies in the ideology of the Pharisees.

THE PHARISEES ON THE AFTERLIFE

Of the Pharisees, three facts are clear. First, they are commonly assumed to have emerged on the stage of history in the second half of the second century BCE. Second, they played a significant role in bridging biblical religion and the talmudic tradition, and hence in shaping what we now identify as the religion of the rabbis. And third, there is little conclusive textual or historical evidence about the origins of that group, its later career, and its distinctive ideology.[6]

There are three sources of information about the beliefs of the Pharisees: The writings of the Jewish-Roman historian of antiquity, Josephus (39–100 CE), in his two major books, *Wars of the Jews* (83–84 CE) and *Antiquities of the Jews* (93–94 CE); the Christian Gospels (which also date from the last decades of the first century CE); and rabbinic sources (most of which date from the second to the sixth centuries CE). In other words, all our sources date to at least two centuries after the Pharisees are thought to have attained a distinctive identity. This accounts for our summary judgement on all of these sources: They agree on the major teachings of the first century CE Pharisees, but tell us little of which we can be certain about their second to first century BCE predecessors.

JOSEPHUS ON THE PHARISEES

At various points in his writings, Josephus describes three Jewish schools of thought which existed in the last decades of the second century BCE: Sadducees, Pharisees and Essenes. Josephus' descriptions of the beliefs of the Pharisees should be read with caution because, as we have just noted, he was writing about the beliefs of a group of Jews which existed roughly two centuries earlier. How accurate is his information? He may have been reading data from his time back into the earlier period. We must also question his objectivity: He was writing in Rome for a Roman audience and he may have been swayed by his own political interests. But Josephus is one of the very few sources we have for details on this period.[7]

In *Antiquities of the Jews*, Josephus describes the Pharisees as promoting the notion of a tradition, parallel to the written Torah, which was transmitted by a "continuous succession of fathers," and which propounds certain laws not written in Scripture. He contrasts this belief with that of the Sadducees who affirm that only the laws in Scripture are authoritative. He adds that while the Sadducees are influential among "the rich," the Pharisees "have the multitude on their side" (13:10:6).[8]

In later rabbinic literature, this notion of a tradition that is independent of Scripture came to be identified as the *Torah She-b'al Peh*, the "Oral Torah." This was also believed to have been revealed to Moses by God at Sinai and is as authoritative as Scripture.

On Pharisaic beliefs about the afterlife, Josephus reports:

> Their belief is that souls have a deathless vigor, and that beneath the earth there are rewards and punishments according as they have been devoted in life to virtue or vice. For the latter everlasting imprisonment is prescribed; but the former shall have the power to revive and live again; on account of which doctrines they are able to persuade greatly the body of the people.... (18:1:3)

In contrast, Josephus reports that "the doctrine of the

Sadducees is...that souls die with the bodies" (18:1:4); and as for the Essenes, "they teach the immortality of souls" (18:1:5).

For Josephus, the Pharisees appropriated doctrines from traditions that were not explicitly Scriptural, they promoted the doctrine of an afterlife for the individual, and they won the loyalty of the masses. An admittedly imaginative integration of these doctrines might suggest that precisely because they accepted the authority of non-Scriptural traditions, they were able to adopt the doctrine of an afterlife (which, as we have seen, is not explicitly in the Torah) as authoritative. Finally, this doctrine helped them win the loyalty of the masses. However suggestive this reconstruction may be, it is not explicitly documented in our sources.

In *Wars of the Jews*, Josephus reports that the Pharisees believe

> that all souls are incorruptible; but that the souls of good men are only removed into other bodies, but that the souls of bad men are subject to punishment. (2:8:14)

And he adds that the Sadducees

> also take away the belief of the immortal duration of the soul, and the punishments and rewards in Hades. (2:8:14)

Finally to the Essenes, Josephus ascribes a thoroughgoing Platonism. Their doctrine is

> that bodies are corruptible, and that the matter they are made of is not permanent; but that the souls are immortal and continue forever;...and are united to their bodies as in prisons...; but that when they are set free from the bonds of the flesh, they then, as released from a long bondage, rejoice and mount upward. (2:8:11)

Josephus explicitly identifies this doctrine as "like the opinion of the Greeks." The few ambiguous references to the afterlife in the Dead Sea Scrolls, commonly believed to have emerged from the Essene community, generally confirm Josephus' version of their belief.[9]

Josephus seems to be defining three alternative positions: The Sadducean denial of the afterlife; the Essene affirmation of a pure Platonic belief in the immortality of the soul; and a middle position which is identified with the Pharisees, and which seems to combine elements of bodily resurrection and spiritual immortality.

The noted historian of antiquity Elias Bickerman evaluates the accomplishments of the Pharisees this way:

> The Pharisees...adopted the Hellenistic doctrine of resurrection, but subsumed it under the principles of the Torah. What to the pagans was an event dictated more or less by necessity, appears among the Jews as the working of the free will of God....[A]mong the Pythagoreans each soul must automatically return to new life after death, each according to its merit. For this fateful and continually operative necessity, the Pharisees substituted the single event of the the Last Judgement, whose day and scope God would determine, and so dovetailed the new Hellenistic idea into the structure of biblical ideas. In its new form the adopted doctrine of resurrection developed into a characteristic element of Jewish belief; it became, with biblical monotheism, its central doctrine.[10]

This is one of a number of claims Bickerman makes to support his broader, somewhat startling thesis that the genius of Maccabean Hellenism rests, not as commonly believed in resisting the onslaughts of hellenistic culture, but rather in knowing what, when and how to assimilate ideas and institutions from that culture, robbing them of their poison and then integrating them into the teachings of Torah.[11]

Bickerman's thesis notwithstanding, what Josephus records is a late-first-century CE historian's version of what a Jewish group from over two centuries earlier believed. By Josephus' time, all three of these groups had disappeared. The Essenes and the Sadducees vanished after the destruction of the second Temple at the hands of Rome in 70 CE, and the Pharisees had become one strand of a broader coalition that formed what we now identify as the rabbinic or talmudic tradition.[12] Is Josephus describing early Pharisaism or rather, as is more likely, that of their successors which he then attributes to their predecessors as well?

Further, even if Josephus' historical reconstruction is accurate, what precisely did the early Pharisees believe about the afterlife? Clearly, they believed in a doctrine of the immortality of the soul. That is recorded in all our sources. But Josephus is far less clear on bodily resurrection. This might reflect Josephus' own predilections as a thoroughly hellenized Jew. Our Josephus texts suggest that the Pharisees combined the doctrine of immortality of souls with Daniel's notion of resurrection. In its "judaized" form, the resurrection "event," brought about, as Bickerman underlines, through God's power and judgement, not simply through natural processes, will be twofold: Bodies will be raised from the grave and then joined once again with their immortal souls.

Further, since Josephus draws a sharp contrast between the beliefs of the Pharisees and those of the Essenes and ascribes to the latter an unambiguously Platonic doctrine of spiritual immortality, we may assume that the Pharisees differed from this latter group by also insisting on bodily resurrection. They also differed from the Sadducees who denied any form of afterlife.

In the chapter preceding, we noted that the two doctrines of bodily resurrection and spiritual immortality entered Judaism at different times and by separate routes, and that early sources emphasize one doctrine to the exclusion of the other. In time, these two doctrines merged. But when did this conflation occur? It is clearly present in our later (200–500 CE) talmudic sources. But if Josephus is correct, it is present at least in the late first century CE, if not earlier.

The Pharisaic doctrine differs from the Greek notion of immortality in one other significant way. In Plato, immortality is achieved through authentic knowledge gained by philosophical activity. For the Pharisees, it is achieved by living a life of virtue, which is defined by obeying God's revealed law. We saw the beginnings of this "judaization" of Plato in The Wisdom of Solomon, roughly half a century before Josephus' writings.

THE PHARISEES IN THE GOSPELS

Our second significant source of information about the beliefs of the Pharisees comes from the Gospels. These sources are contemporaneous with Josephus. (The Synoptic Gospels—Matthew, Mark and Luke—date from roughly 70–100 CE, and John, somewhat later.) In contrast to Josephus, the authors of these texts are not interested in the beliefs of the early Pharisees but rather of the Pharisees of Jesus' time who lived several decades before they wrote their works. Again, two words of caution when using these texts. We can never be confident that their attribution of statements or narratives to the historical Jesus are authentic. Also, we must never forget that these are polemical documents, not dispassionate historical accounts of the life and career of Jesus of Nazareth. They are designed, primarily, to announce a new vision of salvation that can be obtained by faith in Jesus' vicarious death and resurrection.[13]

These texts confirm Josephus' reading of pharisaic teaching about resurrection and clearly identify Jesus with the Pharisees and their doctrine. According to Mark 12:18–27 and Matthew 22:23–33, when the Sadducees challenged Jesus on the doctrine, he responds with his own imaginative proof-text for the source of the doctrine in the Torah. Quoting Exodus 3:6 which identifies God as "the God of Abraham, the God of Isaac and the God of Jacob," Jesus comments: "He is God not of the dead, but of the living; you are quite wrong" (Mark 12:27). Since God is the God "of the living" and of the patriarchs, that must mean that the patriarchs still live, even though they have physically died. To Jesus, then, the Torah teaches resurrection. We will see that the rabbis used equally imaginative interpretations to prove the same point.

Finally in Acts 23:6–7 (also about 100 CE), Jesus' apostle Paul is quite explicit: "I am a Pharisee, a son of Pharisees; I am on trial concerning the hope of the resurrection of the dead."[14]

According to the Gospels, then, Jesus identifies himself with the Pharisees of his day, but as in Josephus, these texts tell us nothing about the beliefs of the Pharisees who existed in the decades following the composition of Daniel.

RABBINIC SOURCES ON THE PHARISEES

As to the evidence from rabbinic sources, the men whose teachings are recorded in talmudic literature nowhere identify themselves as members of a school. After the destruction of the Temple in 70 CE, the Pharisees redesignated themselves as "rabbis," advocating one of several "Judaisms" that competed for authority within the Jewish community. A central belief in their reading of Judaism is a composite doctrine of the afterlife which includes both bodily resurrection and spiritual immortality. Only by the end of the seventh century CE did what we now identify as rabbinic/talmudic Judaism become mainstream. But while it would be historically questionable to view the Judaism of the rabbis as flowing directly from Pharisaism, any listing of rabbinic beliefs, the belief in an afterlife among them, includes what we know of Pharisaic teachings from other sources.[15]

Only one enigmatic source purports to give the history of the origins of the Sadducees and Boethusians (a mysterious group whose existence is reported only in rabbinic sources), and it asserts that these groups "broke away from the Torah" because they had erroneously concluded that there is no resurrection of the dead.[16]

So, despite enormous gaps in our data, it is possible to draw a line connecting our late biblical (Daniel) and apocryphal (II Maccabees and The Wisdom of Solomon) sources with the beliefs of the later (post-200 CE) rabbis. The only possible known connecting link between these is the Pharisees. Of this school, its later (first-century CE) representatives are reported to believe in some combination of bodily resurrection and spiritual immortality. That their first-century BCE predecessors also believed this is not explicitly documented; that is one of the more significant gaps in our data for it precludes an easy transition from Daniel to the later period. It is also clear that the doctrine was controversial and that other schools sharply challenged it.

GOD REVIVES THE DEAD:
THE *GEVUROT* BENEDICTION OF THE *AMIDAH*

An echo of the dispute between Pharisees and Sadducees regarding resurrection can be heard in a text that has had a far greater impact on the later tradition and on Jewish consciousness than any passage yet referred to: The second benediction from the *Amidah*, the prayer recited while "standing," more commonly called the *Sh'moneh Esre*, the "Eighteen" (Benedictions) in its weekday version, or more technically, simply *T'fillah*, "prayer."[17]

In the form currently found in the traditional prayer book, the text reads:

You are eternally mighty, O Lord. You revive the dead; great is Your power to save.

(You make the wind to blow and the rain to fall.)[18]

You sustain the living with compassion; You revive the dead with abundant mercy. You support the falling, heal the ailing, free the captive; and maintain faith with those who sleep in the dust. Whose power can compare with Yours, who is comparable to You O King Who brings death and restores life and causes salvation to sprout!

You are faithful to restore life to the dead. Praised are You, Lord, Who restores life to the dead.[19]

The centrality of this passage to Jewish consciousness cannot be overestimated. To this day, it is recited at least three times daily, every single day of the year, in the traditional worship service.

On the origins of the *Amidah* as a whole, the evidence is confusing. Some traditions locate its origins with the Men of the Great Assembly, an assembly of Jewish notables which dated anywhere from the middle of the fifth to the beginning of the second centuries BCE and of which very little is known.[20] Another tradition claims that a man by the name of Simon the Flaxworker "formulated the eighteen benedictions in the presence of Rabban Gamaliel in the proper order in Yavneh" (Bab. Talmud, *Megillah* 17b). Yavneh was the site of the reconstituted Jewish self-government following the destruction of the Temple in 70 CE, and Rabban Gamaliel succeeded Rabban Yohanan ben Zakkai, the founder of the Yavneh community, as its *Nasi* or Patriarch, the acknowledged head of the Jewish community. This would date our text from the last decades of the first century CE. But the early date is probably too early, and the later date is probably too late.

The issue of dating rests on determining what precisely it is that one is trying to date: The text as we have it today? An earlier version or versions of individual benedictions? The thematic structure as a whole? The "proper order" of the benedictions as in our reference above? The *Amidah* as we know it today is a long and intricately worded text. It is unlikely that the entire *Amidah* was formulated at one time. We must also distinguish between the process of formulating the order and the themes of the benedictions on one hand, and canonizing a specific wording to be used for each on the other. To this very day, different versions of specific benedictions can be found in different liturgical traditions.

In the case of our text, the key is the oft-repeated (six times, if we include the reference to "maintaining faith with those who sleep in the dust"—clearly a reference to Daniel 12:2) claim that God revives the dead. That repetition must reflect a date later than Daniel (post-165 BCE), but also a time when the doctrine was still controversial since if the doctrine were universally accepted, why repeat it so often? We repeat ourselves when we feel we are not being listened to, or when contradictory voices are being raised, or when what we say meets with opposition.

In dating at least the substance of this text, and probably its place in the overall structure of the *Amidah* (though not necessarily its precise final wording), we are led, then, to the period when controversy brewed between Pharisees and Sadducees. This was probably the late first century BCE or early first century CE. In fact, Louis Finkelstein suggests that introducing this doctrine into the liturgy was a political gesture by the Pharisees to ensure that whoever led the community in prayer would be an authentic Pharisee.[21] It is equally possible that the references to resurrection in our version of the benediction were inserted into an earlier text that dealt simply with God's other mighty works listed there.

Daniel 12:2 is in this text and so is Isaiah 26:19. Isaiah's phrase *yehayu metecha* ("let your dead live") becomes the characterization of God as *mehaye hametim* ("...Who restores life to the dead"). In the later tradition, the technical term for the doctrine itself is *t'hiyat hametim* ("the resurrection of the dead").

The name assigned to this liturgical unit as a whole is *Gevurot*, taken from the second word of the text which describes God as *gibor*, "mighty." It recites instances of God's mighty works, and its form reflects a similar (and sometimes parallel) passage in Psalm 146:5–8:

> Happy is he who has the God of Jacob for his help,...
>   maker of heaven and earth,
>   the sea and all that is in them...
>   who secures justice for those who are wronged,
>   gives food to the hungry.
> The Lord sets prisoners free;
>   The Lord restores sight to the blind;
>   the Lord makes those who are bent stand straight;
>   the Lord loves the righteous;
>   The Lord watches over the stranger;
>   He gives courage to the orphan and widow,
>   but makes the path of the wicked tortuous.

Our liturgist knew this psalm and used it as a model for his own work. Yet, because he found the biblical list of God's works too limited, he updated and amplified it by introducing the notion that God also revives the dead. This is another instance of Bickerman's thesis on the use of traditional forms as a vehicle to introduce radically new doctrines.

RESURRECTION BECOMES CANONICAL

By introducing this doctrine into the central portion of the liturgy which rabbinic law mandated Jews to recite daily, our liturgist has accomplished another notable purpose: He has accorded it canonical status. This is a central feature of rabbinic liturgy as a whole: It can be studied as the locus for the authoritative system of Jewish belief. From this date on and for centuries thereafter, every worshipping Jew would proclaim daily that God revives the dead; in the modern era, when Jews ceased believing this doctrine, the liturgy had to be changed.

Our liturgist has also gone beyond Daniel's notion that resurrection is a matter of retribution. He is interested only in God's power. The passage begins with the words *ata gibor,* "You are mighty." The entire liturgical unit is named *Gevurot,* "[God's] mighty works." True, the list as a whole, both in Psalm 146 and in the liturgy, implies retribution. Each item is an instance of reversal. What is now becomes its opposite: The blind see, the hungry have food, the falling stand, the ill are healed, the captives are freed. And the dead live again. Through God's unlimited power, all wrongs can be righted. But retribution is the subtext of the passage; its explicit message is God's power.

If Psalm 146 was indeed the model for our liturgical text, we may be able to solve one of its more puzzling features. In Isaiah 26:19, the phrase is *yehayu metecha* ("let your dead revive!") referring to some event in the future, but our liturgist transposes it into the present tense: *Mehaye hametim.* This transposition may reflect some subtle theological point about the time and nature of the resurrection. More simply, the liturgist may simply have used the model of the psalmist who lists all of God's works in the present tense, indicating that God simply has the power to do all these things, irrespective of when they will actually be done.

If God has the power to do all these things, then resurrection can never be limited to certain groups of Jews. As the mishnah in *Sanhedrin* claims, "All Israel has a share in the age to come." We have gone far beyond Daniel's concern with the resurrection only of the pietists and the evildoers of his age. That further step is the inevitable implication of the move from resurrection as a statement about God's justice to one of God's power, for now even those whose earthly rewards matched their virtue will be resurrected as well.

The mishnaic phrase "All Israel..." also includes all Jews who have ever lived and who will ever live. That expansion was demanded by the sense of Jewish solidarity throughout the generations. Why should previous generations of Israel not share in this triumph of God's power? Again, the liturgical use of this mishnah underlines its importance, for it is recited every Sabbath afternoon during the summer months as a prelude to studying tractate *Avot* between the afternoon and evening worship services.

The phrase "You cause the wind to blow and the rain to fall," which is in parentheses because it is recited only between Sukkot and Passover, the season of rain in Palestine, is introduced at this point in line with mishnah *B'rachot* 5:2, "We mention the 'power of rain' in the benediction of Resurrection." That association is not accidental; it suggests that a model for the resurrection of the dead can be found in God's renewal of the natural cycle.

Finally, though the text seems to reflect a setting when the doctrine of resurrection was still controversial, by the time of the Mishnah that controversy had died. Or had it? One could also claim that the very fact that the Mishnah lists this doctrine as quasi-dogmatic may suggest that it needed reinforcement, that it was still being questioned. But then, what about the doctrine of the divine origins of the Torah, which is also one of the doctrines required for enjoying a share in the age to come? That doctrine was surely not controversial, yet it is there.

Still this uncertainty may explain the two versions of the mishnah text noted above. In our text, the issue is not resurrection itself which is assumed, but rather its textual basis in the Torah. The alternate version which omits the phrase "derived from the Torah" may, as we noted above, reflect an earlier time when the basic issue itself was still under dispute.

127

IS RESURRECTION IN THE TORAH?

While the doctrine of resurrection does not appear in the Torah other than in the passages in Daniel and Isaiah, there is a very strong theological foundation for that teaching in the central doctrines of biblical religion. It was implicit in biblical monotheism and simply needed the proper historical setting to emerge.

This distinction between text and theology is very much a modern invention. The talmudic rabbis knew no such distinction. That the mishnah in *Sanhedrin* insists that one must believe the doctrine to be derived from the Torah reflects the later tradition's determination to read that teaching back into specific passages in the text of the Torah. Religious authorities rarely seek to portray themselves as revolutionaries; they prefer to present their original teachings as rooted in ancient ones, thus assuring their authenticity and facilitating their acceptance.

In our case, the Talmud records a number of attempts to ground resurrection in biblical texts. One is more fanciful than the other, simply because the doctrine is not really in the text. Not surprisingly, both the Daniel and Isaiah texts are used. But what is surprising is that they do not seem sufficient in and of themselves, probably because they are not from the Pentateuch which was considered supremely authoritative. This leads the rabbis into such exercises as:

> R. Meir said, Whence do we know resurrection from the Torah? From the verse, *Then shall Moses and the children of Israel sing this song unto the Lord* (Exodus 15:1). Not *sang* but *shall sing* is written: thus resurrection is taught in the Torah. (Bab. Talmud, *Sanhedrin* 91b)

Or this one:

Raba said, Whence is resurrection derived from the Torah? From the verse, *May Reuben live and not die* (Deuteronomy 33:6) meaning, *may Reuben live,* in this world, *and not die,* in the next. (*Sanhedrin* 92a)

Rabbi Simai taught that there is not a single weekly Torah portion that does not refer to the doctrine of resurrection—if only we had the ability to see it there.[22] When the Sadducees challenged Rabban Gamaliel to prove that resurrection is in the Torah, he cited passages from each of the three units that comprise Scripture: The Pentateuch, the Prophets and the Writings. Not surprisingly, his text from the Prophets is Isaiah 26:19. His pentateuchal text is *"And the Lord said to Moses, 'You are soon to lie with your fathers, and will rise'"* (Deuteronomy 31:16). As the Sadducees quite properly responded, the clear meaning of the verse is not that Moses will rise, but rather, as the conclusion of the verse indicates, that *"your people will rise and go astray after the alien gods."*[23] His text from the Writings, a reference to "sleepers" in Song of Songs 7:10 (not from Daniel 12 as we might have expected), is even more inventive (Bab. Talmud, *Sanhedrin* 90b).

One of my teachers used to remind his students that when a rabbinic argument quotes numerous texts to prove a point, it is clear that none of them by itself is adequate. The hope is that the accumulation of texts will convince. But numerous weak proofs remain an assemblage of weak proofs. They do not together make one convincing proof. If there were one such convincing proof, it alone would be cited.[24]

If anything, the defensive nature of this exercise reflects the fact that, apart from Daniel and Isaiah, the rabbis could not find the doctrine in the Torah, but felt that they must. They understood Torah, Scripture and also the oral Torah, to form one coherent document, all of it the explicit word of God. They did not believe in historical development since an unchanging God does not evolve.

The same with God's teachings.

To be authoritative the doctrine had to be traced back to God's word as delivered at Sinai. If it did not seem to be there, Rabbi Simai notes, that was only because of the blindness of the reader, not because of any inadequacy of the text. Therefore, every effort had to be expended to show that it was indeed there. This underlines the import of the Pharisaic conviction, disputed, as Josephus records, by the Sadducees, that their oral expansion of Scripture was also from Sinai. That was taught in the very first mishnah of tractate *Avot* which represents the Pharisaic claim for divine authority and hence the authenticity of their reading of Torah:

> Moses received Torah from Sinai and transmitted it to Joshua, and Joshua to the Elders, and the Elders to the Prophets, and the Prophets transmitted it to the Men of the Great Assembly. They said three things.... (*Avot* 1:1)

What Moses received from Sinai, the Pharisees said, was not "*the* Torah," but rather simply "Torah," which literally means "instruction" or "teaching." "*The* Torah" could imply Scripture alone; "Torah" implies the entire body of traditional teaching as the Pharisees understood it, for the chain of tradition, as outlined in the continuation of the passage, leads directly to the founding fathers of the Pharisaic movement.[25]

An equally fanciful attempt to read the later tradition back into the Torah can be seen in the midrashic suggestion that the conclusion of the *Gevurot* benediction quoted above, "Praised are You, Lord, who revives the dead," was first recited by Isaac at the climax of the *Akedah* (the binding of Isaac) narrative (Genesis 22). When Abraham's blade touched Isaac's neck, the midrash relates, Isaac's soul left his body. But when Abraham was told to release his son, the soul returned, and Isaac then learned that God resurrects the dead, whereupon Isaac recited the benediction (*Pirke De Rabbi Eliezer*, 31).[26]

What began as a revolutionary expansion of biblical monotheism, created in a specific setting to meet specific theological challenges, now rises above history. It now represents the eternal and unchanging word of God, part of God's original teaching to be accepted by all Jews to the end of time. Such is the power of midrash!

BUT HOW WILL RESURRECTION HAPPEN?

When I teach this material on resurrection to my students, I am invariably asked: Will I be resurrected in the bodily form that I had at the time of my death? Will I be clothed or naked? Will I return with my arthritis or without it? Before my weight-loss or following it? With which one of my spouses will I be living?

These and similar questions reflect an underlying curiosity about what might be called the "mechanics" of resurrection. I usually dismiss these questions with the simple claim that the rabbis were not making a biological/scientific statement about the afterlife but rather a mythic claim. But this, of course, rarely satisfies my questioners.[27]

In fact, relatively little material in Jewish texts deals with these questions. We have noted the constant use of the metaphor of awakening from sleep which has its roots in both the Daniel and the Isaiah texts. Other texts use a metaphor from nature:

> R. Hiyya ben Joseph said: A time will come when the just will break through [the soil] and rise up in Jerusalem, for it is written, *Let men sprout up in towns like country grass....* (Psalm 72:16)

R. Hiyya ben Joseph further stated: The just in the time to come will rise in their own clothes. [This is deduced]...from a grain of wheat. If a grain of wheat that is buried naked [i.e., sown] sprouts up with many coverings how much more so the just who are buried in their shrouds. (Bab. Talmud, *Ketubot* 111b)

To this day, Psalm 72:16, "let men sprout up in towns like country grass," together with Psalm 103:14, "He is mindful that we are dust..." is recited at the end of the burial service while those in attendance pluck blades of grass and toss them over their right shoulders.

In a similar vein, Isaiah 26:19, "Your dew is like the dew on fresh growth," is quoted to teach that the process of resurrection resembles the effects of dew (*Tanhuma Toledot* 19).[28] In line with the prayer for rain in the *Gevurot* benediction, resurrection is also likened to rain (*Genesis Rabba* 13:6). Other analogies are to a potter who fashions his product from clay, to a builder who makes his bricks out of earth and water, or to a mouse which, it was believed, is generated spontaneously from the dust (Bab. Talmud, *Sanhedrin* 91a).

Another text describes resurrection using an anatomical model:

Hadrian [the Roman emperor], may his bones be crushed, asked Rabbi Joshua ben Hananiah, "From which part of the body will the Holy One blessed be He, in the time to come, cause man to sprout forth?" He answered from the nut [in Hebrew, *luz*] of the spinal column [apparently, the tip of the coccyx]. Said Hadrian, "How can you convince me?" He therefore brought one before him; he put it in water, but it was not dissolved; he let it pass through millstones, but it was not ground; he put it in fire, but it was not burnt; he put it on an anvil and began beating it with a hammer, but the anvil was flattened out, and the hammer was split, but all this had no effect. (*Leviticus Rabba* 18:1)[29]

In a similar vein, the description of God's bringing the dry bones back to life in Ezekiel 37:7–10 is used as the model for the final resurrection.[30]

In order that the resurrected be recognized by their contemporaries, it was assumed that they would arise with all of their infirmities, after which, in accord with Deuteronomy 32:39, "I wounded and I will heal," God will heal them (*Ecclesiastes Rabbah,* 1:4).[31]

WHO IS TO BE RESURRECTED?

The mishnah, quoted at the beginning of this chapter, has alerted us to the fact that despite its initial claim, not all of Israel will have a share in the age to come. To the three exceptions quoted in that passage, those who deny revelation, resurrection or providence, the succeeding passages in the mishnah add a number of individuals (such as the evil kings, Jeroboam, Ahab and Manasseh) and groups (such as the generation of the flood and the men of Sodom). But in all of these cases, the exceptions to the rule are guilty of some failure, either of belief or of behavior.

A far different issue is the ultimate destiny of those who are guilty neither of misbelief nor misconduct, preeminently, the nations of the world. On this issue, two late-first-century CE masters, Rabbi Eliezer ben Hyrcanus and Rabbi Joshua ben Hananiah, maintain contradictory opinions. Both appeal to a biblical verse: "Let the wicked be in Sheol, all the nations who ignore God!" (Psalm 9:18). The former reads the first part of the verse, "Let the wicked be in Sheol..." to apply to the wicked of Israel, and the latter part of the verse, "...all the nations who ignore God," to apply to the non-Jewish world. But Rabbi Joshua demurs. He understands the latter phrase to apply only to those non-Jews "who ignore God." The non-Jew who worships the God of Israel will then share in all of the blessings of the age to come as if he were a true Israelite.[32] It is Rabbi Joshua's position which is accepted as law in Maimonides' Code: "The pious of the nations of the world have a portion in the age to come."[33]

This debate between the two talmudic masters is no trivial affair. It deals with no less an issue than the place of the non-Jew in the economy of God's salvation. Though Judaism never once abandoned its conviction that it alone represented God's unwavering will, it nevertheless included within the scope of God's concern, those non-Jews who accepted and lived according to certain basic principles of the Jewish religion, even though they did not formally belong to the community of Israel. The twin doctrines of the "righteous gentile" and of "the seven Noahide laws" were developed to admit into God's salvation all human beings whom Jews considered to be their equal in God's concern. True, Judaism always had its partisan nationalists and its universalists. The debate discussed above pits a representative of each school against the other. But the consensus of rabbinic opinion, here codified by Maimonides, reflects the triumph of the universalist position. It testifies to Judaism's readiness to accomodate the non-Jewish "other" within the scope of God's redemptive work.[34]

TWO DOCTRINES BLEND

From their predecessors, then, the talmudic rabbis inherited two doctrines about the afterlife: The first taught that at some point after death, God would raise the body from the grave. The second taught that, at death, the body disintegrates and returns to dust, but the soul leaves the body and lives eternally. The first, of uncertain

134

provenance, is articulated in three biblical texts. The second, which originated in Greek thought, is not in the Bible. Both appear in the literature of the intertestamental period.

Both these two doctrines are explicit in talmudic Judaism. References to the first are omnipresent in talmudic homilies, but its explicit articulation in the *Gevurot* benediction and in Mishnah *Sanhedrin* constitutes the strongest possible claim for its unquestioned authority. The liturgical phrase, *mehaye hametim,* and the mishnaic phrase, *tehiyat hametim,* are both frustratingly concise and ambiguous. But since both phrases allude to Isaiah 26:19, since the reference in Daniel 12:2 to those "who sleep in the dust" is also in the liturgical piece, and since both biblical texts clearly speak of bodily resurrection, it is fair to assume that the talmudic references carry a similar meaning.

For its part, the doctrine of the immortality of the soul also appears in a talmudic/liturgical text, but it is accorded nowhere as central a position as the doctrine of resurrection.

The *Birkhot Hashahar,* or "Early Morning Benedictions" include this passage taken from the Talmud (Bab. Talmud, *B'rakhot* 60b):

> My God, the soul that You have given me is pure. You created it, You fashioned it, You breathed it into me, You safeguard it within me, and You will eventually take it from me and return it to me in time to come. As long as the soul is within me, I thank You O Lord, my God and God of my ancestors, Master of all things, Lord of all souls. Praised are You Lord who restores souls to dead bodies.[35]

We have no information about the origins of this text apart from its source in the Talmud. The talmudic unit from which it is drawn was originally designated to be recited at home upon awakening, and was only later transferred to the synagogue service.

In its place, a much briefer prayer based on a midrash (*Genesis Rabbah* 78:1) came to be recited at home immediately upon waking:

> I thank You, living and eternal King, for having restored my soul within me with compassion—abundant is Your faithfulness.[36]

The midrash explicitly understands our awakening from sleep as testifying to resurrection.

Both these texts draw upon the biblical model of resurrection as awakening; hence they are to be recited upon awakening from sleep. As an extension of this metaphor, falling asleep was understood as a form of death; this is the explicit message of the *K'riat Sh'ma al Hamitah*, literally, the recitation of the *Sh'ma* "in bed," before falling asleep. If sleep is likened to a form of death, then the liturgies to be recited before falling asleep and upon awakening deal first with dying and then with being revived. It is noteworthy that the prayer to be recited before sleep and the one thanking God for having restored one's soul recited upon awakening, are immediately juxtaposed in their original source (Bab. Talmud, *B'rakhot* 60b). They bracket the experience of sleep and convey the notion that sleep is like death.[37]

There is much of the Greek doctrine in our main text but it is thoroughly "judaized," as it was in The Wisdom of Solomon and in Josephus. The soul enjoys an existence independent of the body; it is an entity in its own right, enters the body at birth, and is taken from the body at death. It continues to exist after the death of the body. But in contrast to Greek doctrine, the soul enjoys these perquisites not because of its inherent non-material nature but rather because that is the way God created it. God creates the soul, fashions it, breathes it into me, guards it, removes it from me and then returns it to me in time to come. It is God Who confers immortality on the soul.

136

That the later tradition fully appropriated the notion of an individualized soul, separate and distinct from the body, is clearly demonstrated in an extended midrashic description of the death of Moses. The biblical description of this death (Deuteronomy 34:5–8) is frustratingly concise, but the midrash expands this narrative into one of the most poignant passages in all rabbinic literature. Most of the passage deals with Moses' refusal to accept death, his challenge that God reverse the divine decree, and his wrestling with the various angels God sent to fetch his soul.

But astonishingly, after Moses finally resigns himself to dying, his soul takes up its own independent challenge. When God calls upon the soul to leave Moses' body, "she still refused and countered with the question: 'Is there a purer body than that of Moses?'" God is then forced to enter into discussion with the soul, promising to raise her to the highest heavens and placing her beneath God's very throne. Still, the soul protests and begs to stay within Moses' body. Finally, "the Holy One, blessed be He, sought out and took his soul with a kiss."[38]

The notion of God's "kiss of death" is a homiletical expansion of Deuteronomy 34:5 which has Moses dying "at the command (in Hebrew, *al pi*, literally, "by the mouth") of the Lord." We are now in an explicitly dualistic framework. Moses is a composite of body and soul; Moses argues and then the soul pursues its own argument independently of Moses' will. And death is the going out of the soul from the body.

In their original form, the two doctrines of the resurrection of the body and the immortality of the soul appear independent of each other. One knows nothing of bodies, the other knows nothing of souls. One ascribes personal identity to the body; the other, to the soul. One teaches that at the end of time, the body will be revived. The other insists that the soul is immortal and needs no revival. But in the liturgy cited just above, the two doctrines are conflated. In fact, in some ancient texts, the concluding blessing of the prayer referred to above reads, "Praised are You, O Lord, Who revives the dead" (in Hebrew, *mehaye hametim*), the identical conclusion which was used in the *Gevurot* benediction, in place of "Who restores souls to dead bodies."[39] This text also repeatedly uses the word "me" (in Hebrew, *bi*) which can only indicate the bodily location of the soul. At the end, the soul will be returned to a resurrected body.

When did that conflation occur? It is not present in the early-first-century CE The Wisdom of Solomon, but it is anticipated in Josephus' description of Pharisaic belief in his late-first-century CE *Wars* and *Antiquities*. What about the earlier and ambiguous reference in the *Gevurot* benediction? The words *mehaye hametim* certainly refer to bodily resurrection, but it is also possible that by this time, they had come to refer to the entire scenario: God resurrects bodies *and* restores souls. After the Mishnah, it surely does have this broader meaning.

The rabbinic description of this broader scenario suggests that at death, the souls of the righteous and of the wicked are separated; the textual basis is I Samuel 25:29:

> [T]he life [in Hebrew, *nefesh*] of my lord will be bound up in the bundle of life in the care of the Lord; but He will fling away the lives [again *nefesh*] of your enemies as from the hollow of a sling.

This text reflects the transformation in the meaning of the Hebrew term *nefesh*. In the biblical text, it means simply "life"; in its rabbinic use, it has come to mean "soul." The souls of the righteous go either to heaven, or to Eden, or more specifically into the treasure house where God preserves souls; the souls of the wicked go to a place of fiery torment. But it is not clear whether these settings represent an intermediate stage prior to the final resurrection, or their final resting place after bodies and souls are reconstituted.

This geographical vagueness reflects a similar vagueness about the chronology of the eschatological drama. Two terms are commonly used to designate the eschatological age: The Days of the Messiah and the Age to Come. Are these identical? Are the Days of the Messiah an intermediate stage between this age and the Age to Come? If the latter, at which point does the resurrection take place? And what happens to souls in the interval? There is no clear resolution of these issues in our material.[40] But Maimonides, for one, distinguishes sharply between the Days of the Messiah and the Age to Come and there are ample talmudic precedents to support such a distinction.

The complete and explicit joining of the two doctrines is reflected in this extended text:

Antoninus said to Rabbi[41]: "The body and the soul can both free themselves from judgement. The body can plead: the soul has sinned, since from the day it left me, I lie like a dumb stone in the grave. The soul can plead: from the day I departed from it, I fly about in the air like a bird." He replied, "I will tell thee a parable. To what can this be compared? To a human king who owned a beautiful orchard which contained splendid figs. He appointed two watchmen, one lame and the other blind. The lame man said to the blind, 'I see beautiful figs in the orchard. Take me on your shoulder that we may take them and eat.' So the lame sat upon the shoulder of the blind, took the figs and ate them. Some time later, the owner of the orchard came and inquired of them: 'Where are those beautiful figs?' The lame man replied: 'Have I feet to walk with?' The blind man replied: 'Have I eyes to see with'? He placed the lame upon the blind and judged them together. So will the Holy One bring the soul, replace it in the body, and judge them together, as it is written: '*He summoned the heavens above, and the earth, for the trial of his people*' (Psalm 50:4). '*He summoned the heavens above*' this refers to the soul; '*and the earth,*' to the body." (Bab. Talmud, *Sanhedrin* 91a-91b)

The resurrection event is twofold: The body rises from the grave, the soul that has never perished is joined with the risen body, and the reconstituted individual human being comes before God in judgement. With few exceptions, this form of the doctrine becomes normative in Judaism until the modern age.

THE DEATH OF DEATH

From the claim that God will resurrect the dead, it would seem to be but a short step to the further claim that God will destroy death itself; why bother resurrecting the dead if people still die? Yet there are frustratingly few rabbinic texts that explicitly take this step. Psalm 48:15 reads:

> For God—He is our God forever;
> He will lead us evermore.

The Hebrew for the word "evermore" is *al-mut*. The translation above reads the word as derived from the Hebrew *olam* or "eternity"; hence the translation: "He will lead us evermore." But a midrash which probably dates from the first or second centuries CE weaves other interpretations of the Hebrew word, including:

> Aquila[42] translated [the word *al-mut*] *athanasia* [Greek for deathlessness, immortality]. [God will lead us to] a world in which there is no death. (*Leviticus Rabbah* 11:9)

The midrash reads the Hebrew *al-mut* as *al-mavet*, "beyond death." In other words, God will lead us to a world in which there is no death.

That God "will destroy death forever" is the claim of Isaiah 25:8, although as we saw above, it is not clear what the author of that statement intended to convey. However, a very clear statement of that belief is in the conclusion of the sixteenth century CE song which concludes the Passover seder liturgy. *Had Gadya* is modeled on a familiar folk ditty, in our culture, known as "The Farmer in the Dell." In its Hebrew version, it chronicles the fate of a kid who is eaten by a cat, who in turn is eaten by a dog, the dog beaten by a stick, the stick burnt by a fire and so on. Each verse repeats the fate of all the preceding characters. Finally, the Angel of Death slaughters the slaughterer and, in the last verse of all,

> Then came the Blessed Holy One and slaughtered the Angel of Death, that slew the slaughterer, that slaughtered the ox....

This song is hardly the creation of the academy. But its provenance in popular Jewish religion testifies to Jews' implicit faith in the ultimate death of death. Here the abstraction "death" is personified as the Angel of Death who is thoroughly under God's mastery. God no longer destroys death in the abstract, but slays its very personification: God's own messenger of death. The very last words of the Passover seder then, appropriately for the celebration of the Festival of Redemption, affirm the ultimate death of death.[43]

INTIMATIONS OF IMMORTALITY

But not only at the Passover seder does the Jew affirm that death is not the final scene in the drama of a human life. From the age of the Talmud on, that affirmation is everywhere in the life of the worshipping Jew. It is explicit in the prayer recited every morning upon awakening; waking from sleep is a prefiguration of wakening from the grave, so the liturgy praises God Who will, in days to come, restore souls to dead bodies. It is equally explicit in every *Amidah*'s sixfold praise of God Who has the power to revive the dead, a text that is repeated by Jewish men and, in our own day, by many Jewish women as well, at least three times every day.

Traditionally, Jewish men, and again in our day, Jewish women, who are called to the reading of the Torah, recite a blessing which praises God for implanting within us eternal life. After every meal, the *Birkat HaMazon* (Grace after Meals) includes a prayer that God make us worthy of life in the age to come.[44] That wish is echoed daily in the liturgy immediately preceding the concluding *Alenu*.[45] Every Sabbath morning, shortly before reciting the *Sh'ma*, the Jew proclaims that one of the powers that makes God incomparable is God's power to resurrect the dead.[46]

Every funeral concludes with the words of the burial *kaddish* which affirms the imminence of an age when God will revive the dead and bring them into eternal life. After the Middle Ages, at every funeral and at every *Yizkor* (Memorial) service, the words of the *El Maleh Rahamim* prayer petition God to shelter the souls of those who have departed this life and bind them in the bond of life. During summer Sabbath afternoons, the weekly review of a chapter of tractate *Avot* begins with the recitation of Mishnah *Sanhedrin* 10:1 which conveys the assurance that all Israel has a share in the age to come.

For worshipping Jews to this very day, life is permeated by these intimations of personal immortality. Such is this doctrine's pervasive power.

VI

MAIMONIDES: THE TRIUMPH
OF THE SPIRITUAL

It is not rare that a person aims to expound the intent of
some conclusions clearly and explicitly, makes an effort to
reject doubts and eliminate far-fetched interpretations,
and yet the unbalanced will draw the reverse judgement of
the conclusions he sought to clarify. Some such thing occurred even to one of God's declarations....If this is what
happened to God's proclamations, it is much more likely
to be expected to happen to statements by humans.[1]

THE FRUSTRATION OF these opening words from Maimonides' *Essay
on Resurrection*, written in the author's fifty-sixth year—he was born
in 1135 in Spain and died in Egypt in 1204—captures the tone of
this, his third attempt to articulate his views on the doctrine of the
afterlife. Few other issues in the entire body of his thought haunted
him, tormented him, and engendered such controversy as this one.

But there is one other issue to which he returns again and
again, repeating and clarifying his position, denouncing his critics
and adducing new supporting evidence for the truth and authenticity of his claims. That issue was the portrayal of God in corporeal
terms, which, for Maimonides, was the cardinal theological sin.
Perhaps that ongoing debate may serve as a clue to the impulse that
underlies his writings on the afterlife. The two issues may well be one.

MAIMONIDES' AGENDA

Maimonides inherited two intellectual traditions. He was passionately committed to both and spent his entire lifetime trying to reconcile them. One was Torah, not only Scripture but also the Oral Torah as recorded in the Babylonian and Palestinian Talmudim, together with the entire body of interpretation and commentary on these texts to his own day. The second was Greek philosophy, primarily in its neo-Platonic and Aristotelian forms, which, in Maimonides' time, was accessible to the Jewish world in Arabic, the common language of the medieval world.

Maimonides was convinced that truth is one. It was inconceivable to him that these two traditions, each of which claimed to be true and both of which he accepted as true, could be contradictory. If they appeared to be contradictory, it was because the reader failed to understand them.

On another level, motivating Maimonides' attempt to integrate these two sources of truth was his commitment to reason as the distinguishing crown of the human being, and to rationality as the ultimate source of truth.

For Maimonides, reason is the image of God in which, according to Genesis 1, human beings were created. God is intrinsically reason, Maimonides believed, and since we are created in God's image, it is reason which distinguishes us from the rest of creation. The full development of our rational powers is our distinctive mandate, our most noble accomplishment, and the mark of human perfection. It is also the ultimate goal of the human endeavor. Of this image of human perfection, Maimonides writes in the last chapter of his monumental *Guide of the Perplexed,*

> This is in true reality the ultimate end; this is what gives the individual true perfection; a perfection belonging

to him alone; and it gives him permanent perdurance; through it man is man.[2]

If reason is our ultimate distinction, then exercising our rational powers is a divine command. The underlying agenda of all of Maimonides' writings is to demonstrate that truth can only be reached through using reason, and therefore that the teachings of Torah are inherently rational. Torah and reason differ only in the idiom in which this single truth is articulated and it becomes the task of the Jewish teacher to translate one idiom into the other. Again, if we miss this dimension of Torah, it is because of our limitations and it is the responsibility of the authentic teacher of Torah to help overcome these limitations.

From this flows the classical Maimonidean conclusion that authentic Judaism demands an authentic belief structure. Not for Maimonides is the frequently voiced claim that Judaism is simply a religion of deeds, not of beliefs; that what counts is how we behave as Jews and that our beliefs are of secondary importance. For how is it even possible to know what God commands us to do without an underlying philosophy? Two claims are included in this position: That a belief system is indispensable for Jews, and that there are both correct Jewish beliefs and idolatrous ones. It then becomes the responsibility of the teacher of Judaism to inculcate the correct beliefs and to uproot the idolatrous ones.

That is precisely what Maimonides was trying to accomplish when he opened his *Mishneh Torah,* a code of law, by discussing at length the central beliefs that Jews have held, and stipulating precisely which are correct and which idolatrous. That enterprise was offensive to some Jews for three reasons: It granted the status of law to beliefs; it stipulated which beliefs are authentically Jewish and which are not; and it offered Maimonides' sometimes idiosyncratic version of what these correct beliefs actually mean.

It was primarily the last of these that agitated some of his readers when they learned of his views on the afterlife, specifically on the respective merits of the two doctrines of bodily resurrection and the immortality of the soul. Maimonides' primary concern was to uproot the idolatrous notion that God has a body, and to brand one who believes this a heretic, indeed "a hater, an enemy and an adversary of God."[3] It is this rejection of the notion of divine corporeality that impels his equally obvious discomfort with the doctrine of bodily resurrection as the ultimate stage in the afterlife.

The need to integrate or reconcile the apparently divergent conclusions of these two traditions impels Maimonides to read their major texts in startling new ways. Most important, it impels him to reformulate the substance of Torah as a body of thoroughly rational truths. To put this another way, what Maimonides produces is an elaborate midrash, both on Aristotle and on Torah, but mainly on Torah, because it is precisely the inherent rationality of the teachings of Torah that appears most questionable.

To put it still another way, both Moses and Aristotle (but mainly Moses) would be absolutely stunned to read the version of their teachings as Maimonides understood them.

MAIMONIDES' WRITINGS ON THE AFTERLIFE: THREE STATEMENTS

Maimonides dealt with the issue of the afterlife on three separate occasions. The first is in his *Commentary on the Mishnah* which he began writing in 1158 at the age of 23.

Though the Mishnah predates the compilation of the Babylonian Talmud by roughly three centuries, it was typically published as part of that larger work and was rarely studied as an independent text.[4] Maimonides' purpose is to view the Mishnah as an introduction to talmudic literature and a summary of its contents. Typically, his commentary consists of brief notations on individual words or clauses in the text which convey the gist of the talmudic discussion to follow.

But occasionally, Maimonides departs from the commentary format and presents more extended discussions on issues arising from the text. One of these is his introduction to *Helek* that precedes his commentary to chapter 10 of tractate *Sanhedrin.* The opening words of that chapter's first mishnah which we discussed at length in chapter 5 above read: "All Israel has a portion [in Hebrew: *helek*] in the Age to Come." Hence, the title of this introduction which has assumed an independent standing in the Maimonidean *corpus.* Since this mishnah deals with the notion of the Age to Come, Maimonides devotes this broader inquiry to interpreting Judaism's teachings on this topic.[5]

The second is his *Mishneh Torah,* written between 1168 and 1178, which, together with his *Guide to the Perplexed,* represents his most towering achievement. The *Mishneh Torah* is a comprehensive codification of the entire body of Jewish law from Scripture, through talmudic literature and including all responsa, codifications and commentaries on this legal tradition to his day. It was the first such comprehensive survey of the entire body of Jewish law since the Mishnah that had been compiled roughly 1000 years earlier.

Harvard professor Isadore Twersky, the consummate master of Maimonidean literature, lists five features of this work which account for its authoritative standing to our own day: It was written in mishnaic Hebrew, thereby departing from biblical Hebrew and talmudic Aramaic, the languages in which the material had originally been written; it ignores the sequence of the Mishnah and adopts a new "topical-pedagogical" arrangement; it eliminates debate and conflicting interpretations and formulates the law as a unilateral, undocumented decision, resting solely on the author's authority; it is all-inclusive, containing rulings even on issues such as agricultural laws and the laws of the Temple cult which had long been inapplicable to Jewish life; and it fuses law and philosophy, for Maimonides insists that the two cannot be separated, that Jewish law rests on theological or philosophical assumptions which demand their own elaboration and are as binding on the Jew as the law itself. Twersky's claim that the *Mishneh Torah* "changed the entire landscape of rabbinic literature" is amply justified.[6]

The *Mishneh Torah* is divided into fourteen books. In the first, called *Sefer HaMaddah* or *The Book of Knowledge,* Maimonides articulates the theological and philosophical assumptions that underlie all of Jewish law. It thus serves as a preface to his work as a whole. One of the sub-books included here is called *Hilkhot T'shuvah* (*The Laws of Repentance*). Chapter 8 of this book is devoted exclusively to Maimonides' codification of Jewish beliefs about the afterlife.

Maimonides' third discussion of the afterlife is his *Essay on Resurrection*. Written in 1191, it is one of several monographs in which Maimonides addresses specific questions on which he was consulted by Jewish communities or, as in this case, in which he clarifies some of his teachings which had been attacked and which he felt had been misunderstood.

Notably missing from this list is Maimonides' *Guide of the Perplexed,* completed around 1190, his most elaborate and extensive attempt to resolve the apparent philosophical contradictions between Torah and Greek philosophy. By any criterion, the *Guide* is the single most significant philosophical work ever penned by a Jew. Yet on the issue of the afterlife, it is totally silent, probably because Maimonides did not view resurrection as a philosophical issue, but rather as a miracle that has to be accepted on faith alone.[7]

The core issue in each of these discussions is the tension between the Greek notion that ultimate eternity is for the soul alone and the Torah's teachings that it also pertains to bodies after resurrection. We saw earlier that despite the later tradition's attempt to conflate these two doctrines, they can seem to be working at cross-purposes. The first ascribes eternal life to souls alone; the second to bodies. The talmudic doctrine ascribes eternity to both, but Maimonides is clearly uncomfortable with that resolution for it offends his commitment to the Greek notion that nothing material can be eternal. On the other hand, he is also bound by the teachings of Torah which clearly says what it says. Here, then, is one of those instances where his determination to reconcile his two commitments is explicitly challenged.

Each of these three accounts of Maimonides' teachings on the afterlife deserves attention. They represent three attempts to reconcile the tension between the two traditions, Torah and Greek philosophy, as reflected on the issue of the afterlife. We will have to see whether these three statements represent an evolution in Maimonides' thinking on these issues, or whether they simply restate his personal beliefs in different language.

INTRODUCTION TO HELEK

When Maimonides claims in his *Essay*, that he had expounded his views on Jewish eschatology "clearly and explicitly," he is being disingenuous. Whether or not his later writings on the issue indicate a significant change of heart, it is hardly the case that this first attempt to do so is in any way clear and explicit. If, as he claims, his readers misunderstood him, there is ample justification for that misunderstanding. The failure is Maimonides' own, possibly because he was fully aware of the controversy that an explicit statement of his views would arouse.

What Maimonides has to say here on the doctrines of resurrection and immortality is couched in an overview of Jewish eschatology as a whole. To get a sense of how his thought on these two issues fits into the larger pattern, it is useful to outline the overall structure of the work which covers six broad themes:[8]

1. A summary of the views of the "masters of Torah" on the rewards due one who obeys God's commands;
2. The broader issue: Should one expect a reward in the first place? (Ideally, no!)
3. The central (in all of Maimonides' writings) methodological issue: Should one interpret the language of the sages literally or metaphorically?
4. Materialist and spiritual interpretations of the afterlife;
5. Ideally, we should serve God without expectation of reward;
6. The Thirteen Principles of Jewish Belief.

The heart of Maimonides' argument lies in his discussion of the third and fourth of these themes. Two points are central: The first is his classical methodological attack on religious literalism. It is the key to everything else in this statement and, indeed, to all of Maimonides. The community that Maimonides is addressing is the "few and scattered" Jews who know

> that the words of the sages contain both an obvious and a hidden meaning,...that they were employing the style of riddle and parable which is the method of truly great thinkers.[9]

Maimonides dismisses those who believe that the words of Torah should be understood literally as simply beyond help.

Then, applying this methodological thrust to the issue at hand, Maimonides presents his totally spiritualized view of the afterlife. Just as the blind cannot imagine color, so bodies can never attain spiritual delight. Bodily delights are inferior and discontinuous, but spiritual delight is eternal and uninterrupted. Angels know this kind of delight and those of us who have purified ourselves in our lifetime will be like them after death. We will be like a king who has no interest in playing ball with children as he did before he became king.

The bodily delights that formerly satisfied us will do so no more.
We will neither experience bodily delight nor crave it.

> In the age to come our souls will become wise out of the
> knowledge of God the Creator....[10]

For proof, Maimonides quotes a talmudic passage to which
he will return again and again:

> In the age to come there is no eating, drinking, wash-
> ing, anointing, or sexual intercourse; but the righteous
> sit with their crowns on their heads enjoying the radi-
> ance of the Divine Presence. (Bab. Talmud, *B'rakhot* 17a)

He then proceeds to give his own interpretation of the passage in line with the principle that the text must not be understood
literally. The phrase "with their crowns on their heads" signifies "the
immortality of the soul being in firm possession of the Idea which
is God the Creator." The "crown" is "precisely the Idea which great
philosophers have explicated at length." The expression "they delight in the radiance of the Divine Presence" means that

> the souls enjoy blissful delight in their attainment of
> knowledge of the truly essential nature of God the Crea-
> tor, a delight which is like that experienced by the holy
> angels who know His existence first-hand.[11]

This is the "ultimate good," the "final end," the "incomparable good, for how could that which is eternal and endless be
compared with anything transient and terminable?"

Then comes one solitary paragraph on resurrection:

> The resurrection of the dead is one of the cardinal prin-

ciples established by Moses our teacher. A person who does not believe this principle has no real religion, certainly not Judaism. However, resurrection is for the righteous. This is the meaning of the statement in *B'reshit Rabbah*[12] which declares: "The creative power of rain is for both the righteous and the wicked, but the resurrection of the dead is only for the righteous." How, after all, could the wicked come back to life, since they are dead even in their lifetimes? Our sages taught: "The wicked are called dead even while they are still alive; the righteous are alive even when they are dead" (Bab. Talmud, *B'rakhot* 18b). All men must die and their bodies decompose.[13]

The paragraph makes three points: Resurrection is a cardinal principle of the Torah which all Jews must believe; it is for the righteous alone; and "all men must die and their bodies decompose."

Three further statements in this work touch upon the afterlife. The first is a mysterious sentence at the heart of Maimonides' discussion of the Days of the Messiah: "But the Messiah will die, and his son and his grandson will reign in his stead."[14] We will return to the link between resurrection and the Days of the Messiah below.

The second statement is the last of his Thirteen Principles with which he concludes the work as a whole. This listing of principles follows a statement of the author's intent to write a book collecting all the sages' teachings on this subject, showing which should be understood literally, which metaphorically, and which are "dreams to be interpreted by a wakeful mind." His goal is "to teach those with no training in theology, a subject which not every man can understand."[15]

The Thirteen Principles frequently appear in traditional prayer books as one of a series of texts to be recited after the end of the formal morning service.[16] As Maimonides explains, they represent his listing of the minimal credal commitments required of every Jew, even those "with no training in theology." A Jew who believes these principles, even should he commit every possible sin, is a member of "Israel"—the "Israel" referred to in the first words of the mishnah—and has a share in the Age to Come.

That explains why this listing appears as the climax of this particular treatise; belief in the principles is the gateway to immortality, even for the masses.

In their original context, each principle is followed by a brief explanation. But the thirteenth reads simply:

The Thirteenth Fundamental Principle is the Resurrection of the Dead which we have already explicated.[17]

When Maimonides claims, decades later in his *Essay on Resurrection*, that he has expounded his thinking on the afterlife "clearly and explicitly," this introduction is one of the two texts to which he refers. In this version, the ultimate goal of a human life is to know God, to achieve eternal contemplation of God's essence, a passionate, intellectual vision which we can never fully attain during our bodily existence on earth. Knowing God is for souls alone, and for the souls of the righteous alone. If we strive to attain that goal during our lifetime, and if we live righteously, we will be granted it in perpetuity after our death.

But how does his rhapsodic description of a totally spiritualized Age to Come relate to the resurrection of the dead? If, in the Age to Come, there is no eating, drinking, washing, anointing or sexual intercourse, then what form of bodily existence is there? More generally, admitting that resurrection is a "cardinal principle" that every religious Jew must believe, how does Maimonides understand this event? And what about that mysterious concluding sentence: "All men must die and their bodies decompose." We can easily see why Maimonides' critics accused him of denying the doctrine of resurrection.

That, at this stage of his writings, Maimonides seems to be ambivalent about bodily resurrection is confirmed in the opening lines of *Helek,* the third of the three tangential references to the afterlife in this text, where he lists five different views on the afterlife held by the "masters of Torah," the third of which is "the resurrection of the dead." He describes that view in these words:

> By this they mean that a man will live after his death and return to his family and dear ones to eat and drink and never die again. According to this opinion the evil is that a man may not live after his death among those who are resurrected. Here, too, proof is adduced from many sayings that are found in the words of the sages and from Biblical verses whose literal meaning seem to teach this, wholly or in part.[18]

In this context, Maimonides simply lists the five views on the afterlife while offering no further comment on their validity. Yet he proceeds to complain that few people think seriously about resurrection or inquire about its real meaning. It is safe to assume that he does not think much of any of the five positions listed here, and it is also obvious from his later treatment of the issue that the doctrine is far more complex than in this version.

Most important, compare the tone and the rhetoric of Maimonides' statement on the bliss that souls will enjoy after death with his treatment of bodily resurrection. The first is passionate, elegiac, extensive and detailed; the second is brief, matter-of-fact, almost trivialized and obscure. If anything, what *is* clear and explicit is that Maimonides cares desperately that Jews understand the afterlife in terms of spiritual immortality. He cannot ignore the traditional material on resurrection simply because it is there. But there is no passion here. The thrust of this statement is that when the liturgy has us recite that God revives the dead, what it means is the kind of afterlife associated with the soul. But then what happens to resurrected bodies?

Finally, at the very end of this work, when he lists the thirteenth principle as "the Resurrection of the Dead which we have already explicated," he again seems to imply that we should understand resurrection in this spiritualized form. This, he seems to claim, is what the doctrine of resurrection teaches. In contrast to the Talmud which combines the two doctrines while preserving the integrity of each, Maimonides seems to fold one into the other; resurrection *means* spiritual immortality. That this is not what he means, that in fact he is prepared to view bodily resurrection as an independent event within the broader eschatological scenario, emerges explicitly only years later in the *Essay*.

If the central tension in all of Maimonides' work is between the claims of Torah and of Greek philosophy, then this statement suggests that on this issue, at least, philosophy has triumphed over Torah.

THE *MISHNEH TORAH*

Maimonides does nothing to clarify any of these issues in his statement in Chapter 8 of The Laws of Repentance. If anything, this statement is even more problematic because, in this text, he says not one word about resurrection.

The context is Maimonides' discussion of the Torah's view on what constitutes the disinterested service of God and of the almost unlimited power of repentance to right our relationship with God. This leads to Chapter 8 where he describes the reward due one who serves God in this way. The opening words of the chapter convey the thrust of what follows:

> The good that is hidden for the righteous is the life in the Age to Come. This is the life which is not accompanied by death and the good which is not accompanied by evil. The righteous will enjoy this eternal and entirely good life; the evil will be cut off from it.[19]

Then comes an almost verbatim review of what the author wrote about the delights of spiritual immortality in his *Introduction to Helek,* including an elaboration of the statement in *B'rakhot* 17a that in the Age to Come there will be no bodies but only souls who neither eat nor drink nor engage in other bodily activities.

This discussion has only two significant original points. The first is a technical distinction in his definition of the soul. The second is the claim that the Age to Come will not arrive in the future following the end of the present age. Rather, it is present now in a different dimension than our familiar material world. What it does "follow" is the death of the individual. In other words, Maimonides seems to say that the righteous enter the Age to Come immediately after death.[20]

We have contemporaneous evidence of the controversial nature of this version of Maimonides' position in the comment of Rabbi Abraham ben David of Posquieres, known as "the *RAbaD,*" an acronym formed by the first letters of his Hebrew name. The *RAbaD's* comments on specific points in Maimonides' work are inserted as sidebars in the printed edition of the Code.

On the paragraph dealing with the absence of bodies in the Age to Come, the *RAbaD* notes:

> This man's words are in my eyes near to those who assert that there is no resurrection of the body but only of souls. But by my life, this was not the opinion of our sages....

He proceeds to quote various talmudic statements that clearly state that it is the body that will be resurrected and he continues:

> All of which is conclusive proof that the dead will arise with their bodies and remain alive. Nevertheless, it is possible that the Creator will set them in strong, healthy forms as are the forms of angels, and is the form of Elijah....[21]

To the *RAbaD,* then, Maimonides denies the doctrine of resurrection. Indeed, what else should the *RAbaD* have concluded given Maimonides' total silence on resurrection in this text? True, there was the claim in *Helek* that resurrection is a cardinal principle of the Torah, but the cumulative impact of that earlier statement could be taken to suggest that resurrection should be understood as spiritual immortality alone. Finally, if Maimonides does believe that the Age to Come exists now in a different dimension, and if the dead enter that world immediately following death, then in principle, a doctrine of bodily resurrection seems to be superfluous.

But the *RAbaD* was not the only voice that challenged Maimonides' teachings. Hence, his need to return to the issue, some decades later, in the *Essay on Resurrection.* Here, finally, we are to learn just what he believes on all of these issues.

THE *ESSAY ON RESURRECTION*

Professor Twersky suggests that there are three possible approaches to this work: It may be a forgery, a genuine summary of Maimonides' thought, or an "intentionally distorted composition designed to mollify his critics and gain adherents."[22]

None of these options is totally satisfactory. The first has never been conclusively documented, and the third would be counterproductive, since Maimonides' conclusions here would continue to be profoundly offensive to his critics. As to the second, the *Essay* may well represent a summary of Maimonides' *thinking* on the issue, but it is hardly a representative summary of his published writings.

The *Essay* should be understood as Maimonides' only attempt to do what he says he has done previously but had never really done: "To expound the intent of some conclusions clearly and explicitly."

What is most striking about the *Essay* is its tone. This is the writing of a frustrated, embittered, angry teacher. Maimonides does not understand why he has to return again to the issue of resurrection. There is

> absolutely nothing more in it [the *Essay*] about this theme than I wrote down in the commentary on the Mishnah or in my major work [the *Mishneh Torah*] and some further comment, which even women and ignorant folk will understand.[23]

Those who misunderstood his conclusions are "unbalanced." His critics are "boors" and "simpletons." An essay on the theme by the incumbent head of the Academy in Baghdad is dismissed as

> a collection of the homilies and legends...of the sort that women tell one another in their condolence calls.[24]

Those sages in Israel who interpret these homilies literally

> are in fact the most ignorant, and more seriously astray than beasts, their minds filled with the senseless prattle of old women and noxious fantasies....[25]

What prompts Maimonides to write the *Essay* are three reports that reached him from Damascus, Yemen and Baghdad. Two claimed that Maimonides had denied the doctrine of resurrection and dismissed traditional sources that affirm it as entirely metaphorical. The third was the essay by the head of the Baghdad academy in which he calls some of Maimonides' views erroneous and sinful, though others are defensible.

Maimonides then turns to resurrection, whose meaning, all agree, is "the return of the soul to the body after separation [death]."[26] This is the first mention of this definition in all of his writings. Had he said this in his earlier works, our attempt to understand his position would be much easier. His proof text is the familiar passage from Daniel 12:2 which, he will note later, is the single unambiguous biblical reference to resurrection and all we need. This text, he insists, cannot be understood as a metaphor. Though Ezekiel 37 (the vision of the dry bones) may be metaphorical, Daniel is not.

Then comes the core statement of the work as a whole:

> (T)he individuals who will return to their bodies will eat, drink, marry, and procreate, and they will die after a long life, like those who live during the messianic age. The life, however, that is not followed by death, is life in the world to come, since it will be bodiless.[27]

Life in the world to come will be bodiless because "God creates absolutely nothing in vain." Since (and here returns the familiar passage from B'rakhot 17a) in the world to come there will be no eating, drinking or sexual intercourse, what need is there for bodies? What misleads "the masses" is that "they do not recognize existence except of a body or of what is in a body." This is the link between Maimonides' view of resurrection and of God's corporeality; his focus on the totally spiritual nature of immortality reflects his concern that "the masses" will view God as also corporeal. But resurrection is a miracle and "the denial of miracles is a denial of God and a defection from the Law."[28]

For the first time now, Maimonides is clear and explicit. What he is expounding is the doctrine of a "double dying." We die once, our bodies return to the earth and our souls leave the body. Then we are resurrected with our bodies and souls coming together again. Next we die a second time, after which the souls of the righteous enjoy the totally spiritualized and eternal life in the world to come. This is Maimonides' synthesis of Torah and philosophy, of bodily resurrection and spiritual immortality. They do not contradict each other. They are both true, Maimonides insists, but they occur sequentially. The eschatology of the individual is a drama in two acts: First, resurrection of bodies reunited with souls; and then, after our second death, spiritual immortality alone.

Why, he asks, has he treated these two doctrines at such different lengths? Because immortality is a "hidden" matter which has to be explained and elaborated; its meaning is obscure. But resurrection is a miracle; its truth is neither hidden nor difficult. Nothing more is required than to believe in it; it cannot be proved rationally. It is simply to be accepted "and that is that."[29] To deny miracles is to deny God's freedom and power, and that would lead to a denial of the entire structure of Judaism.[30]

THE DAYS OF THE MESSIAH AND
THE AGE TO COME

Maimonides' distinction between resurrection and spiritual immortality depends on a further distinction in his broader eschatology. Beginning with *Helek* and continuing through the *Essay*, he insists that the coming of the Messiah will be a totally natural event, that nothing miraculous will occur, that the world will continue to pursue its normal course. One difference alone will result: Israel will be freed from its exilic bondage. For proof, Maimonides quotes an oft-repeated talmudic passage in the name of Samuel, the early-third-century CE teacher:

> The only difference between this world and the days of the Messiah is that [Israel's] bondage to foreign kingdoms will be abolished. (Bab. Talmud, *B'rakhot* 34b; *Shabbat* 63a, 151b; *Pesahim* 68a; *Sanhedrin* 91b, 99a)

Maimonides elaborates: In the days of the Messiah, there will still be rich and poor, strong and weak, though it will be easier for people to make a living. Wisdom will increase and it will be easier to fulfill the commandments. As a result, more people will ultimately enjoy the Age to Come—which still lies ahead, in the indefinite future—but people will live longer.[31]

There follows the statement that the Messiah will die, and his son and grandson will reign in his stead. What all of this has to do with resurrection, however, does not emerge clearly until he takes up the issue again in the *Essay* where he notes that the resurrection of the dead will take place "in the lifetime of the Messiah, or before him, or after he dies."[32]

By identifying resurrection as roughly contemporaneous with the coming of the Messiah and distinguishing between the age of the Messiah and the Age to Come, Maimonides is thereby freed to separate resurrection from the totally spiritual form of immortality which will take place in the latter age alone.

WHY IS THE TORAH SILENT ON RESURRECTION?

With this elaboration of his views, Maimonides considers the main purpose of the *Essay* to be accomplished. But lest we think that this work is "bereft of benefits, because it contains nothing more than repetition of what is written in my commentary to the Mishnah and in my major composition," he takes up two new problems relevant to the subject matter: Clarifying those many passages in the Bible that deny that there will be a resurrection, and determining why the Pentateuch does not mention the doctrine.

What follows is the most fascinating part of this unusual document. Maimonides now resorts to his familiar role as teacher of his community. Sarcasm and bitterness are left behind; in their place comes a clear exposition of some basic tenets of Maimonidean thought.

Maimonides explains that the writings of the prophets and the Hagiography (more familiarly called the "Writings," in Hebrew, *Ketubim*),[33] seek to portray only the familiar, customary or natural patterns of existence. The "way of nature" is that what dies never returns, just as it is the way of nature that from a rock one cannot draw water. Yet a miracle occurred and Moses did draw water from a rock. Similarly, resurrection is a miracle. When the biblical texts deny resurrection, they deny that resurrection can occur as a familiar pattern of nature. That should not affect our belief in its miraculous nature.

To the second question, Maimonides resorts to what is, for his day, a startling account of the evolution of biblical religion. Since the Torah is believed to come from God, the proper question is why did God not teach the doctrine of resurrection in the Torah itself? Simply put, the answer is that the people of that age were not ready to accept this doctrine. They did not believe in miracles and in prophecy, only in the predictable course of nature. Teaching them about the miracle of resurrection would have led to its rejection and even to the rejection of revelation as a whole. Eventually, however, the basic principles of religion

became firm and valid with no doubts about the veracity of the prophets and the performance of miracles. After that, when the prophets informed us of what they were told of the Resurrection, its acceptance was facilitated.[34]

After digressing briefly on the nature of miracles, Maimonides concludes on a defensive note. He should not be blamed for the repetitions, additions, or "the extensive clarification of what does not really require further light." He has written not only for the common people but also for those who reproached him for the brevity of his treatment of resurrection in his earlier works. But "those who are truly learned" need neither repetition nor prolonged exegesis. Finally for a teacher, "the right thing to do is to address each group according to its capacity."[35]

THE IMPACT OF ISLAMIC FUNDAMENTALISM

I have interpreted the *Essay on Resurrection* as an extension and clarification of the position Maimonides held from his earliest writings on the issue. Professor Twersky suggests the possibility of an alternative interpretation of this document, namely that here Maimonides is retreating from his earlier dismissal of resurrection and tailoring his views to mollify his critics.

But if that was indeed his purpose, Maimonides could have offered a much more thorough reformulation of his position, bringing it, for example, more closely into line with the talmudic conflation of the two doctrines with which, of course, he was completely familiar. He does not do that here. He still insists on the notion of a double dying and that resurrected bodies will not enjoy eternal life. Finally, there is sufficient coherence between the earlier and the later statements to suggest that he felt no need to drastically alter the basic thrust of his thinking.

One further consideration may clarify Maimonides' purpose in affirming his belief in resurrection more explicitly now than he had done earlier. Maimonides lived in an Islamic world that was relatively open; Muslim, Christian and Jewish thinkers spoke and read Arabic, read each other's books, and borrowed freely from each other's thought. Each, too, had its religious rationalists and its fundamentalists who engaged in bitter polemics. Further, in the years in which Maimonides wrote his major works, he not only lived under Islamic rule but also served as a physician in the court of the caliph Saladin. Finally, bodily resurrection was one of the burning issues that sharply divided Muslim rationalists who dismissed it, and their fundamentalist opponents who embraced it as dogma.

We have evidence that in the years preceding and coinciding with the writing of the *Essay*, Saladin championed Islamic orthodoxy and persecuted thinkers who departed from that approach. We also know that Saladin thought that Maimonides' *Guide* undermined all faiths.[36]

Thus, Maimonides was vulnerable to attacks from not only Jewish fundamentalists, but even more seriously, from Muslims on whose favor he depended. It was imperative, then, that he lessen his vulnerability by saying explicitly what he had only hinted at earlier: He *did* believe in bodily resurrection. It was not the ultimate destiny of the individual and he never once recanted his view that the ultimate reward was for the soul alone. But at least resurrection did appear as part of his eschatological scenario. He hoped that this would placate his opponents, both Jewish and Muslim.

Finally, one further perspective on Maimonides' writings as a whole may illuminate his purposes in this material. In his seminal *Persecution and the Art of Writing,* the noted twentieth-century political philosopher Leo Strauss suggests that some thinkers, notably Maimonides and Spinoza, wrote simultaneously on two levels, an exoteric and an esoteric level; that they were addressing two audiences, a public, political or religious orthodoxy and a private

164

heterodoxy. Strauss suggests that these authors wrote—and that we have to read them as writing—"between the lines."[37]

If Strauss is correct, the tension in Maimonides' writings on this issue is deliberate. He wants to reassure traditionalists that he believes in resurrection, and to instruct the "few and scattered" of his students in what he believes is the authentic teaching about the totally spiritual nature of immortality, and to do both at the same time. He trusts the latter group to be perspicacious enough to read "between the lines" and to unearth what he really believes is true.

This may well be the covert message of the concluding sentences of the *Essay*. He reminds his readers that he

> wrote this tract only for the common people who had begun to doubt what I had stated explicitly, and for those who reproached me for brevity when I spoke of the Resurrection. Those who are truly learned are satisfied with a suggestion; they need neither repetition nor prolonged exegesis; they need only summary statements....

And finally,

> the right thing to do is to address each group according to its capacity.[38]

This is Maimonides' most explicit acknowledgement that he is writing for two audiences simultaneously, for "the common people" and for "the truly learned." We should then not be surprised if the author's conclusions are ambiguous: This was his intent from the outset.

The *Essay* is neither a forgery nor a recantation of Maimonides' earlier views. It may be his first attempt to say clearly and explicitly what he had only alluded to much more enigmatically in his earlier works, refining his views sufficiently to mollify his critics. Or, as

Strauss suggests, together with his earlier writings, it may be a deliberately ambiguous statement designed both to placate the Orthodox and to instruct the enlightened.

THE TRIUMPH OF THE SPIRITUAL

In assessing this body of teaching, the first point that must be emphasized is that Maimonides believed we should not expect any reward for serving God. His ideal was that we serve God out of love and in a totally disinterested way. But since most human beings need and expect some form of reward, what should motivate us is the spiritual reward awaiting us in the Age to Come.

What he cannot tolerate is the masses' vulgar belief that the *ultimate* reward is material or bodily delight, that

> the expected good is the Garden of Eden, a place in which one eats and drinks without any physical work or effort...

and where

> houses are made of precious stones, beds of silk, rivers flow with wine and fragrant oils....[39]

At the heart of his rejection of this eschatological materialism lies his commitment to Greek philosophy's dualistic view of the human being. It claims that we are composed of two substances: A material body and a spiritual soul. Of these two, the "real me," my genuine identity, is the soul. The body cannot be a genuine reality because it can be destroyed. But since spiritual substance is indestructible, it is eternal, and hence—and this is the most important conclusion—the ultimate value. The body distracts us from intellectual striving and tempts us to seek the demeaning satisfactions of

166

the body instead of the spiritual delights of philosophy.

The ultimate conclusion of that position is that death is the final, longed for liberation from the demands of the body. That is why philosophers welcome death.

We traced what we called the "judaization" of this doctrine in the apocryphal The Wisdom of Solomon, in Josephus's version of Pharisaic ideology and in later rabbinic literature. But of all Jewish thinkers, Maimonides is the sharpest dualist. He cannot go quite as far as Plato does because much in Judaism's traditional texts exalts the body and attaches value and significance to bodily pleasures. Nor can he claim that death is a liberation to be welcomed. But he is uncomfortable with any suggestion that the body outranks the soul in value. This is the impulse behind his denial of divine corporeality and of his embarrassment at the notion that our ultimate destiny is tied to bodily existence. From this perspective, how could he possibly believe that our bodies will remain eternal?

Torah confronted Maimonides with two challenges: Its notion that there is a reward for service to God in the first place. And equally problematic, its manifold descriptions of that reward in material or bodily terms.

Maimonides would have loved to avoid the whole issue of resurrection. That is amply documented by the way he treats it in all of his writings. But the charge that he denied the doctrine *in toto* is also clearly inaccurate. It was impossible for him to do so: After all, he did recite the *Amidah* with its benediction that God revives the dead, at least three times daily. But what he could do was shape resurrection within his broader view that emphasizes the eternal life of the soul. Though his earliest statement of his position seems to imply that resurrection *means* spiritual immortality, this final statement suggests that the two are distinct: Resurrection comes first, spiritual immortality follows.

This was clearly not sufficient to pacify his critics. The controversy over Maimonides' writings raged for two centuries after his death, and led to condemnations, book-burnings and even excommunications. One of the many issues that fueled the battle was this one. But the sense of loneliness that pervades the *Essay on Resurrection* was simply his destiny, the almost inevitable outcome of his primary commitment which was to teach his community to serve God as he did.

Finally, Maimonides may have been a lonely voice in his own time, but centuries later, when Jews entered the modern age and began to question bodily resurrection, they turned to Maimonides' affirmation of spiritual immortality as a "purer," by which they meant more rational, yet still authentically Jewish alternative. While controversial in his time, his views would eventually have a far greater impact in the modern age than those of his more traditional contemporaries.

MAIMONIDES' PHILOSOPHICAL COLLEAGUES

The medieval period in the history of Jewish thought is commonly dated from the tenth to the fifteenth centuries. Maimonides stands roughly at the center of this period. By any criterion, this work marks the high point of the period as a whole. No other thinker treated the issue of the afterlife as extensively as he did. But he was writing against the background of his predecessors, and his work influenced the thinking of his successors, some in support of his views and others in opposition. He serves as a standpoint from which we can survey the rest of the field.[40]

The first in the line of medieval Jewish rationalists was Saadia ben Joseph (882–942) who was born in Egypt and later served as Gaon or head of the Babylonian academy in Sura. Saadia was a prolific author whose contributions to Jewish philosophy, biblical exegesis, the codification of Jewish law and liturgy, and the study of the Hebrew language were monumental.

Saadia's *Sefer Emunot Ve'Deot* (*The Book of Beliefs and Opinions*), written two centuries before Maimonides' *Guide*, was the first systematic attempt to present the beliefs of Judaism in rational terms and to show that there is no fundamental discord between Torah and reason.

For Saadia, that God has the power to resurrect the dead is the logical implication of God's power to create the world out of nothing. We first encountered that argument in the speech of the mother of the seven sons in II Maccabees. His biblical proof texts are Daniel 12:2, Ezekiel 37 (the vision of the dry bones), Isaiah 26:19, all of which are familiar to us, and Deuteronomy 32:39 (which he translates as "I deal death and give life"). This view raises no philosophical problem for Saadia since he believed that matter is never destroyed but simply preserved in other forms; whatever happens to the body after death, God simply restores it to its original form.

But for Saadia, there are two resurrections: The resurrection of the righteous of Israel at the time of the Messiah, and the resurrection of other persons at the dawn of the Age to Come. The impulse behind this view is Saadia's wish to insure that all righteous Israelites will participate in the national redemption of their people which will take place with the coming of the Messiah. He thus interprets the familiar passage from Daniel 12:2, "many of those who sleep in the dust will awaken," to include not only the righteous Israelites who died as martyrs in the reign of Antiochus IV, but also all past righteous Israelites.

But Saadia understands the conclusion of that passage which prophesies also the resurrection of evildoers "to everlasting abhorrence," in a totally counter-intuitive way. The evildoers, Saadia claims, will not be resurrected but will be marked for eternal shame in their graves. Finally, Saadia interprets resurrection as the return of the soul to the body from which it was separated at death. The individual, reconstituted as body and soul, then faces God for judgement.[41]

The medieval thinker whose views most closely approximate Maimonides' was his slightly older contemporary, Abraham Ibn Ezra (1092–1167). It is not clear what Maimonides knew of Ibn Ezra's writings or when he learned of them, but in his commentary to Daniel 12:2, Ibn Ezra writes:

> In my opinion, the righteous who died in exile will be resurrected when the Redeemer comes.... They will then partake of the Leviathan, Ziz, and the Behemoth and die a second time, only to be again resurrected in the Age to Come, in which they will neither eat nor drink but luxuriate in the splendor of the Shekhina [God's Presence].[42]

Ibn Ezra, here, anticipates Maimonides' notion of the double dying, but is more circumspect about the nature of the ultimate reward to come. He seems to suggest that the ultimate afterlife would be bodiless as Maimonides claimed, but he is not nearly as explicit on that point as was his colleague.

On this issue, Maimonides' arch-antagonist was Moses ben Nahman (commonly known as Nahmanides or through the acronym, the *RaMbaN*). Nahmanides, who wrote and taught in Gerona in the mid-thirteenth century, insisted that after the resurrection, the body and the soul will live for eternity.

To Maimonides' claim that there will be no need for bodies in the hereafter, Nahmanides retorts that since bodies are needed in this world, they will be present in the future world as well. But this future bodily existence will not be identical to the one we know in this life. Our bodies in the Age to Come will be spiritually refined and will not experience physical need. This view was suggested by Abraham ben David of Posquieres as noted above, but derided by Maimonides in his *Essay*.

Nahmanides also rejects Maimonides' theory of "double dying," by quoting Isaiah 25:8, God "will destroy death forever." Thus, the resurrected bodies will live eternally.[43]

An equally fervent denunciator of Maimonidean intellectualism was Hasdai Crescas (1340–1444). For Crescas, what leads to immortality is not knowledge but rather love of God, the ultimate commandment and the goal of all the other commandments. The soul that has achieved this love of God will gain immortality, or eternal union with God, a view which Crescas concedes is not explicit in the Bible but implied there. Since in our lifetime body and soul co-exist, it is fitting that there will be an ultimate reward and punishment for both as well. Hence the need for bodily resurrection.

Echoing Saadia, Crescas taught that resurrection will take place after the coming of the Messiah, and the resurrected dead will then return to inform the living how they fared when their souls left their bodies. But Crescas insists that contra Maimonides, bodily resurrection must be affirmed, first because it is of the essence of human life to be lived in a body, and second, echoing the author of Daniel's concern with the problem of retribution, to affirm God's ultimate justice.[44]

Finally, as the age of medieval Jewish philosophy draws to a close, the last systematic review of the issues of the period was provided by Joseph Albo (1380–1444) in his *Sefer Ha-Ikkarim*, or *Book of Principles*. On most issues he reiterates the teaching of one or the other of his predecessors. His main interest lies less in defending philosophy and more in propounding what he understands to be authentic biblical/talmudic teachings.

Albo echoes Maimonides. He accepts the notion of the "double dying" and agrees that ultimate reward is spiritual only. He also echoes his master's disdain for Nahmanides' view that the resurrected body will be transformed into a spiritualized entity. As a reward, the soul will join with other spiritual beings in apprehending the glory of God. However, the erring soul will rest in limbo, striving for material reward which it can no longer attain while yearning for spiritual bliss which it can never achieve. That state of tension will constitute its ultimate punishment.[45]

This is but a sampling of some of the representative positions on the afterlife in medieval Jewish philosophy. Nothing in this summary overview is strikingly original. The overriding tension in the medieval era was between faith and reason, between Torah and philosophy; and on the afterlife, between bodily resurrection and spiritual immortality. Philosophers marshalled the few explicit and other implicit biblical texts and the weight of the rabbinic tradition in defense of one or the other of the doctrines, and tried to reconcile them with their favored philosophical teachings.

By the close of the fifteenth century, this entire range of issues became moot, only to be revived with the dawn of the Jewish enlightenment at the close of the eighteenth century.

VII

THE MYSTICAL JOURNEY
OF THE SOUL

BY ANY CRITERION, the impact of medieval Jewish philosophy—even of a Maimonides—on the masses of believing Jews was limited. Only the sophisticated elite among the community could digest these writings or even cared about the issues they addressed. Even more, this body of thought had remarkably little impact on Judaism as it was lived and practiced by generations of Jews throughout this period and thereafter. Very few traces of medieval philosophical thinking can be found in our liturgy, for example, or in the rituals and customs of Jewish life.

In contrast, the impact of Jewish mysticism, or *Kabbalah* (Hebrew for "tradition"), as it is commonly called, is omnipresent in Jewish religion to this very day. Countless liturgies, rituals, and doctrines which became part of Jewish practice originated in mystical teachings. So deeply have these practices penetrated the Jewish consciousness that most Jews are not even aware of their origins or their initial meaning.

One example of this influence is the hymn *Lekha Dodi*

("Come, my beloved...") which is now the centerpiece of the Friday evening *Kabbalat Shabbat* service everywhere in today's synagogues, and was written by the sixteenth-century mystic, Simon Alkabez. It emerged out of the practice of the Safed school of Jewish mystics who would go to the outskirts of their city on Friday afternoon to greet the Sabbath bride with songs of praise.[1] A second is the increasingly popular practice of spending the night of the *Shavuot* festival—the festival that celebrates God's revealing the Torah to the Jewish people—in Torah study.[2]

Or note the recent appropriation of the notion of *tikkun olam,* or "repairing the world," to justify a wide range of Jewish social and political activities. The notion that humans are responsible for perfecting the world does appear in talmudic texts. But its more recent use also stems directly from the Safed kabbalists, for whom the performance of God's *mitzvot* "repairs" the metaphysical state of brokenness that pervades the world, and ultimately brings the Messiah.[3]

To put this another way, if medieval Jewish philosophy and Jewish mysticism are both midrashim on earlier Jewish texts and thought, if they are both reformulations of the original content of Torah, then the midrash of the mystics was infinitely more relevant to the needs of the community than its philosophical counterpart.[4]

For a definition of mysticism, we can borrow the suggestion of the scholar of religion, Dr. Rufus Jones. Mysticism, to Jones, is

> [t]he type of religion which puts the emphasis on immediate awareness of relation with God, on direct and intimate consciousness of the Divine Presence. It is religion in its most acute, intense and living stage.[5]

The agenda of Jewish mystical literature is twofold: In its theoretical mode, it describes what the world must look like for this experience to take place. It provides its own distinctive answers to the central questions posed by all forms of religious expression. It discusses, for example, the nature of God and the human being, how God created the world, and how God relates to the created world. In its practical mode, mystical literature instructs one on how to achieve the true mystical experience.

Intimations of this kind of "direct and intimate consciousness" of God can be found in certain biblical texts. For example, Exodus 24:9–11 claims that certain Israelites

> saw the God of Israel: Under His feet there was the likeness of a pavement of sapphire, like the very sky for purity...; they beheld God, and they ate and drank.

Or when the prophet Isaiah claims, "I beheld my Lord seated on a high and lofty throne..." (6:1). Or the prophet Ezekiel's vision of a divine chariot on which there perched "the appearance of the semblance of the Presence of the Lord" (Ezekiel 1:28). The Israelites may have eaten and drank when they perceived God, but both prophets are overwhelmed by their experience. Isaiah cries out, "Woe is me; I am lost! For I am a man of unclean lips.... Yet my own eyes have beheld the King Lord of Hosts" (6:4). And Ezekiel reports, "When I beheld it [the Presence of the Lord], I flung myself down on my face" (1:28).

Or reflect on the psalmist's suggestion, "Taste and see how good the Lord is" (Psalm 34:9). The very suggestion of this almost tangible relationship with God reflects a far more intimate experience than the terms "seeing" God or "hearing" God's voice, which are commonly used to characterize the human experience of God. The metaphorical suggestion that we can "taste" the Lord captures perfectly the texture of the experience the mystic strives to achieve.

Echoes of the mystical experience can also be found in many talmudic narratives, such as the account of the four talmudic masters who entered the *pardes* (literally, the "orchard") of mystical speculation (Bab. Talmud, *Hagigah* 14b).[6]

175

If the language used by mystics to capture the mystical experience seems to recall the language used by the ultra-rationalist Maimonides to characterize the ultimate philosophical experience, that is no accident. Frequently, in philosophy as elsewhere, opposites meet. Rationalists and mystics may follow very different paths, but their ultimate destinations may turn out to be identical. Indeed, the very distinction between Jewish philosophy and Jewish mysticism is a creation of modern scholarship. In all likelihood, medieval mystics and philosophers were not aware that they represented two differing approaches to understanding Judaism. In fact, they were probably unaware that they were doing midrash in the first place; they felt that they were simply articulating what seemed to them to be the plain meaning of Scripture.

WHAT TRANSPIRES BETWEEN DEATH AND RESURRECTION?

Though prefigurations of Jewish mystical experiences are as old as the Bible, and though the emergence of specific mystical doctrines among Jews is usually dated from the first century CE, the crystallization of this understanding of Judaism in a more systematic form and in specific books is a medieval phenomenon. Gershom Scholem, the acknowledged master of the field of Jewish mysticism, claims that the earliest work that adopts "the specific approach and symbolic structure characteristic of kabbalistic thinking" is *Sefer haBahir*, "The Book of Illumination," which made its first appearance in southern France at the end of the twelfth century.[7]

Sefer haBahir is important for our purposes because it sets the agenda for the discussion of the afterlife in the Jewish mystical literature that follows. The issue is not the grand resurrection to come. The fact that God will resurrect the dead is assumed. What is of primary concern to the mystics, however, and what remains their most distinctive contribution to the development of afterlife doctrines in Judaism, is their portrayal of the fate of the soul in the period between death and resurrection. Here, the central doctrine is that of metempsychosis, the transmigration of souls, or to use the popular term, reincarnation. In Hebrew, the term is *gilgul,* or literally, "revolving."

Whenever I lecture on the afterlife before lay audiences, I am invariably asked about reincarnation. I am tempted to dismiss the doctrine as a popular superstition, but that would seriously underestimate its importance both in Judaism and for many of our contemporaries. Though the notion of reincarnation is not found in talmudic literature, and though it was opposed by major medieval Jewish philosophers such as Saadia and Albo, and ignored by others such as Maimonides and Yehudah Halevi, it becomes omnipresent and of increasing importance in medieval kabbalistic literature and thereafter. And it clearly persists in the popular Jewish imagination to this day.[8]

Jews probably inherited the doctrine of reincarnation from some Christian sects who learned of it from Oriental religions or from early medieval versions of Platonic teachings.[9] The Greek philosophical assumptions of the doctrine are obvious. The kabbalists believed in the pre-existence of souls, and that the soul survives the death of the body. Following Aristotle, they understood the three biblical terms that, we saw earlier, came to characterize this independent part of the human person—*nefesh, neshamah* and *ruah*—to define three distinct parts of the soul. *Nefesh* came to mean life itself, the vital part of the person; *neshamah* is that part of the soul which is concerned with mystical cognition; *ruah* involves the power of ethical discrimination.[10]

The doctrine of reincarnation, as its name implies, teaches that after death, some souls that depart the body in which they were "housed" enter into other bodies—how many depends on the stage in the development of the doctrine over time—until the resurrection.

WHY DO THE INNOCENT SUFFER?

The impulse behind the doctrine is familiar to us from our study of the first appearance of resurrection in Daniel. It is the most radical challenge facing monotheism: How can a just and compassionate God permit the innocent to suffer and evildoers to triumph? The kabbalistic answer to that challenge is that the innocent suffer because of sins committed in earlier incarnations. Thus, reincarnation appears as an expression of both God's judgement and God's mercy: Judgement, because human sin must be purged before resurrection; and mercy, because God gives the individual soul manifold opportunities to perfect itself before it reaches its ultimate destiny.[11] When will that take place? When will reincarnation cease? At the time of resurrection.

A sense of the impulse behind the doctrine of reincarnation in *Sefer haBahir* can be captured in this passage:

> Why is there a righteous person who has good, and [another] righteous person who has evil? This is because the [second] righteous person was wicked previously, and is now being punished. Is one then punished for his childhood deeds?...
>
> I am not speaking of his present lifetime. I am speaking about what he has already been, previously.... Go out and see. What is this life? A person planted a vineyard and hoped to grow grapes, but instead, sour grapes grew. He saw that his planting and harvest were not successful so he tore it out. He cleaned out the sour grape vines and planted again. When he saw that his planting was not successful, he tore it up and planted it again.[12]

In *Sefer haBahir* and the early kabbalistic literature, the sins which reincarnation purges are limited to offenses against the law of procreation and sexual offenses.[13] By the time of *Sefer haZohar* (literally, "The Book of Splendor"), the classic of kabbalistic literature, compiled in Spain toward the end of the thirteenth century, the doctrine has expanded to deal with all human sins. It becomes a universal law of retribution governing all creatures.[14]

But if, in the course of achieving its destiny, the soul inhabits many bodies, then what will be the ultimate fate of all of these bodies through which the soul has passed until the grand resurrection to come? Ostensibly, only the final bodily habitation of the soul will be resurrected. But God's justice demands that all these other bodies which the soul had inhabited and which helped it achieve its state of purity should also share in the final judgement. The answer to this question led the kabbalists to the theory of "soul sparks" (in Hebrew, *nitsotsot*). According to this doctrine, any one human body may acquire sparks of many different souls. Thus, the resurrection of any one human affects the fate of the many other bodies which housed this particular soul. This doctrine will become central in the later evolution of the doctrine of reincarnation.[15]

Three centuries later, in the middle of the sixteenth century, this doctrine achieves its most expanded statement in the kabbalistic teachings of the Safed school of Rabbi Isaac Luria.

First, some general background. Gershom Scholem claims that Lurianic *kabbalah* developed as a response to the expulsion of Jews from Spain and Portugal at the close of the fifteenth century. At its core, it is a stunning myth of exile and redemption. The history of the Jewish people becomes a symbol of a far grander drama where not only Jews, but the entire world, and even God, are in exile and await redemption.

The four cornerstones of the Lurianic myth are the doctrines of *tzimtzum*, or "contraction"; *shevirat hakelim*, or "the breaking of the vessels"; *yeridat hashefa*, or creation through emanation; and *tikkun*, or "restoration." The colorful character of these metaphors captures the imaginative way in which these mystics reformulated the content of Torah and helps us understand the power of the Lurianic myth in particular. It is clearly far more striking than any doctrine penned by medieval Jewish philosophers.

The most imaginative aspects of Lurianic mysticism deal with events that took place prior to the creation of the world as described in Genesis, so to speak, in the silence prior to Genesis 1:1. Before the beginning of creation, God was everywhere and everything. In order to create the world, God had to contract, to limit God's self, so as to prepare the primordial space in which the world would come to be. Thus, the teaching that the first stage in God's creation of the world was an act of contraction, or self-limitation, by God and within God.

Creation itself took place by emanation of one dimension of God into this primordial space. However transcendent God may be, however "Other" than the created world, God is also within creation, immanent throughout the world. This is a revolutionary understanding of creation which seems to depart radically from the implications of the account of creation in Genesis. At the conclusion of the Genesis account of creation, God and God's created world are substantively distinct; a gap exists between God and the world. Of course, that gap is constantly bridged by God's revelation, for example, or by human prayer, but no aspect of God is identical with creation. Indeed the notion that God and the world are identical leads to pantheism, long considered heretical in Jewish circles. The kabbalists avoided pantheism by espousing the notion that God had two "faces" or two dimensions, *En Sof,* literally "Without End" or "Infinity," God in God's self, God's essential nature, and that aspect of God that emanated into creation, the "finite" God as opposed to the infinite *En Sof.* It is only this second dimension of God's nature that is identified with the created world.

In other words, the kabbalists skirted one heresy, pantheism, by embracing a different heresy, dualism, that is, the belief that there are two Gods. But when accused of dualism, the kabbalists would insist that these two dimensions of God are but two aspects of the one God. These pantheistic and/or dualistic implications of mystical teachings helped to fuel the tensions that persisted between Jewish mystics and their opponents.

If creation is by emanation, then God pervades creation. God is literally "within" the created world. This notion becomes indispensable to Luria's view of redemption.

The process of emanation resulted in the emergence of "vessels" that were designed to contain the light of creation so that the creative process would proceed in an orderly way. But these vessels shattered when they could not hold the light of God's emanation. The divine light returned to its source, God, but the fragments of the vessels became embedded in *kelipot* or "shells" scattered throughout the primordial space. This cosmic catastrophe accounts for the presence of evil in God's created world. The primary symbol for this chaotic element in the world is Exile. And because God is immanent in creation, God too is in exile, in a state of imperfection. Or, to use Lurianic terminology, the two dimensions of God's nature, the infinite, transcendent God and the finite, emanated God became alienated one from the other.

Finally, Luria taught that the process of redemption is one of *tikkun*, literally a cosmic "repairing" of the fragmented vessels thereby restoring the original order intended by God. A major part of that process of repair is entrusted to Jews through their observing God's commands. Each command, fulfilled with the proper intent, repairs the shattered vessels, restores the harmony of creation, and knits together God's two dimensions. In other words, Jews' repairing of the world even redeems God, and brings the Messiah.[16]

A liturgical reflection of this last notion is in a series of *kavvanot* (Hebrew for "intentions" or "focusings"), brief prayers uttered prior to performing a *mitzvah,* and designed to help focus the worshipper's attention on the larger, cosmic purpose of the *mitzvah* to be performed. A typical version of this passage reads

> For the sake of the unification of the Blessed Holy One, and God's Presence [in Hebrew, *Shekhina*], in fear and love to unify the Name [here follows the four-letter name of God, but with the first two letters split from the last two], in perfect unity, in the name of all Israel.[17]

Here, the splitting apart of God's two dimensions is symbolized by the split between the first two and last two letters of God's name. The performance of the *mitzvah* with the proper intent reunites or repairs God's name and restores God's original unity. For Luria, reincarnation becomes an integral part of this broad process of restoration. The idea of retribution for sin is pushed into the background. In its place, Luria teaches that every soul is given unlimited opportunities to work through its own individual *tikkun*, to fulfill more and more of God's commands, until it reaches its state of perfection. In achieving this goal, the individual soul is assisted by all of the soul sparks which have adhered to it in the course of its career. Scholem notes that this complex of soul sparks associated with each individual, captures "a certain expansion of the psychophysical unity of the individual, through its transformation into a unified field of energy."[18] At the same time, the *tikkun* of each reincarnated soul contributes to the broader process of cosmic restoration which leads to the ultimate redemption of Israel, the world, and God.[19] In Scholem's words,

> Lurianic Kabbalah placed the Jew in an ineluctable entanglement of transmigrations....(A)ll things are in exile,...all things must wander and transmigrate in order to prepare, through a combined effort, for redemption.[20]

182

EXILE AS A METAPHYSICAL CONDITION

As in our study of the historical setting for the emergence of the doctrine of resurrection in Daniel, the existential setting for the emergence of this complex myth is crucial. In Daniel, it was the martyrdom of pious Jews at the hands of Antiochus IV. If Scholem's thesis is correct, the complex Lurianic myth and its reformulation of the doctrine of reincarnation reflected the situation of a generation of Jews who had experienced anew the trauma of dispersion and homelessness. The myth in its entirety was designed to provide a measure of consolation to that generation; not only are they in exile, but so is the world and so is God. Exile is no longer simply a historical event; it becomes a metaphysical symbol of all that is not right in creation. Fragmentation is everywhere in the world. But the myth also accomplishes one further significant goal. It provided Jews with the resources to repair the fragmented world, to end the exile and hasten the redemption: Perform God's commands.

Is it any wonder then, that, as Scholem claims, this doctrine of reincarnation extended its influence, after 1550, with startling rapidity and became what it is to this day, an integral part of Jewish popular belief and folklore? It could achieve this standing because, as Scholem claims, it was central to a body of teachings that

> explained, transfigured and glorified the deepest and most tragic experience of the Jew in *Galuth* [exile], in a manner which appealed most strongly and directly to the imagination. Formerly it had been regarded either as a punishment for Israel's sins or as a test of Israel's faith. Now it still is all this, but intrinsically it is a mission: its purpose is to uplift the fallen sparks from all their various locations.[21]

From the sixteenth century on, reincarnated souls were

everywhere in the Jewish imagination. They populated folktales, hasidic stories and the liturgy. The prelude to the *Sh'ma* recited upon going to sleep at night, for example, reads:

> Master of the Universe, I hereby forgive anyone who angered or antagonized me or who sinned against me ...whether through speech, deed, thought, or notion, whether in this transmigration or another transmigration...[22]

Reincarnated souls could appear as a temporary benign possession, designed to allow the soul to accomplish one specific test (the doctrine of *ibbur,* or "pregnancy"). The doctrine of *ibbur* was at the core of the doctrine of "chains of transmigration." The mystics believed that one can trace the journey of a soul through a series of specific reincarnations. Considerable exegetical skill was exercised, for example, in proving that certain biblical figures incorporated the souls of specific predecessors.

The mystics also believed that one could be possessed by a *dybbuk* (literally, "cleaving" or "clinging"), a soul that, because of its sins, is not even allowed to transmigrate and seeks refuge in the body of a living person. A *dybbuk* had to be exorcised and the later literature is replete with liturgies and rituals designed to exorcise these demonic souls.[23] These traditions persist to this day in hasidic circles, even in non-hasidic circles, and, in a largely attenuated form, in popular Jewish superstitions.[24]

Scholem weaves an intriguing and startling thesis regarding the ultimate impact of Lurianic mysticism on Jewish history in the centuries following. This thesis claims that the complex myth of exile and redemption taught by Luria and his disciples was so effective and had such a broad impact that it is thoroughly understandable why masses of Jews came to believe, a century later, that the ultimate *tikkun* had been achieved, that redemption was at hand, and that the Messiah had finally come in the personage of Sabbatai Zevi.

This traumatic episode in Jewish history reached its climax in Sabbatai Zevi's conversion to Islam in 1666. This step forced his disciples to choose between two equally painful conclusions: Either his apostasy was part of the divinely ordained messianic scenario, and he would reappear in triumph as the true Messiah. Or he was a false Messiah from the outset and the entire Sabbatai Zevi phenomenon was a tragic mistake. The first reaction led to the Sabbatian movement which Jewish authorities branded heretical, and its adherents relentlessly pursued for generations.[25] The second reaction was one of the factors that led to a radical reformulation of the Lurianic myth which emerged, a century later, as Hasidism.

Scholem contends—the claim is highly controversial among scholars of the field—that Hasidism is Lurianic kabbalah without its messianic or redemptive thrust.[26] Lurianic messianism had become destructive and dangerous. The new hasidic ideal becomes *devekut* (literally, "clinging" to, or "communion" with God), which is achieved through inner concentration or contemplation. No longer does the performance of the *mitzvot* alone lead to the redemption of Israel, the world and God. Indeed, the entire notion that Jews can collectively redeem the world by their behavior becomes of secondary importance. The new emphasis is on a more personal impulse whereby one's achievement of *devekut* redeems his or her individual soul sparks through communion with God. That in itself becomes the ultimate religious ideal. In this last stage of its development, the doctrine of reincarnation provides the individual Jew with the means of achieving personal redemption.[27]

Finally—and this is by far the most controversial of the claims associated with Scholem's thinking—Scholem suggests that the messianic thrust in Lurianic mysticism did not simply disappear. It went underground for generations and later emerged, in a thoroughly secularized form, in political Zionism. Once again, Jews came to believe that they could "bring the Messiah" by dint of human activity, now, not through performing the ritual *mitzvot* of Judaism, but through political and diplomatic efforts. They did not use the religious language of *mitzvah*. But what the first generation of Zionist ideologues was re-affirming, now in secular language, was the Lurianic program, namely the redemptive power of human activity.

This far-ranging thesis is one of those grand, imaginative patterns that only the most accomplished masters of a discipline can perceive. Whether or not it is correct in all of its details, its stunning accomplishment is to integrate the history of the Jewish people and of Jewish thought over four centuries into one coherent scheme. This may well be the most far-ranging of Scholem's many accomplishments.

THE TRIUMPH OF THE SPIRITUAL

Not unexpectedly, the teachings of Jewish mysticism were derided by the scholars of the Jewish enlightenment. These teachings were perceived as a primitive, embarrassing, almost pagan composite of beliefs, practices and superstitions, not worthy of Judaism in general, and certainly not a subject for serious scholarly investigation. The noted nineteenth-century historian of the Jews, Heinrich Graetz, for example, begins his discussion of the teachings of Isaac Luria by writing of "the darkness of medievalism" which settled upon Jewry while the rest of Europe beheld "the dawn of a new day." Luria, he claims, "infected an ever growing circle with [his] vagaries and ecstasies."[28] Not until Gershom Scholem began his scholarly career in the 1920s did the Jewish world take note.[29] Ironically, while nineteenth century Jewish historians were energetically deriding the mystics, their contemporaries were reaffirming the very same triumph of spiritual immortality that the mystics had celebrated, but now, in the much more rarified form that it took, for example, in the writings of Maimonides.

186

In our own day, Scholem's work, together the impact of the new, cross-cultural concern with spirituality, this entire tradition has been reappropriated by many Jews. If anything, they perceive it to represent Judaism at its most authentic. It is not surprising, then, that the doctrine of reincarnation has awakened widespread contemporary interest. It addresses many of the issues of the age: The upcoming millennium, the dread of mortality, the search for the meaning of a human life, the current interest in Eastern religions (which was probably the original source for Jewish teachings on reincarnation), the New Age movement, and the rejection of modernity's reliance on science and technology as the ultimate arbiters of human achievement. Theology, as we have seen, never exists in a vacuum; it invariably responds to an existential situation, to issues posed by the life-experience of a community. Jewish theology has clearly done so again, in our day.

On the issue of the afterlife, then, the mystics were not overly concerned with bodily resurrection. That doctrine was well-established and accepted as canonical. What did fascinate them was the soul. The mystics were obsessed with the nature and destiny of the soul, both before and after death. They clearly understood it to be the "real" person, the source of our distinctive identity. They explored its origins, its structure, and the twists and turns of its journey toward that "direct and intimate consciousness of the Divine Presence" which constituted the core of the mystical experience. For the mystic, the journey began even before the birth of the individual, and one's entire lifetime was preparation for that ultimate encounter. Death marked the onset of the final stage of the journey. Mystical eschatology, then, was essentially the eschatology of the soul.

This could also serve as an excellent summary statement on the treatment of the afterlife throughout the Middle Ages, both in philosophy and in mysticism. Plato and Aristotle permeate this material. True, medieval thinkers were able to draw upon a long and rich tradition of what we have called the "judaization" of Plato, dating back at least to the first century CE. But in contrast with the literature of the Talmud where platonic traces are scattered and diffuse, in medieval philosophy and certainly in the *kabbalah,* that process is systematic and all-encompassing.

Torah had its place in the picture—how could it be otherwise? But by and large, thinkers shaped the teachings of Torah to fit conceptual schemes whose origins lay far from biblical and talmudic teachings. Again, we marvel at the power of midrash!

VIII

THE ENCOUNTER WITH MODERNITY

HISTORIANS COMMONLY DATE Judaism's encounter with modernity to the late eighteenth century. This is when Jews encountered the two movements that transformed Judaism and the Jewish people and continue to shape the Jewish agenda to óur day: The Enlightenment (or *Haskalah,* from the Hebrew root for "understand"), and its political counterpart, the Emancipation.

Enlightenment and Emancipation represented two facets of one single process: Judaism's gradual accommodation, in fits and starts and not always with great enthusiasm, to the political, socioeconomic, cultural and intellectual currents of Western civilization, first in Western Europe and America and eventually in Eastern Europe as well.

Enlightenment refers to the cultural or intellectual dimension of that process, when Jews begin to absorb the intellectual currents in the community at large, to enter universities, read books in foreign languages, and study new disciplines. They begin to think like their non-Jewish contemporaries; even more important, they begin to apply these new ways of understanding to Judaism. Emancipation refers to the political dimension of the process: Jews become citizens of emerging national states—France in 1789, America in 1791—with the same rights and responsibilities as all citizens of these states.

In short, the Jewish encounter with modernity led to the collapse of the intellectual and political walls that had separated the Jewish community from the rest of the world. In the process, it would transform everything Jewish—particularly Judaism's beliefs and practices—for it was the distinctive character of the Jewish religion that had established these walls in the first place.[1]

The encounter with modernity reveals a progressive disenchantment with the doctrine of bodily resurrection and a growing emphasis on the immortality of the soul. The belief in resurrection is judged to be primitive, out of synch with sophisticated Western thinking; and even, astonishingly, not grounded in classical Jewish tradition. In contrast, the doctrine of spiritual immortality is praised as more intellectually respectable, as more "elevating," as more in tune with the enlightened spirit of the age.

THE MODERN TRIUMPH OF THE SPIRITUAL

This triumph of spiritual immortality is not new in Jewish intellectual history. It had appeared, centuries earlier, in the thought of some medieval Jewish philosophers, Maimonides in particular, and in Jewish mysticism. Enlightenment thinkers may have ignored the mystical tradition, but the belated impact of Maimonides' writings on the afterlife is omnipresent here, sometimes implicitly, but frequently quite explicitly. More radical thinkers simply expunge resurrection and replace it with spiritual immortality; others, who are more sensitive to tradition, impose the latter on the former so that resurrection

190

comes to mean spiritual immortality. Only within recent decades has this process begun to be reversed.

A forecast of this triumph of spiritual immortality as Judaism encountered the modern temper can be seen in the thought of Moses Mendelssohn (1729–1786), who was arguably the model of the enlightened Jew. He advocated the integration of his fellow Jews into the broad cultural milieu in which they lived and provided a personal role model for how that could be achieved. He encouraged Jews to master German so that they could gain access to the best scientific, philosophical and literary writings of the day. What kept him—in contrast to his descendants and later disciples, most of whom eventually converted to Christianity—solidly within the Jewish community was his fervent commitment to Jewish law which he understood had been revealed at Sinai and was hence eternally binding. The assumption which made it possible to integrate his Jewishness and his enlightened modernism was his conviction that all Jewish beliefs, indeed all religious beliefs, are rational and hence universally compelling, and that no philosophical teaching could undermine Jewish faith and practice.

The book that initially established Mendelssohn's renown was his *Phaedon or On the Immortality of the Soul in Three Dialogues* (1767). Widely read, it was reprinted many times and quickly translated into many languages. As the title implies, this work is based on Plato's dialogue of the same name, both in its form, which replicated the dialogue format that Plato used, and in its substance.[2]

As in Plato, Socrates, facing death, expounds to his disciples the arguments for the immortality of the soul. The dialogue form lends a measure of drama and poetry to what would otherwise be a dry philosophical treatise. The author characterizes his work as "something intermediate between a translation and a work of my own."[3] On substance, Mendelssohn admits that he puts arguments in Socrates' mouth that the Socrates of history could never have

191

known. His Socrates is a modern, enlightened contemporary, and his arguments are thoroughly consistent with the best philosophical thought of the Enlightenment.

Briefly, Mendelssohn argues that all "simple" (that is, non-composite) substances are indestructible, and that since the soul is a simple substance that unifies the composites that form the body, the soul is also indestructible. But to claim that the soul is indestructible does not mean that it is immortal, that it retains its conscious, rational nature after death. Mendelssohn demonstrates this further claim by arguing, first, that it is inconceivable that the Supreme Being would encourage humans to pursue perfection here on earth, and then deprive them of the opportunity to achieve it with their death; second, that only through the doctrine of immortality can we reconcile God's providence with the actual fate of humans during their earthly existence; and finally, that since the impulse for human perfection may demand that individuals sacrifice their lives for the sake of others, they must continue to exist in some other way after death in order to make that sacrifice legitimate.

Mendelssohn avoids any discussion of the nature of life after death. He also does not raise the issue of bodily resurrection, though he acknowledges that in that life to come, we may retain some bodily functions. What is important is that the main issue is spiritual immortality, and that the truth of that doctrine is demonstrated through thoroughly rational arguments. The rationalism of the age, carried into religion, demanded the advocacy of spiritual immortality.

Phaedon is in no way a "Jewish" book; its audience was the philosophical elite of the day. Though Mendelssohn did write a Hebrew version of the dialogues that was published after his death, it is questionable how many of Mendelssohn's Jewish contemporaries could deal with the type of argumentation he mustered. But the currents that produced a Mendelssohn were at work in the Jewish community at large and could not be avoided.

we hope you will enjoy this book and that you will find it useful and use it to enrich your life.

Book title: _____

Your comments: _____

How you learned of this book: _____

Reasons why you bought this book: (check all that apply) ☐ Subject ☐ Author ☐ Attractive Cover
☐ Attractive Inside ☐ Recommendation of Friend ☐ Recommendation of Reviewer ☐ Gift
If purchased: Bookseller _____ City _____ State _____

Please send me a JEWISH LIGHTS Publishing catalog. I am particularly interested in: (check all that apply)

1. ☐ Spirituality
2. ☐ Mysticism
3. ☐ Philosophy/Theology
4. ☐ History/Politics
5. ☐ Women's Issues
6. ☐ Environmental Issues
7. ☐ Healing/Recovery
8. ☐ Children's Books
9. ☐ Limited Edition Books
10. ☐ Haggadahs
11. ☐ Audio Tapes of Books
12. ☐ Audio Tapes of Author Lectures

Name (Print) _____ Phone _____

Street _____

City _____ State _____ Zip _____

Please send a JEWISH LIGHTS Publishing catalog to my friend:

Name (Print) _____ Phone _____

Street _____

City _____ State _____ Zip _____

JEWISH LIGHTS PUBLISHING

P.O. Box 237 • Sunset Farm Offices, Rte. 4 • Woodstock, VT 05091 • Tel: (802) 457-4000 Fax: (802) 457-4004
JEWISH LIGHTS Publishing books are available at better booksellers

JEWISH LIGHTS PUBLISHING
P.O. BOX 237
SUNSET FARM OFFICES, RTE. 4
WOODSTOCK, VT 05091-0237

MODERN LITURGICAL REFORMS

The evolution of these currents of thought can be traced in the theological/ideological writings of modern Jewish thinkers. More particularly, they can be traced in their prayer books, first in the ways they translated the traditional rabbinic liturgical texts into German, and later into English, and eventually in the outright changes they introduced into the Hebrew text of their liturgies.

These liturgical changes are significant because it is primarily through liturgy that the distinctive Jewish sensibility was shaped. Theological statements and ideological platforms have their place and must be read carefully, but the very large majority of caring Jews rarely consulted these documents. What they did encounter, weekly or even daily, was the prayer book. Even in antiquity, it was particularly the liturgical use of selected biblical and rabbinic texts which brought certain classical Jewish doctrines to the fore and impressed them on the consciousness of every Jew. In our case, it was the Pharisaic and later rabbinic incorporation of the doctrine of resurrection into the *Gevurot* benediction of the *Amidah* that lent that doctrine canonical status. Reject that doctrine on theological or ideological grounds and the liturgical text becomes problematic.

There are three possible strategies for handling a liturgy that no longer reflects your theology: Replace the Hebrew with a more palatable alternative; keep the Hebrew text and shade the translation to accommodate your new interpretation of the doctrine; or provide options which allow the worshipper to choose a text that reflects his or her particular belief.

The last of these strategies, the most recently adopted, is used in the Reform movement's 1975 *New Union Prayer Book* (more commonly called *Gates of Prayer*), more sparingly in the Conservative movement's *Siddur Sim Shalom* (1985), and in *Kol Haneshamah*, the 1994 prayer book of the Reconstructionist movement. The first strategy—replacing the original Hebrew—was adopted by the early

193

American Reform movement in its 1895 *Union Prayer Book,* and by Mordecai Kaplan in his first liturgical publication, the *Sabbath Prayer Book* (1945), designed for his then-nascent Reconstructionist movement.

The second strategy, keep the original but shade the translation, was preferred by those who were reluctant to reject a traditional formulation, yet felt sufficiently uncomfortable with it to impose their own interpretation on the traditional text through the translation. A few early European Reform texts use this strategy, but it eventually became the characteristic approach of prayer books published in recent decades by the Conservative movement.

Each of these strategies has its merits and its problems. The first, the most radical approach, has the merit of honesty, but it profoundly offends the traditionalist. The precise wording of the core portions of the liturgy, particularly the *Amidah,* had become mandated by the *halakhah* as early as the first century CE. These very words had achieved a unique sanctity. Changing them, for whatever reason, was a grave affront to traditional Judaism.

But beyond this, this strategy deprives the worshipper of an encounter with the central themes of the classical tradition, and the experience of struggling with their content. The editor of the prayer book does that work on behalf of the worshipper, and typically presents the conclusions of the inquiry without tracing the process that led to that conclusion. A student of mine, raised in a Reform synagogue, protested that she had never seen a traditional prayer book, never knew what it taught, and was thereby deprived of her own opportunity to decide how she felt about the traditional doctrines.

The second strategy, keeping the original Hebrew but modifying the translation, rests its case on the indeterminacy of meaning in poetic or liturgical language. Statements such as that God revives the dead can mean many different things and we should not feel ourselves bound to an excessively literal interpretation of the text. That may be true, but in fact, this strategy works as long as the worshipper understands Hebrew, and can appreciate the varying meanings of the original text. But most American Jews do not understand the Hebrew of the prayer book. The strategy may be effective for the editor but not for the worshipper.

Providing a series of optional versions of the prayer in question seems to meet all these objections, but this makes the prayer book somewhat confusing and deprives the liturgy of one of its most significant functions: Providing a predictable structure for the experience of prayer.

In practice, most recent non-traditional prayer books adopt a mix of all these strategies. Reform's *Gates of Prayer,* for example, provides the congregation with ten different versions of the Sabbath Eve service, but each of these adopts most of Reform's characteristic liturgical changes, and rarely does its English capture the precise literal sense of the Hebrew text that was adopted.

For the rest of this chapter, we will focus on the various strategies modern liturgists have used for dealing with the wording of the *Gevurot* benediction of the *Amidah* (to be referred to as "our benediction") discussed at length above, specifically in its closing words which praise God Who "...revives the dead" (Hebrew, ...*mehaye hametim*). This specific text affirms the canonical status of the doctrine of resurrection. Because of its antiquity, its prominence in the core portion of the liturgy, its omnipresence in every single worship, and its halakhic status (since it uses the traditional formula, *Baruk Atah Adonai...*, "Praised are You, Lord...," which incorporates the name of God, the use of which was strictly regulated by Jewish law),[4] modern liturgists could not ignore it. It was an affront to their deepest theological convictions, but changing the original text was a radical move.

The phrase *mehaye hametim* is frustratingly concise and enigmatic. What did the liturgist mean in penning these words? Bodily resurrection alone? Restoring the soul to the resurrected body? We don't really know. It is precisely this indeterminacy of meaning which gave modern liturgists the latitude to interpret the words in ways consistent with their own convictions.

Here is a literal translation of the traditional text of our benediction:

> You are eternally mighty, Lord, you revive the dead, You are abundantly able to save.

> You sustain the living with kindness, You revive the dead with great mercy. You support those who fall, heal the sick, set the captives free, and keep faithfulness with those who sleep in the dust. Who is like You, Lord of power? Who resembles You, O King Who brings death and restores life, and causes salvation to flourish?

> You are faithful to revive the dead. Blessed are You, O Lord, Who revives the dead.

REFORM'S AMBIVALENCE ABOUT RESURRECTION

The Reform movement was the first to deal systematically with the full range of challenges posed by modernity. It is impossible to over-estimate the impact of the early nineteenth century German Reformers on modern Judaism. They were deeply devoted Jews. They cared desperately about the future of Judaism and the Jewish people. They were convinced that their reforms were the only way to save Judaism for the ages. They also faced unprecedented challenges. Much of Jewish intellectual history in the nineteenth and twentieth centuries can only be understood as a reaction to the agenda of these early Reformers, who influenced the shape of all modern Jewish movements.[5]

196

It is no accident that Reform focused its first, tentative attempts to change Jewish religious life on the worship service. That was where most Jews encountered Judaism. Further, in contrast to the home, the synagogue represented the public face of Judaism to the world, and these men cared deeply about the non-Jewish community's perception of Judaism. Finally, if you want to transform Jewish beliefs, you must modify the liturgy.

Yet, somewhat surprisingly, the early German Reform ideologues were reluctant to tamper with the traditional liturgy. They did concentrate on the externalities of the service: They wanted more decorum in the synagogue and they introduced choral singing, the sermon in the vernacular and German translations of selected prayers. But with very few exceptions, they retained the traditional liturgy. This was but one expression of a far deeper controversy among the early Reformers regarding the substance, the pace, and the manner of reform. What was to be changed? Just the externalities of the worship service, or substantive beliefs and practices? How quickly and in what manner were these changes to be effected? Immediately, by decree of rabbinic authorities? Or by gradual evolution?

On the issue of liturgical change, and specifically on the issue of resurrection in the *Gevurot* benediction of the *Amidah*, Rabbi Jakob Petuchowski, the master historian of liturgical reform in modern times, notes:

> Not a single one of the rituals under consideration here found it necessary to change the Hebrew text, although many of them (but not all!) substituted the concept of Immortality in their vernacular translation or paraphrase.[6]

In the 1841–42 edition of the *Forms of Prayer* of the West London Synagogue of British Jews, this reluctance to expunge references to resurrection was justified on the ground that it had its origins in the Bible which was divine.[7]

The most celebrated prayer book controversy in this period was prompted by the 1841 publication by the Hamburg Temple, the first congregation to be founded (in 1817) explicitly on Reform principles, of a revised version of their original 1819 prayer book. Though this 1841 edition proclaims its Reform character by opening from left to right rather than right to left as do traditional Jewish books, it limited its liturgical changes to omitting the prayer for the return to Zion and the restoration of the Temple cult. Our benediction appears in its traditional form and is given a literal translation.[8]

But in 1844, at a conference of Reform rabbis meeting in the German city of Brunswick, Abraham Geiger (1810–1874), the acknowledged ideological father of European Reform, spoke on the issues involved in creating a new prayer book. He notes that during its long history, Judaism had "attracted to itself ideas and sentiments which have become entirely foreign to our time, which in fact have been strongly rejected by it." Some of these concepts have taken on "a more spiritual character and, therefore, their expression in prayer must be more spiritual." One of these is the hope for an afterlife which "should not be expressed in terms which suggest a future revival, a resurrection of the body; rather they must stress the immortality of the human soul."[9]

Geiger was later to serve congregations in Breslau, Frankfurt, and Berlin. In 1869, Geiger addressed a memorandum to his Frankfort congregation on the publication of a new prayer book. Again, he lists specific guiding principles, one of which reiterates his belief that immortality should not be restricted to physical resurrection, but should also include the concept of spiritual immortality.[10]

In line with this position, the 1854 prayer book that Geiger compiled while serving in Breslau, and its later version, published in Berlin in 1870, retains the Hebrew of our benediction but translates its concluding passage *"der Leben spendet hier and dort,"* literally, "who bestows life here and there." A free translation of that last phrase would probably be "in this world and the other," that is, in this age and in the age to come. The Hebrew original remains, but the vernacular disposes of resurrection and replaces it with a vaguely-worded promise of eternal life.

Geiger's attempt to justify the changes he proposes is typical of what we will encounter in much of the literature that follows to the middle of our century. Whatever we might feel about the conclusions of Mendelssohn's proofs, they serve as an exemplar of a sustained argument for the doctrine of immortality. There is nothing in Geiger that even begins to approach that kind of inquiry. There is an intuitive sense that physical resurrection is not worthy of serious consideration and it is just dismissed. Nor is there a clear exposition of what the alternative doctrine really says, not to mention a consideration of the new problems it creates. It will take a full century before those broader questions are even posed, let alone seriously discussed.

If a single figure shaped the history of liturgical change in Reform, that man was Rabbi David Einhorn (1809–1879). Einhorn served as rabbi of various Reform congregations in Germany and later in America. At the 1845 Frankfurt Conference of Reform rabbis, he advocated introducing German into the worship service and eliminating prayers for the return to Zion and the restoration of the Temple cult. Those and similar positions established him as the champion of the more radical wing of German Reform, but the opposition he aroused convinced him that he would find a more congenial audience for his views in America. In 1856, he was appointed Rabbi of Har Sinai Temple in Baltimore, and later served in Philadelphia and at New York's Temple Emanu-El.

Einhorn's expectation that American Jews would be more open to his radical approach to Reform than their European counterparts was amply justified. The first Reform congregation to be established on American soil had been The Reformed Society of Israelites in Charleston, South Carolina in 1824. In 1826, the founding members of this congregation adopted a ten-point creed, loosely based on Maimonides' Thirteen Principles. One of its paragraphs reads:

> I believe, with a perfect faith, that the soul of man was breathed into him by God, and is therefore immortal.[11]

The historian of the Reform movement, Michael Meyer, notes that the Society's 1825 prayer book was "the first radical liturgy produced by a Reform congregation anywhere." The order of the service was rearranged and shortened, many traditional prayers (such as the restoration of sacrifices, the anticipated advent of the Messiah, and the return to Zion) were excised, and most of the service was recited in English. But despite the credal statement noted above, the liturgical passage dealing with resurrection remained.[12]

As in Europe, these early decades of the Reform experience in America were marked by a good deal of controversy over the substance and the pace of reform, and the liturgical voice of the Charleston congregation did not go unopposed. The year 1857 saw the publication of *Minhag America,* a prayer book authored by the institutional father of American Reform, Rabbi Isaac Mayer Wise. And in 1871, Rabbi Marcus Jastrow of Baltimore published his *Abodath Yisrael.* Both reflected the more conservative wing of American Reform, and both maintained the traditional form of our benediction.

But it was Einhorn's vision that was destined to shape the future course of the Reform movement. In 1856, Einhorn published *Olat Tamid: Book of Prayers for Jewish Congregations,* a prayer book which embodied all of his liturgical reforms, and which stated as one of its guiding principles, the

> clear and undeniable fact that the traditional service has no charm for the present generation; the old prayers have become for the most part untruths for present

conditions and views....Salvation will come only from a complete reform of the public service which, founded on principle, will enable the worshipper to find himself and his God in the sacred halls.[13]

In line with this principle, Einhorn's prayer book eliminates prayers for restoring animal sacrifices and for the return to Zion, and replaces the doctrine of resurrection with "the idea of a purely spiritual immortality." His version of our benediction replaces the traditional closing with a new Hebrew phrase which praises God "Who has planted immortal life within us."[14] *Olat Tamid* later became the basis for *The Union Prayer Book* (1895), which became standard in all American Reform congregations until 1975 when it was replaced by *The New Union Prayer Book*, more popularly known as *Gates of Prayer.*

The New Union Prayer Book retains Einhorn's formulation of our benediction. For its part, *Gates of Prayer* adopts the more recent practice of providing several options for the evening and morning service. Of all these options, only the eighth version of the Shabbat eve services and the Yom Kippur afternoon service in Reform's High Holiday *Gates of Repentance* retain the traditional Hebrew closing of our benediction (but translate it "whose gift is life, whose cleansing rains let parched men and women flower toward the sun"). All other options replace it with the Hebrew phrase *mehaye hakol*, variously translated as "Source of life" or "Creator of life." In the accompanying *Gates of Understanding* (1977), which discusses Reform's approach to liturgical change and annotates the changes made in *Gates of Prayer*, we are told simply that the doctrine of resurrection was eliminated because "it is not accepted by Liberal Judaism."[15] The prayer book adopted by Israeli Reform congregations uses the Hebrew wording of *Gates of Prayer* without a translation.

Einhorn's influence was further advanced by the work of his

son-in-law, Rabbi Kaufman Kohler (1843–1926). Also European born and educated, Kohler quickly became the ideological spokesman for the radical wing of American Reform. Einhorn and Kohler had participated in the conferences of Reform rabbis in Germany, and they shaped the statement adopted at the first such conference to be held in America in Philadelphia in 1869. The sixth article of the Philadelphia statement reads:

> The belief in the bodily resurrection has no religious foundation, and the doctrine of immortality refers to the after-existence of the soul only.[16]

This statement is significant, not only in its own right, but also because it served as the backdrop for a more influential statement of the principles of American Reform, the Pittsburgh Platform adopted by a group of Reform rabbis in 1885.

The Pittsburgh Conference was Kohler's idea. He issued the invitations for the conference, planned its agenda, and brought with him a draft of a statement of principles for American Reform which was based on the 1869 Philadelphia statement. The final version of the Platform, composed of eight paragraphs, included the following statement:

> We assert the doctrine of Judaism, that the soul of man is immortal, grounding the belief on the divine nature of the human spirit, which forever finds bliss in righteousness and misery in wickedness. We reject as ideas not rooted in Judaism the belief both in bodily resurrection and in Gehenna and Eden (hell and paradise), as abodes for everlasting punishment or reward.[17]

The discussion that followed the first formal reading of the Platform, refers to Maimonides as "the best authority corroborat-

ing the spiritual conception of Retribution expressed in the platform."[18] Subsequently, the entire Platform, including the paragraph
on immortality, was adopted.

In 1918, Kohler published his *Jewish Theology: Systematically
and Historically Considered*.[19] In the three full chapters devoted to
Jewish teachings on the afterlife, Kohler traces the history of the
doctrines of resurrection and immortality from their earliest manifestations through rabbinic and philosophical sources. He concludes
that those of his contemporaries who see "God's greatness...revealed
through miracles, that is through interruptions of the natural order
of life" will cling to the doctrine of resurrection. But

> he who recognizes the unchangeable will of an all-wise,
> all-ruling God in the immutable laws of nature must find
> it impossible to praise God according to their traditional
> formula as the "reviver of the dead," but will avail him-
> self instead of the expression used in the Union Prayer
> Book after the pattern of Einhorn, "He who has im-
> planted within us immortal life." (296–297)

Note the subtle theological shift here. The benediction deals
with God's limitless power, but for Kohler, that power is best revealed not in the "miracle" of resurrection, but rather in God's
creation of the immutable laws of nature, which decree that everything material must die, that this death is final, and that everything
spiritual must live eternally. This is the closest Kohler comes to a
serious theological inquiry into the weight of the two doctrines.

Fifty years later, American Reform rabbis drafted a new platform of principles in Columbus, Ohio in 1937. In the intervening
years, both the world at large and the Jewish world had changed
drastically: Zionism had become a powerful religious and political
force, Hitler was expanding his rule in Europe, and American Jewry
had grown considerably and had a very different set of concerns than

had its predecessors in 1885.

The Columbus Platform reflects all these transformations, particularly in recognizing the enduring power of the hope for the return to Zion. But on the afterlife, little had changed. Paragraph three of the Columbus Platform reads:

> Man. Judaism affirms that man is created in the image of God. His spirit is immortal. He is an active co-worker with God. As a child of God, he is endowed with moral freedom and is charged with the responsibility of over-coming evil and striving after ideal ends.[20]

In its early decades, the American Reform movement may have been uncertain about its distinctive ideology, but the Pittsburgh Platform of 1885 marked the triumph of the movement's radical wing. The century to follow, which came to be known as the age of "Classical" Reform, was shaped by the Einhorn/Kohler vision of a radically transformed Judaism, a vision which dictated, among other things, that the doctrine of resurrection be replaced by the "spiritually purer" notion of spiritual immortality.

Reform's progressive dismissal of bodily resurrection in favor of spiritual immortality took all of four decades, from the German prayer books of the 1840s that shade the vernacular to reflect the new thinking, to the 1885 Pittsburgh Platform which dismisses resurrection as a belief that "is not rooted in Judaism."

In recent years, many Reform rabbis have called for a reappraisal of classical Reform liturgy and a return to more traditional forms, now freed of their literal meanings. In this spirit, the power of praising God for resurrecting the dead is beginning to be appreciated once again. These voices are few in number and they have to confront the full weight of a century of Reform practice. But the traditional formula may yet reappear in Reform publications to come.

CONSERVATIVE JUDAISM
ON SPIRITUAL IMMORTALITY

The Pittsburgh Platform was directly responsible for the break-up of the Reform coalition of the early decades of the 19th century. The more conservative members of that coalition could stomach neither the principles of that Platform nor the Einhorn/Kohler reading of Judaism. Literally within weeks, they met in New York and announced the formation of a rabbinical school "in conservative Jewish principles." A year later, in January 1887, The Jewish Theological Seminary of New York (later to become The Jewish Theological Seminary of America) welcomed its first entering class. With that, the movement, eventually known as Conservative Judaism, was born.[21]

Reform began as a congregational movement; Conservative Judaism began as a school. Not unexpectedly, it was some decades before the movement could spawn a congregational arm, and even more time until it produced a movement-wide prayer book. When it did, it predictably took a more "conservative" approach to liturgical change than did Reform.

In 1927, the Conservative movement published the *Festival Prayer Book,* its first liturgical publication intended for movement-wide use.[22] The main edition of the *Festival Prayer Book* preserves the traditional liturgy intact. The closing phrase of our benediction is translated "who quickenest the dead."[23]

Some twenty years later, the Conservative movement published its *Sabbath and Festival Prayer Book* (1946) which quickly became omnipresent in Conservative congregations until the publication of *Siddur Sim Shalom* (1985) which was designed to replace it. A brief statement next to the title page of the *Sabbath and Festival Prayer Book* announces that it is based on a manuscript submitted by Rabbi Morris Silverman of Temple Emanuel, West Hartford, Connecticut, who, in 1936, had published a prayer book with the same name for the use of his congregation. Both the original Silverman and the *Sabbath and Festival* texts are equally modest in their liturgical innovations. Both preserve the traditional Hebrew closing of our benediction, though Silverman translates it "Author of life eternal," and *Sabbath and Festival* uses "Who callest the dead to life everlasting."

The Foreword to *Sabbath and Festival*, written by Rabbi Robert Gordis, Chairman of the Joint (i.e. United Synagogue and Rabbinical Assembly) Prayer Book Commission that produced the volume, informs the worshipper that three principles guided the Commission in preparing the prayer book: Continuity with tradition, relevance to the needs and ideals of the current generation, and intellectual integrity. It justifies the strategy employed in our case:

> The rendering of the phrase *mehayyai hameitim* [*sic*] "who calls the dead to life everlasting" is linguistically sound and rich in meaning for those who cherish the faith in human immortality, as much as for those who maintain the belief in resurrection.[24]

This captures Conservative Judaism's predilection for the second strategy for handling troublesome liturgical passages: Wherever possible, retain the Hebrew but shade the English translation to reflect a more modern sensibility. The strongest argument for this strategy is that liturgical language, like all poetry, should be permitted a certain indeterminacy of meaning, that it should be open to many possible interpretations, and that any attempt to impose one specific meaning robs it of its poetic quality.

But in this context, the argument is disingenuous. To properly appreciate the indeterminacy of meaning of the Hebrew text, the worshipper must be able to understand the Hebrew, which is precisely what most contemporary Conservative Jews cannot do.

Whatever its merits, this strategy has been followed in the

Conservative prayer books published in recent decades. The 1961 *Weekday Prayer Book,* the 1972 *Mahzor for Rosh Hashanah and Yom Kippur* and the 1985 *Siddur Sim Shalom,* currently in use in many Conservative synagogues, all retain the traditional Hebrew closing for our benediction, but translate it "Master of [or over] life and death." Somewhat puzzlingly, though, the phrase immediately preceding the closing benediction is translated as "Faithful are You in bringing the dead to life again," or as "Faithful are You in giving life to the dead."

Finally, still one more recently published prayer book, not officially produced by the Conservative movement, but used almost exclusively in Conservative congregations, is *Siddur Hadash.* This prayer book follows the usual Conservative practice of retaining the traditional Hebrew for our benediction but using the translation to introduce a deliberate note of ambiguity. Its translation reads: "...who confers immortality upon the departed."[25]

Robert Gordis, who chaired the Commission that edited *Sabbath and Festival,* was to become one of the movement's elder statesmen. A congregational rabbi and a respected scholar, Gordis was an articulate defender of the movement's ideology and, on both theological and halakhic issues, as close to its center as possible. His views were an accurate barometer of main-line Conservative ideology, and certainly of the Conservative rabbinate, at mid-century.

Gordis' *A Faith for Moderns,* originally published in 1960, is his most personal theological statement, and reflects his wide-ranging knowledge of the entire Jewish tradition, as well as his cautious, middle-of-the road position. His chapter, "Immortality—An Unconquerable Hope" concludes with a tortuous personal statement that captures the author's ambivalence about what a modern Jew can believe on this issue.

He concedes that the one principle that Judaism clearly affirms is *"the conviction that physical death does not end all for man, that in some sense man's life is indestructible and his spirit is endowed with immortality.*"[26] Every individual must determine whether he or she can accept this principle. But what does the principle mean? Gordis backs off: "[A] man will be wiser to accept the limitations of existence and knowledge...and not seek to peer behind the veil." Yet, Gordis does "peer behind the veil" and cautiously recommends the doctrine of spiritual immortality: "The facet in man's nature which is deathless, the vital spark, the breath of life, we call the soul."[27]

Gordis concedes that most modern interpretations of the doctrine of the afterlife prefer the notion of spiritual immortality over that of resurrection. In fact, when he shifts from a historical overview to an advocacy position, resurrection is never mentioned. There is no question that if Gordis' contemporaries in the Conservative rabbinate had been polled, they would have found this statement to be entirely congruent with their own views at that time.

MORDECAI KAPLAN'S RELIGIOUS NATURALISM

By the mid-point of our century, both the Conservative and Reform Movements had settled on spiritual immortality as the only acceptable doctrine for modern Jews.[28] So did Mordecai Kaplan's Reconstructionist Movement.

Conservative Judaism may have flaunted its "pluralistic" character, and the deliberate ambiguity of its ideology. But there is absolutely no ambiguity about the ideological position of that controversial shaper of modern Jewish thought, Mordecai Kaplan (1881–1983). Though Kaplan taught at The Jewish Theological Seminary from 1909 to 1963 and thereby decisively shaped the thinking of many Conservative rabbis, and though he was widely read in Reform circles, he is known primarily as the founder of Reconstructionism, a movement created to institutionalize Kaplan's reading of Judaism.

Kaplan was a thoroughgoing religious and theological

naturalist. He believed that all religions are the natural creation of a community, not, as traditionalists believe, divinely revealed by a God who transcends the natural order. Judaism is the outcome of one people's attempt to understand how the world came to be the way it is, where this community came from, what it stands for distinctively, and its unique destiny among the peoples of the earth.

From this follows Kaplan's conclusion that Judaism or Jewish religion is a function of the Jewish people, that the community, as the center of authority for what Judaism teaches, has the ongoing right and responsibility to reshape Judaism's teachings so that its adherents may participate creatively in the life of the community. To put it more sharply (and to paraphrase one of Kaplan's more memorable comments), if religion involves behaving, believing and belonging, then behaving and believing should serve the purposes of belonging.[29]

This justifies Kaplan's radical transformation of many of Judaism's traditional beliefs and practices including his radical approach to liturgical change. The introduction to his 1945 Reconstructionist *Sabbath Prayer Book,* which clearly reflects Kaplan's thinking (and was probably written by Kaplan himself), decries the apathy which many modern Jews feel about prayer, insists that the traditional service has not preserved the spirit of worship among Jews, and claims that other (read Reform Judaism's) attempts at new liturgical expression have failed to rekindle in Jews the spirit of worship "by reason of their theology and their conception of the Jewish people."[30]

We are thereby prepared for the extensive changes that follow.

Listed in a section of this introduction titled "Modification of Traditional Doctrines," they include the doctrines of the chosen people, revelation, the personal Messiah, the restoration of the sacrificial cult, retribution and resurrection. On the last of these, the introduction says:

Men and women brought up in the atmosphere of modern science no longer accept the doctrine that the dead
will one day come to life. To equate that doctrine with
the belief in the immortality of the soul is to read into
the text a meaning which the words do not express. That
the soul is immortal in the sense that death cannot defeat it, that the human spirit…transcends the brief span
of the individual life and shares in the eternity of the
Divine life can and should be expressed in our prayers.
But we do not need for this purpose to use a traditional
text which requires a forced interpretation. This prayer
book, therefore, omits the references to the resurrection of the body, but affirms the immortality of the soul,
in terms that are in keeping with what modern-minded
men can accept as true.[31]

In this spirit, Kaplan substitutes a new Hebrew text, taken
from the High Holiday liturgy, for the closing of our benediction
and translates it literally as, "Who in love rememberest Thy creatures unto life." In a different context, Kaplan concedes that the
wish for immortality stems from a "divine urge in man not to live
only for himself and for the moment, but also for mankind and its
future." He continues, "Insofar as the good we do while we live
bears fruit after we are gone, we have a share in the world to come."[32]
That is about as much immortality as Kaplan is prepared to concede.

In 1994, the Reconstructionist movement published a new
prayer book, *Kol Haneshamah,* which restores some of Kaplan's
deletions and reformulates many of his original proposals. In this
text, the new Hebrew closing for our benediction is *mehaye kol hai.*
This is translated as "…Who gives and restores life," though it should
be noted that literally, the Hebrew means "…Who gives life to all
living things"; there is no reference to "restoring" life in the original Hebrew.[33]

Kaplan's most theologically sophisticated disciple was Rabbi Milton Steinberg (1903–1950).[34] Many of Steinberg's writings dealing with the issues that confronted American Jewry in the 1940s, are now somewhat anachronistic. But what is still widely read is his *Basic Judaism* (1947), one of the most attractive introductions to Judaism in print, partly because of Steinberg's elegant style, but also because he conveys the full spectrum of opinions on each issue, from the most traditionalist to the most liberal.

Steinberg's discussion of "The World-to-Come" addresses immortality, and understands it primarily to mean that "man contains something independent of the flesh and surviving it; his consciousness and moral capacities, his essential personality: a soul."[35]

He concedes that "some few modernists" claim that neither resurrection nor immortality is "integral to the Jewish religion." Others may retain faith in "the deathlessness of man's spirit" but "they abandon the doctrines of the Resurrection of the body, at least in any literal sense; of an actual, spatial Heaven and Hell; and of eternal damnation." Though elements of the traditional doctrines may survive, Jewish modernists "continue to believe that though he die man lives on, and that the scales of cosmic equity always end up in balance."[36]

What is startling in this statement is that Steinberg, a competent theologian, dismisses resurrection "in its literal sense," but makes no attempt to consider it in any "non-literal" sense. Yet it is precisely the non-literalness of the doctrine that will commend itself to the next generation of Jewish liberal theologians. That Steinberg could not conceive of this possibility reflects the temper of the age in which he wrote.

RESURRECTION IN CONTEMPORARY
ORTHODOXY

Finally, no prayer book designed for Orthodox Jews through-out this period could even contemplate changing the traditional liturgy or use the translation to hint at some discomfort with the traditional doctrine. Hence, the three versions of the prayer book most widely used in the American Orthodox community, *The Traditional Prayer Book,* edited by Rabbi David De Sola Pool (Behrman House, Inc., 1960), the various editions compiled by Philip Birnbaum (Hebrew Publishing Company) and those under the *ArtScroll* imprint (Mesorah Publications, Ltd.) all retain the traditional text of our benediction and translate it literally. De Sola Pool and Birnbaum translate it as "...Who revives the dead," and *ArtScroll,* "...Who resuscitates the dead."

In the *ArtScroll* edition, the commentary draws our attention to three forms of "resuscitation":

Man's awakening every morning after deathlike slumber; the rain that has the life sustaining quality of making vegetation grow; and the literal resuscitation of the dead that will take place in the Messianic age.[37]

This observation is attributed to the fourteenth-century Spanish student of the liturgy, Rabbi David Abudraham. It provides us with two thoroughly natural models for understanding the messianic resurrection of the dead: Awakening from sleep and the revival of nature each year. To the editor, then, the doctrine literally means what it says: At the end of days, all dead bodies will come to life again, just as we awaken from sleep every morning and just as nature comes to life again each spring.

But it is abundantly clear from this overview that, by the middle of the twentieth century, the entire liberal wing of the contemporary religious community had abandoned the doctrine of resurrection, either explicitly or implicitly. But abandoning resurrection did not lead to rejecting all notions of an afterlife. Judaism had provided an alternative, the doctrine of spiritual immortality. In most of our texts, this latter doctrine either replaces resurrection or is read back into it. The fact that the talmudic tradition does preserve this doctrine, that it is present in the daily liturgy, and most important, that it is affirmed as quasi-dogmatic by Maimonides, all contributed to lend it an authority which modern liberal Jews gratefully embraced.

OPTIONS FOR MODERN JEWS

It is worth noting that contemporary Orthodoxy embraces resurrection and liberal Jews reject it *for the very same reason*: They all understand it as a literal statement. All of these thinkers believe that the doctrine can only be interpreted as describing, in literal, objective terms, an event that will occur exactly as described in some future time. That is why Orthodox Jews affirm it and liberal Jews reject it. There is no attempt to consider the problem of the language in which the doctrine is phrased in traditional literature, or of the epistemological status of eschatological thinking, or even more broadly, of theological language in its entirety.

So the broader questions remain: Is there an alternative to theological literalism? Must all our descriptions of God's activity be understood only in objective, literal terms? Are there alternative ways to understand how human beings can speak of God? Can human beings have an objectively accurate picture of God and of what God does? And if not, does that relegate all other positions to pure secularism? To put it somewhat crudely, is religious/theological fundamentalism the only available option for modern religious Jews?

What is also missing throughout much of this material from all branches of modern liberal Judaism, is a serious, systematic

213

inquiry into the theological weight of the doctrine of resurrection, what it might mean to contemporary Jews, and precisely why it is unacceptable today. Apart from vague and sweeping generalizations, there is no interest in even considering its possible relevance to the contemporary mind. No one asks just what it means for human beings to "have" a body in the first place, or why God endowed us with bodily existence, or what theological weight this bodily existence may assume.

Equally striking is the absence of any serious inquiry into the theological thrust of the alternative doctrine of spiritual immortality. Everyone seems to assume, for example, that it is absolutely clear just what the soul is, that human beings do, in fact, have souls, and that this soul is somehow related to the body.

Finally, not one of these thinkers asks about how these issues affect our understanding of God and of God's relation to creation and to humanity. Claiming that God resurrects the dead is very different than claiming that God confers immortality on the soul. The first is an event, a singular manifestation of God's ultimate power over death. The second demands no intervention by God. As Plato clearly understood, souls are immortal simply because that's what souls are: Spiritual substances never die.

Changing the balance between these two doctrines involves more than a change in our eschatologies. It also represents a significant change in our understanding of God, and this should not to be undertaken lightly.

All of these questions are now being addressed by a new generation of Jewish theologians, who collectively have effected a radical transformation in Jewish teachings on the afterlife.

THE RETURN TO RESURRECTION

THE LAST DECADES of the twentieth century have witnessed a renewed interest in eschatology in general, in the afterlife in particular, and still more narrowly, in the doctrine of bodily resurrection. The tension between the doctrines of bodily resurrection and spiritual immortality is being reappraised, and the theological and religious power of the former is being acknowledged anew, even by modern liberal Jews.

What has led to this reappraisal? Part of the story is the approach of the millennium. Significant chronological milestones—a turn-of-the-century, for example, or even more, a new millennium—have always generated eschatological visions. When else should the tensions inherent in human life and history be resolved than at such a mathematically determined marker? True, the imminent new millennium is a Christian, not a Jewish milestone, but most modern Jews live in a Christian culture and have begun to be caught up in the fervor that it inspires.[1]

Another part of the story is the unanticipated flowering of

traditionalism in all religious communities, Jewish and otherwise. Equally significant is a renewed interest in the distinctive language of theology and liturgy, for example in Jewish thinkers' appropriation of the notion of myth as the way to characterize much of theological thinking and speaking. As we have seen, the surest way to dismiss eschatology is to understand it in literal terms.

Finally, it is clear that our age has brought with it a renewed concern for meaning-of-life issues. The reigning scientific/technological/rationalist temper of the past two centuries has been exposed as a singularly inadequate resource for dealing with the twin issues that lie at the core of human existence: What is the meaning of a human life? And, how are we to live it?

THE POSTMODERN IMPULSE

A useful way to characterize this new sensibility is to refer to our age as "postmodernity." Rabbi Eugene Borowitz has aptly characterized this notion of the postmodern as "an intuition seeking self-understanding."[2] This intuition has been used to unify a wide range of recent developments in fields as diverse as art, architecture, literature, philosophy, the social and physical sciences, and in religion and theology.

As its name implies, postmodernism signifies a distancing from, and ultimately a critique of the age that preceded this new one, the age of "the modern," of what we call "modernity." Characteristic of modernity was a basic confidence about our ability to understand and control the world and human existence, a reliance on science and technology as uniquely qualified to teach us about how the world works and how we should conduct our lives, and the exaltation of human reason as the most sublime expression of our humanity. Postmodernism implies the very opposite: A renewed humility about human powers and impulses, a vision of science and even mathematics as themselves resting on fragile and arbitrary foundations, and a recognition of the limits of reason as a resource for dealing with the most significant dimensions of human experience.

We have learned to be humble about human powers and impulses because they have been the source of untold devastation. We now understand that mathematical systems rest on axioms that are themselves unprovable and are chosen simply because they create the system we wish to use. Even science itself, as evidenced by quantum theory, the principle of indeterminacy and astronomy, has abandoned the view that it is uniquely gifted to render a "true" picture of the "real" world, that it, too, like theology deals with entities and events that elude direct perception and verification. Finally, we have realized that far from defining our essential humanity, reason alone can just as easily demean it, and that what is most essentially human about our identities lies elsewhere.

If there is one event that precipitated the death of Jewish modernity, it was undoubtedly the Holocaust. That event, precipitated by a culture that was the birthplace of Jewish modernity and embodied the very best of the modern temper, has led to a profound disillusionment about the perceived accomplishments of the past two centuries. If this is the best that modern culture can produce, then of what value was this culture? Add to that Israel's "miraculous"—the term is only slightly hyperbolic in this context—return to Zion and the events of the 1967 Six Day War. The understanding of Jewish identity that worked for the past two centuries now demanded reformulation.[3]

Even beyond these events, forces were at work in Jewish life and thought that produced new expressions about how to live and think as a Jew. The search for a Jewish model of spirituality has become a central preoccupation of many committed Jews. The traditional movements and their institutions, mainly the classic, suburban "cathedral" synagogue and its formalized service of worship, are viewed as cold and impersonal. By contrast, the new generation of spiritual seekers have either turned to traditional synagogues, or created smaller, more intimate and more informal religious communities (called *havurot*), or embraced mysticism and hasidic forms of prayer and ritual. In the extreme, they have embraced Eastern religions, cults and New Age faiths.

A similar spirit has transformed the academic study of Judaism. Since the dawn of the Enlightenment, the reigning paradigm for the academic study of Judaism was *Wissenschaft des Judentums* (literally, the "Science of Judaism"), an approach which emphasized a critical, detached, objective, or "scientific" stance toward everything Jewish. That approach was deemed indispensable if the study of Judaism was to win its place within the curriculum of the Western academy, and by extension, if Judaism was to be recognized as a legitimate modern form of religious expression. That approach to Jewish study was enthroned in the curricula for training rabbis in Reform and Conservative seminaries; in turn, it created a model of the rabbinate which had its own impact on Jewish religious life.

RE-ENCHANTING THE WORLD

Wissenschaft may well have been indispensable in its time, but its goals have now been realized: Departments of Jewish studies are omnipresent on American colleges and universities. More recently, it has been exposed to be as subjective as the traditional forms of learning embraced in Eastern European *yeshivot* (academies), and as singularly inadequate for the crucial task of making our classical texts speak to contemporary concerns.[4]

The new Jewish feminism has been a catalyst for reappraising the role of ritual in Jewish religious life and for creating new liturgies and rituals that serve the specific needs of Jewish women.[5] Healing services are spreading, books about angels and meditation practices abound, and God has returned to the synagogue pulpit and its classrooms. Theology is "in," rabbis discuss prayer, sin, death, feelings, ritual and *mitzvot*, all of which had been taboo topics in Judaism's liberal wing for generations. The Jewish mystical tradition, dismissed by the Jews of the Enlightenment as primitive and unworthy of serious study, has been rediscovered. Sophisticated Jews now talk and write about the reincarnation of souls. Hasidic approaches to worship are now incorporated into the culture of the modern liberal suburban synagogue. The most flourishing of these include singing and even dancing as part of their worship services. Jews are now asking what Judaism has to say about ecology, the human body, sexuality, aging, and also about eschatology and life after death.

Beyond the synagogue and the rabbinic communities, Jewish postmodernism has become a topic of intense scholarly interest. An on-line network brings these scholarly voices together and academic conferences have become annual events. The writings of men such as the late Emanuel Levinas, who toiled for decades in relative obscurity in France, have been translated into English and are taught and studied throughout Jewish academia.[6]

Most postmodernists insist that they do not indulge in a wholesale rejection of modernity. Nor do they wish to return to the pre-modern. There is little nostalgia in their writings for a pre-scientific, pre-industrial revolution, pre-emancipatory or pre-Enlightenment culture. The achievements of modernity are real and acknowledged. What is questioned is modernity's imperialism, its lack of awareness of its limitations, its self-aggrandizement, its claim to legislate even meaning and values. The new goal is to appreciate modernism's inherent limitations, the partiality of its visions, the one-sidedness of its truths, the issues which it simply could not deal with.

One student of the postmodern sensibility captures its essence:

After all, postmodernity can be seen as restoring to the

world what modernity, presumptuously, had taken away; as a *re-enchantment* of the world that modernity tried hard to *dis-enchant*. It is the modern artifice that has been dismantled; the modern conceit of meaning-legislating reason that has been exposed....[7]

If the goal of the postmodern is to re-enchant the world, then it is clear that the fathers of Jewish postmodernism are Martin Buber and Franz Rosenzweig, because they emphasized interpersonal relations as the source of meaning and insisted that this relation has to be lived, not thought; and Abraham Joshua Heschel, because of his view that the core of religion lies in an experience of "radical amazement," amazement not only at one facet of the world but "in the startling fact that there are facts at all."[8]

Neither Buber, Rosenzweig nor Heschel was overly preoccupied with the afterlife. But if the new temper seeks to re-enchant the world, then talk of the end of days and of the ultimate destiny of human beings after death seems almost inevitable. Also inevitable is a reappraisal of the doctrine of resurrection, since it deals with central issues on the agenda of postmodernism such as death, the human body, and the mythical, enchanted realm that follows the end of history, and precisely because it is such a scandal to reason.

RESURRECTION IS "OUTRAGEOUS": WILL HERBERG

An early anticipation of this new interest in the afterlife can be found in one of the most influential contemporary interpretations of Jewish religion: Will Herberg's *Judaism and Modern Man*.[9]

Herberg (1901–1977) was a former Marxist who broke with the Communist party in the late 1930s and began studying Judaism. His book attempts to render the existentialist thought of Martin

Buber and Franz Rosenzweig and the Protestant theologian Reinhold Niebuhr in terms that would be understandable to modern American Jews. Its wide impact was helped by Herberg's powerful presentation of his thinking on campuses throughout the country.

In a book that begins with a ringing denunciation of the follies of modernism and its idolatries such as scientism, Marxism, psychoanalysis, nationalism and racism, the richest chapter deals with Jewish eschatology. As a former Marxist, Herberg appreciates the power of eschatology, and one of his more fascinating claims is that Marxist eschatology effectively transmutes biblical thinking into secular terms. Marxism understands history as a three-phase process beginning with a primal state of innocence, proceeding through a "fall" into a middle period of social evil, which is to be overcome by a "new age" of harmony in the future. This final culmination is preceded by a great catastrophe, the "Revolution," which purges the evils of the middle age and opens the way for renewal. The "structural analogy" with biblical thinking, Herberg insists, could not be closer.[10]

The major difference between the two scenarios is that in Marxism, the impetus for realizing the eschatological vision lies within history itself: "History is...its own redeemer." But for Herberg, that is the ultimate Marxist "illusion." In Judaism, however, the impetus lies in God's power. God alone has the power to transform history into eschatology.

Herberg reviews the major themes of Jewish eschatology including the two doctrines of the resurrection of the dead and the immortality of the soul, the first of which he calls "outrageous" but which he insists is indispensable and which should not be confused with the latter:

> The symbol [note well!] "resurrection of the dead" expresses the depth and dimensions of Hebraic religion in relation to the destiny of mankind more adequately perhaps than any other concept.

It does that for three primary reasons: First, because it affirms

> that man's ultimate destiny is not his by virtue of his own nature—by possession of an "immortal soul"...—but comes to him solely by the grace and mercy of God, "who wakes him from the dead."

Second, because it affirms that what is destined to be fulfilled

> is not a disembodied soul...but the *whole* [emphasis Herberg's] man—body, soul and spirit—joined in an indissoluble unity.

Finally, because it affirms that God's promise of salvation

> is not a private, individual affair...but the salvation of mankind, the corporate redemption of men in the full reality of their historical existence. The whole point of the doctrine of the resurrection is that the life we live now, the life of the body, the life of empirical existence in society, has some measure of permanent worth in the eyes of God, and will not vanish in the transmutation of things at the "last day."

We cannot dispense with the doctrine of the resurrection of the dead, Herberg insists,

> no matter how impatient we may be with the literalistic pseudo-biological fantasies that have gathered around it through the centuries.[11]

Herberg's disdain for the doctrine of spiritual immortality is rooted in his disdain for the otherworldly and antihistorical outlook of Greek and Eastern thought. In contrast to biblical historiography, that view denies that there is any meaning or even reality to history itself:

> The actual world of events—indeed, everything that is involved in time—is regarded as either unreal, a mist of illusion, or else as hopelessly caught in an endless cycle of recurrence that leads nowhere.

For the idealist, true meaning does not lie in this familiar world of space and time, but rather in some eternal, immutable alternative world, the world of Plato's Ideas or the All-Soul of Hinduism. The ultimate aim of existence—redemption—lies in liberating ourselves from our familiar world and uniting with or contemplating this ideal reality. To Herberg, this impulse means that

> [t]he actual world is written off as worthless. It does not matter what history may bring....I will pursue truth, cherish beauty, fulfill my obligations....(I)n other words, it does not matter what happens to men!... The one true reality is the timeless ideal, and the true meaning of life is singleminded devotion to it.

This view, Herberg continues, is rooted in a matter-mind dualism

> in which matter is devaluated as evil, intrinsically unreal and impotent, while mind is exalted as spiritual and eternal, the very heart of all that is real and good.[12]

For "matter" and "mind" in that sentence, read "body" and "soul," and we can grasp the source of Herberg's dismissal of spiritual immortality. For at the heart of that doctrine lies the assumption that what is "really real" and valuable about the human person is not the material body, but the spiritual soul which will persist after death. Redemption is understood as the perfect actualization of the ideal to be pursued here on earth. If we perceive a critique of Maimonides in these paragraphs, it is by no means accidental since, as we have seen, much of Maimonidean thought on the afterlife was rooted in his appropriation of this Hellenistic world-view.

It is now clear why Herberg values the doctrine of bodily resurrection. Indeed, the

> whole point of the doctrine of resurrection is that the life we live now, the life of the body, the life of empirical existence in society, has some permanent worth in the eyes of God and will not vanish in the transmutation of things at the "last day."[13]

It is ultimately an affirmation of the value of history and society, of the only life we know of, life as embodied individuals in space and time.

Note that for Herberg, resurrection is a "symbol." Herberg will have nothing to do with the "literalistic pseudo-biological fantasies" either of traditionalists who buy the doctrine or of reformers who reject it. To say that the doctrine is a "symbol" is to adopt the language of myth current in recent theological writing, for one definition of myth views it as a series of symbols, extended and systematized.

Symbols are representations of some other, more elusive reality which cannot be captured in simple thought and language. According to Paul Tillich, symbols have the quality of "pointing beyond themselves," and of "participating in" or nursing from the power of the reality to which they point. That's why symbols cannot be created in conventional ways and cannot be easily replaced; a national flag is an excellent example of this kind of political symbol. Finally, symbols "open up levels of reality which are otherwise closed to us" and also "open up hidden depths of our own being."[14]

The doctrine of resurrection is a symbol because it points beyond itself to an event that is beyond time and space; it participates in that reality because it draws its emotional thrust from that event; it opens up levels of reality and hidden dimensions of our soul by revealing the ultimate destiny which we all face as human beings.

What is most significant in Herberg's appropriation of the doctrine is that, in contrast to the superficial thinking of liberal theologians of the past two centuries, it comes as the outcome of a rigorous, systematic theological inquiry into the fundamental assumptions of Judaism, particularly the Jewish understanding of history. Note also that he affirms the doctrine precisely because it is "outrageous." Affirming a doctrine because of its outrageousness to reason and to the scientific temper is perfectly attuned to our postmodern sensibility.

RESURRECTION IS "SCANDALOUS": ARTHUR A. COHEN

An equally powerful reappraisal of the doctrine of resurrection has been proposed by Arthur A. Cohen in the anthology *Contemporary Jewish Religious Thought: Original Essays on Critical Concepts, Movements and Beliefs,* edited by Cohen and Hebrew University Professor Paul Mendes-Flohr.[15]

Cohen, a skilled and articulate Jewish theologian, who, like Herberg, was strongly influenced by the writings of Buber and Rosenzweig, reviews the tortuous history of the doctrine through modernity and concedes that it is "unpersuasive" because it is "alogical" and "antirational." Yet the more one thinks about the

225

doctrine, he notes, "the more one is obliged to wonder at its theo-logical persistence and its mythological power. Why does it endure?"

The principle difficulty with the doctrine, Cohen asserts, is that "it wrests from God a promise that distorts the acceptable char-acterization of his nature and behavior." God's ways are supposed to be compatible with reason, rather than eccentric and capricious. But all eschatology is, at its very heart, miraculous.

> Resurrection in the flesh is a miracle that God works for the individual.... What fails within nature and dies is restored in the kingdom, transformed, strained of the agitations of the flesh, and purified by miraculous grace.[16]

Cohen appeals, in conclusion, to the last words of the *Alenu* prayer, the prayer that brings every Jewish service of worship to a close, and which quotes the prophet Zechariah: "On that day the Lord shall be One and his name One"(14:9). Until the end of days, "the consciousness of God is rent, his person still distinguishable from the seal of his name." But then, when God supplants the cre-ated order with a perfection it has not known, "the finality of death...is overcome by the same overcoming that ends the division within God." For human beings as well,

> death is now conquered and God bestows upon the dead a unity analogous to that which he has won for himself— a unity of illuminated consciousness and perfected flesh.[17]

Three dimensions of Cohen's statement should be noted. The first is his insistence that it is precisely the paradoxical, alogical, antirational—what Herberg referred to as the "outrageous"—na-ture of the doctrine of resurrection that recommends it. This is another reflection of the postmodern temper: If God is truly God, then God can work paradoxes.

> Resurrection remains a mystery, scandalous to reason, obnoxious to those with a deficient sense of the deep mythos of consciousness, embarrassing to those who believe divinity reasonable and sufficient.[18]

If for Herberg, resurrection is a symbol, for Cohen it is part of the classic Jewish myth.

Second, as in Herberg, and reflecting the theological impulse behind the *Gevurot* benediction, it is God's power that is ultimately at issue, that underlying the doctrine is the presupposition that "eternal life in the presence of God is indeed an immense and unmerited generosity." The doctrine of resurrection is the ultimate affirmation of God's unlimited power, the last stage in the triumph of monotheism, the fulfillment of Zechariah's prophecy that God will indeed be totally "One," for God will have triumphed over death.[19]

Finally, note Cohen's appeal to the power of an eschatological vision that respects our concrete individuality as we know it in this life. This theme will return repeatedly in all contemporary reappraisals of the doctrine.

Still a third reconsideration of resurrection on philosophical/ theological grounds is provided by the late Professor Steven Schwarzschild (1924–1989). German-born, educated in America and ordained at the Hebrew Union College, Schwarzschild served for many years on the faculty of Washington University in St. Louis. He was an extraordinarily rigorous scholar and prolific author on a wide range of philosophical issues, both general and Jewish.

His essay, "On Jewish Eschatology," is a detailed reconstruction of the eschatological scenario as understood by Maimonides.[20] In fact, Schwarzschild's exposition is infinitely more detailed than anything Maimonides ever committed to writing, and his arguments are technical and well beyond the reach of anyone not trained in rigorous philosophical inquiry. But what is important for our purposes here is Schwarzchild's personal conclusion:

> [W]e require the doctrine of resurrection, therewith to assert what is nowadays called the psychosomatic unity, or the embodiedsoul [sic]/ensouled-body, of the human individual and the infinite ethical tasks incumbent upon him or her.[21]

The doctrine of resurrection is necessary then as an affirmation of God's power and of the value of our embodied existence, the only existence of which we are aware.

Many of these arguments for resurrection are echoed in still another statement by the prominent Orthodox theologian/philosopher, Michael Wyschogrod.[22] Wyschogrod's paper was originally delivered at a conference on Holy Week and Easter, sponsored by a Christian Seminary, and his primary concern is to compare Jewish and Christian views of resurrection, which he finds remarkably similar, and both of these with Plato.

On the Jewish teachings, Wyschogrod insists, first, that "because God is a redeeming God, it follows that death cannot be the last word.... Either death wins or God saves." He reads the text of the *Gevurot* benediction in the *Amidah* as summarizing God's redemptive work. "God redeems whatever bad things happen to people"—illness, imprisonment, bondage, slavery:

> So redemption is this broad pattern of liberation, and one of the forms of redemption is the conquest over death, though of course it is the most dramatic redemption because death is the one triumph of the negative over which we have not yet seen any triumph.[23]

For the record, it should be noted that this reappraisal of

bodily resurrection on the part of contemporary Jewish thinkers is far from unanimous. One significant exception is Rabbi Louis Jacobs, a Conservative rabbi serving a congregation in London, England, but better known for his voluminous scholarly publications in all areas of Jewish studies.

Jacobs' *A Jewish Theology* is an exemplary review of both the history and substance of classic Jewish beliefs. His chapter titled "The Hereafter" surveys the evolution of Jewish doctrines of the afterlife, and concludes that though to reject belief in the hereafter would be "to impoverish and despiritualize Judaism itself," the general tendency among modern Jews who do believe in an afterlife "is to place stress on the immortality of the soul rather than on the resurrection of the dead."

Jacobs acknowledges the recent renewed interest in resurrection (citing Will Herberg, among others), but insists that

> unless we are prepared to accept the biological details of an actual recomposition of the physical body, we are still affirming a version of the immortality of the soul even when we affirm the doctrine of resurrection.... We ought to be frank enough to admit that all the speculations regarding life here on earth after the resurrection simply do not "ring a bell" for us whereas the more spiritual interpretation of a Maimonides does.

Jacobs argues further that there has been a sufficient number of Jewish thinkers from Philo onwards who have preferred to understand immortality in spiritual terms "to make [this doctrine] completely respectable from the Jewish point of view." But as to the details of the eschatological scenario, Jacobs, citing Maimonides, falls back on "religious agnosticism" which, he claims, is "not only legitimate but altogether desirable." Once the basic affirmation of faith in the hereafter is made, "it is...narrow to project our poor, earthly imaginings on to the landscape of heaven."[24]

But among contemporary theologians, Jacobs' reluctance to consider anything but a literal reading of the doctrine of resurrection is more an exception than the rule.

As we saw in the case of Moses Mendelssohn two centuries earlier, the impact of these philosophical statements on behalf of bodily resurrection is probably limited. Herberg, however, was, and continues to be widely read by Jewish intellectuals (this writer among them) and was responsible for guiding many of us into a serious encounter with Judaism. But the currents of thought that impelled these theoretical statements are also at work in the broader community and, more important, among Conservative and Reform rabbis. If the doctrine of resurrection is being considered anew, it is more because of the work of these men and women who, as in the past, are singularly responsible for shaping Jewish thinking.

REFORM RECONSIDERS RESURRECTION:
EUGENE BOROWITZ

In 1975, when the Reform movement celebrated the centennial of the founding of the Union of Hebrew Congregations of America and the Hebrew Union College, it issued a statement describing the movement's current "spiritual state," the third such statement in the course of its history.[25]

Recall that in both the 1937 Columbus Platform and its predecessor, the Pittsburgh Platform of 1885, Reform had disavowed resurrection and supplanted it with spiritual immortality. That shift, we have seen, was reflected in all American Reform liturgies from the middle of the nineteenth century through our own day.

On the face of it, the one sentence accorded to the afterlife in the *Centenary Perspective* promises no significant departure from that position. The sentence reads:

Amid the mystery we call life, we affirm that human beings, created in God's image, share in God's eternality despite the mystery we call death.[26]

That sentence does not suggest much of an advance over the two brief sentences of the 1937 Platform:

Judaism affirms that man is created in the Divine image. His spirit is immortal.[27]

What is significant, however, is the elaboration of that one sentence included in an extensive interpretation of the *Perspective* in *Reform Judaism Today*[28] by Rabbi Eugene B. Borowitz. Borowitz is Reform's reigning theologian, a prolific author, a teacher of generations of Reform rabbis and educators and a moving force in the writing of the *Perspective*.

Borowitz begins by noting that the modern temper cannot ignore the reigning scientific view that death is simply the breakdown of a chemical structure: The chemicals that make up the human body may survive in other forms, but the individual human life has come to an end. Nor do we have any accurate evidence about what happens to us after our death. But despite the reluctance of the drafters of the *Perspective* to say anything about the afterlife, they determined that the issue could not be avoided.

Significantly, Borowitz then distances himself from the prevailing notion that what survives is the human soul.

Our present difficulty is that the notion of such a substance as a soul is no longer intellectually tenable for most modern thinkers.

Nor is the synonymous "spirit."

We still use both words—but only poetically, to point to what we think we believe but have very little idea of.[29]

Yet life, to Borowitz, has a mysterious quality which seems to surpass mere chemistry: We have consciousness. We are aware of God and of our ability to respond to and participate in God's reality. We share in God's purposes and powers. We are coworkers with God in creation. We are partners with God both in life and thereafter.

> There is something God-like about human beings and God does not die.

Though death is even more mysterious than life,

> we cannot believe that having shared so intimately in God's reality in life we do not continue to share it beyond the grave.[30]

And then,

> [h]aving reached such heights precisely in our personhood, our individuality, we trust that our survival will likewise be personal and individual.[31]

That cautious statement is not much more than an elaboration of the one-sentence statement in the *Centenary Perspective*, though Borowitz's insistence on the preservation of human individuality hints at a move toward bodily resurrection.

A year later, Borowitz goes significantly further in *Liberal Judaism*, a comprehensive statement of his personal theology.[32] His chapter on life after death reviews the history of doctrines of the afterlife and repeats some of the claims in his 1983 statement. But in his concluding "Life-After-Death, a Personal Statement," he restates what prompted classical Judaism to insist on an afterlife for each individual, and notes that this doctrine gives him continued hope for furthering God's purposes on earth, even facing despair, and bolsters his trust that his efforts on God's behalf will be rewarded "in another existence." The lives of believers "will be fulfilled no matter what happens in this world for they have a life with God yet to come."

Finally, Borowitz confesses that, while he has no knowledge of what awaits him after death, he is yet

> inclined to think that my hope is better spoken of as resurrection than immortality for I do not know my self as a soul without a body but only as a psychosomatic self.[33]

His trust in God's generosity is captured best in the concluding verse of the hymn *Adon Olam*:

> In God's hand I place my soul both when I sleep and when I wake
> And with my soul, my body. God is with me. I shall not fear.

This is a stunning statement. Stunning, because it comes from the heart of contemporary Reform. Stunning, because it represents the current thinking of a man who has devoted a lifetime to an intensive inquiry into how Jewish theology can speak to the modern Jew. And stunning because it represents a departure in the thought of a theologian who was very much identified with Jewish modernism.

That it also marks the beginning of a more comprehensive turnabout in Borowitz's own thinking is fully explicit in his most recent book, *Renewing the Covenant: A Theology for the Postmodern Jew*, referred to above. Though this volume deals only incidentally with our doctrine, it is, as its subtitle implies, a thorough reworking of Borowitz's theology along postmodern lines.

Borowitz remains a somewhat lonely voice among contemporary Reform Jews, but not entirely. The Fall 1982 issue of the *Journal of Reform Judaism* includes an article, "Upon Arising: An Affirmation of *Techiyat Hameitim*," by Richard N. Levy, a Reform rabbi and the Executive Director of the Los Angeles Hillel Council, which makes a frontal attack on Reform's practice of defining itself through the doctrines that it does *not* accept. Levy calls this practice "a kind of medievalism in reverse." Reform, he notes, should encourage

> its members to address the full spectrum of belief and practice we received at Sinai—either by a personal response to a call from God...or by a choice emerging out of study and experience.

In this spirit, Levy advocates a reappropriation of resurrection for three reasons:

> It is faithful to the nature of our being as creations of God;
>
> It is compatible with the basic covenantal promise that has bound our people with God...;
>
> And by its connection with the messianic promise, it binds us to Eretz Yisrael in a manner that political and cultural Zionism fails to do.[34]

On the first of these, Levy argues that from the outset of the Jewish tradition, "humanity and the earth...are inextricably combined." We are created from the dust of the earth, we return to the earth, and we are promised (in Isaiah 26 and Daniel 2) that those who sleep in the earth will awaken. Levy finds the most exalted expression of that faith in the *Elohai Neshamah* prayer which promises a reunion of our bodies and our souls in our full individuality. In a striking coda to this portion of his argument, Levy suggests that we view burial as an act of planting, "not at all brutal, but an act of love, of cosmic hope."[35]

Second, Levy argues that God's covenantal promise (in Genesis 13:16) compares Israel to the dust of the earth. As the dust is eternal, so is Israel eternal: "The dust which we become after death shall be transformed into the uncountable people we were promised to be."

Third, Levy pleads that embracing the doctrine of resurrection will lead to Reform's more thoroughgoing engagement with the land of Israel than will political and cultural Zionism:

> If it is the adama [earth] of [the land of] Israel whose reclamation transcends the curse of Adam's toil, then it is upon that earth that the miracle of techiyat hameitim, the miracle of the fulfillment of the covenant, will take place.

Finally, Levy argues that if Reform believes its own doctrines, then it would want them to be known by Jews who lived before the Enlightenment as well:

> Just as the tradition describes Moses visiting Akiba's classroom and being reassured that what the sage was teaching was from Moshe MiSinai [i.e. divinely revealed to Moses at Sinai as recounted in Exodus], we should yearn for Moses and Akiba and Maimonides and the Vilna Gaon to visit our classrooms as well and to help them draw the same conclusions.[36]

All three of Levy's arguments are original and imaginative extensions of traditional thinking, but the first is most compelling.

It echoes Herberg, Cohen, Schwarzschild and Borowitz in its claim that whatever God's ultimate plan for us may be, that plan should deal with us in our full concrete individuality as body and soul indissolubly linked together. Again, from the very heart of contemporary Reform, comes a plea to reappraise the doctrine of resurrection.

Finally, also emerging out of the Reform movement is a slim anthology, *What Happens After I Die? Jewish Views of Life After Death,* edited by two Reform rabbis, Rifat Soncino and Daniel Syme.[37] Part I of this volume is a brief restatement of classical Jewish positions on the issue. Part II consists of eight personal statements by thinkers ranging from Orthodox to Reform. There is little that is original in these cautiously agnostic statements. What is significant is that the question posed in the title of the book is being asked in a new and urgent way, precisely from within the Reform movement.[38]

CONSERVATIVE JUDAISM RECONSIDERS THE AFTERLIFE

In contrast to American Reform, Conservative Judaism has been reluctant to issue ideological platforms. It was not until 1988 that it issued *Emet Ve-Emunah: Statement of Principles of Conservative Judaism,* its first such statement.[39] There are a number of plausible explanations for this reluctance. The movement sought to be inclusive and was created as a broad traditionalist coalition designed to stem the growth of Reform. Attempting to define its ideology was viewed as potentially fatal to the coalition. But on theological and ideological issues, the rabbinic arm of the movement was sharply divided between traditionalists and liberals. Not only was it strategically unwise to write a statement that would win the assent of its membership, it was in fact almost impossible.

Emet Ve-Emunah's 40 pages, drafted by a Commission of

academicians, rabbis and lay representatives of the various wings of the movement, include a four-page statement titled "Eschatology: Our Vision of the Future," which states, in part:

> For the individual human being, we affirm that death does not mean extinction and oblivion. This conviction is articulated in our tradition in the two doctrines of the bodily resurrection of the dead and the continuing existence, after death and through eternity, of the individual soul.

The statement asserts that these doctrines have been understood by some as "literal truths which enable us to confront death...with equanimity," and by others, in "a more figurative way." It then proceeds to spell out some of the "figurative" understandings of these two doctrines: Resurrection affirms the value Judaism accords to "our bodily existence in our concrete historical and social setting"; the doctrine of the immortality of the soul affirms that "our identities and our ability to touch other people and society does not end with the physical death of our bodies."[40]

Emet Ve-Emunah was never approved by any formal meeting of representatives of the movement apart from the members of the Commission that wrote it. It has been criticized as being either excessively traditional or excessively liberal, too discursive or too compact, too rigid or too pluralistic, all of which suggests that the statement is probably positioned just where it should be. But it remains Conservative Judaism's single ideological statement.

Individual Conservative rabbis have also addressed the afterlife, notably the late Rabbi Hershel Matt, close friend and disciple of Will Herberg, in an article titled "An Outline of Jewish Eschatology."[41] The article is a close study of our two doctrines and an affirmation of the power of the doctrine of resurrection.

Matt notes that Judaism affirms the reality of death, but

denies its finality because "to believe in the Creator-God...is to trust in a fulfillment of our life that is beyond history," that is, in a life that continues beyond history's record of only partial fulfillments. That fulfillment assumes the possibility of my ultimate and personal responsibility and accountability for my life before God. It there-fore also demands the reality of a personal life after death. That is why classical Judaism must affirm the revival of the body "a trans-formed body, perhaps, but a genuine and recognizable body."[42]

But why stress bodily resurrection rather than immortality of the soul? For many reasons: Because the notion of immortality tends to deny the reality of death, of God's power to take my life and to restore it; because the doctrine of immortality implies that my body is less precious, important, even "pure," while resurrec-tion affirms that my body is no less God's creation and is both necessary and good; because the notion of a bodiless soul runs counter to my experience of myself and of others; because immor-tality implies the absorption of my soul into an All-Soul thus denying my individuality; and because resurrection affirms the significance of society.

What is most striking about Matt's article is an extended foot-note in which the author discusses the meaning of theological statements, such as that God revives the dead. It reads:

> We are speaking not in terms of literal truth, but "mythi-cal" or poetic truth. A "mythical" or poetic statement seeks to point to a truth and to affirm a truth which is beyond the power of science to demonstrate, beyond the power of experience fully to confirm, beyond the power of logic to prove, beyond the power of rational discourse to convey.

He continues:

The truth here being affirmed by the concept of *t'hiyat ha-metim* includes these affirmations: that God's purpose for man is not ultimately fulfilled in this life; that it is not ultimately defeated, however, by death; that the ultimate fulfillment is beyond death and beyond history; and that this fulfillment involves full awareness by a real person that, being in God's presence and under His judgement, he must accept the full responsibility and full consequences for his life. I am aware of no better concept than *t'hiyat ha-metim* for conveying these affirmations.[43]

Though Matt uses the term "myth" here, he is simply spelling out what Herberg alludes to by calling the notion of resurrection a "symbol." Both terms indicate that this teaching must not be taken scientifically or literally, but as an attempt to use human language to capture an infinitely elusive truth.

JEWISH RENEWAL REAPPROPRIATES THE AFTERLIFE

The impact of these new currents of thought has led, finally, to the publication of a book-length study on our topic by a rabbi/psychologist who is associated with the Jewish Renewal movement. This movement encourages the exploration of more spiritual expressions of Judaism than are commonly provided by mainstream synagogues.

Simcha Paull Raphael's *Jewish Views of the Afterlife* is a thorough review of Jewish teachings on the afterlife with emphasis on kabbalistic and hasidic sources.[44] His concluding chapter, "A Contemporary Psychological Model of the Afterlife" draws heavily on this mystical tradition, on contemporary thanatology, the study of death and dying as exemplified in the writings of Dr. Elisabeth

Kübler-Ross, on Buddhist and Hindu teachings on life after death, and on the transpersonal school of psychology.

In this chapter, Raphael describes the journey of the soul after death. He uses kabbalistic and hasidic teachings on reincarnation, and shows how reports of near-death experiences and the teachings of Eastern religions can elaborate and often parallel the Jewish sources. Raphael's conclusions are also explicitly practical; he advocates the preparation of a manual on dying, and a program for training practitioners who would function for the dying much as midwives do for women who are giving birth.

In line with Jewish Renewal's reappropriation of Jewish mystical doctrines, it is not surprising that Raphael's emphasis on the journey of the soul after death plays a more significant role in his thinking than bodily resurrection. But what remains significant about his work is the fact that we now have a book-length study of Jewish views of the afterlife. This reflects the renewed and intense interest on the part of Jewish thinkers in what Judaism has to teach about what happens to people after they die.

THE POSTMODERN STRUGGLE AGAINST LIBERAL THEOLOGY

In recent decades, then, all the essential questions posed at the end of our previous chapter have begun to be addressed: The nature of theological and eschatological language and thought, the theological importance of the human body, the full implications of an individual eschatology that stresses the life of the soul alone, and the central issue in all of Jewish theology, the nature of God.

In one way or another, most of these authors reaffirm the doctrine of resurrection because it alone testifies to God's ultimate power; because it alone ascribes value to our embodied existence and hence to history and society; and because it alone makes it possible to preserve the sense of our individuality even after death. Many of them also affirm the further methodological point that the surest way to dismiss resurrection is to understand it in literal/biological terms. It is precisely the "outrageous" or "scandalous" nature of the claim—scandalous to the modern rationalist/scientific temper—which makes it most attractive to Jewish postmodernists.

None of this should be understood as implying that postmodern Jews have done away with the doctrine of spiritual immortality. Indeed, Jewish postmodernity is permeated with discussion of the soul and its destiny. Louis Jacobs and Simcha Paull Raphael provide ample testimony to the continuing power of that doctrine as part of the legacy of Jewish mysticism and hasidism, both of which Jewish postmodernists have eagerly embraced. What is striking, however, is that in contrast with their nineteenth- and early-twentieth-century predecessors, our contemporaries have rediscovered the doctrine of bodily resurrection and have found it worthy of serious consideration. That is new and quite recent.

What further distinguishes this material is the quality of its arguments. They are infinitely more rigorous and serious than the superficial and casual dismissal of resurrection in the writings of their predecessors. A plausible explanation for this difference is that our contemporaries are fighting to overthrow nearly two centuries of liberal theology and the inherent resistance of powerful religious institutions which were created precisely to embody this reading of Judaism. In this context, nothing casual or superficial could even hope to be effective. And they have been largely successful. The issue of the afterlife of the individual is now back on the agenda of the Jewish religious community and bodily resurrection figures prominently in these discussions.

X

WHAT DO *I* BELIEVE?

MOST OF THIS book has reviewed Jewish teachings on the afterlife from the Bible to our own day. The tone was deliberately dispassionate; our goal was to study the most significant Jewish statements on the afterlife, to come as close as possible to unearthing their literal meaning, and to trace the evolution of the doctrine through the centuries.

That part of our task has been accomplished. What remains is a very different kind of inquiry. We now must ask: What does all of this mean for us today? How are we to understand it? What are we to believe?

These questions demand not dispassionate objectivity, but existential testimony. The believing Jew must present his or her own beliefs about the afterlife as clearly and coherently as possible and argue for their validity. Others must then determine whether this personal statement works for them as well.

MY DATA

One of the unexpected results of my delving into this issue has been my growing awareness that the theological and philosophical literature on the afterlife by Jews and non-Jews in the past two decades is simply overwhelming. No single volume can encompass it all. Before I proceed to discuss my own conclusions, the reader deserves to know what data I have chosen to ignore—and why.

First, I have chosen to ignore many of the arguments for and against human immortality that are couched in the language of academic philosophy and psychology. These arguments deal with an analysis of how moderns can speak meaningfully of the human soul, its possible relationship or non-relationship with the human body, its origins and its ultimate destiny, and the implications of all of this for notions of bodily resurrection and spiritual immortality. This kind of argumentation, however interesting it may be in a scholarly setting, assumes a grounding in classical philosophical literature and is difficult to convey to readers without such a background. It is primarily the intelligent and concerned lay reader that this volume hopes to reach.[1]

Second, I have chosen, with a much greater sense of guilt, to ignore the literature that finds convincing arguments for immortality in the wide range of experiences commonly denoted as "New Age." I concede the value of being open to the entire range of human experience, yet I remain unconvinced by the evidence of parapsychology, near-death experiences, and alleged communications between the dead and the living. I acknowledge the bias that leads me to be skeptical of these claims. But fortunately for the reader who does not share this skepticism, there is a wealth of easily accessible, published material that does take this data seriously.[2]

Third, I tend to minimize the popular notion that one's immortality rests in the memories one leaves behind, in the impact of one's life on friends, family and community, in children and grandchildren, in the institutions one helped build, the students one taught or the books one published.

I am fully aware that my identity has been shaped by biological factors that predate me by millennia. I know that my more immediate ancestors had a decisive impact on my psychological makeup. I also share a Jewish communal memory that dates back, at least, to the biblical Abraham and Sarah. Some of those who succeed me on earth will in turn be shaped by who I was, by the life I lived and the values I affirmed. This is a kind of immortality, and for many, it is quite sufficient.

It is not sufficient for me, however, largely because this view does not acknowledge my concrete individuality as I experience it during my life here on earth. According to the view that my immortality is fulfilled through succeeding generations, my immortality merges with that of the countless others who share in shaping the identity of those who follow us. Judaism, on the other hand, provides me with a doctrine of the afterlife that affirms that despite the influence on me of countless others, I remain a totally distinct and individualized human being. It is precisely this individualized existence that is most precious to God and that God will preserve for eternity. We shall quote, below, the claim of the Mishnah that though we are all shaped in the image of the single person that God created at the outset, each of us is different from the other. Each of us can then say: "For my sake was the world created." Moreover, when that individual person dies, he or she dies, and there will never be another precisely like him or her. The burning question remains: Is that death the final word on the destiny of that individual? Judaism argues that it is not, and I agree.

I will construct a Jewish understanding of the afterlife out of our classical sources, but one that is also congruent with our contemporary understanding of religious thinking and language. Also, in much of what follows, I will be drawing on the work of the contemporary thinkers that I discussed in the previous chapter.

THE REALITY OF DEATH

To deal with the question of the afterlife means, first of all, to accept the reality of death. This may appear incongruous because, at least in the popular imagination, notions of an afterlife seem to be designed precisely to challenge the reality of death. Not so! The very opposite is the case. What doctrines of the afterlife do challenge is the *finality* of death, the view that death represents the end point of our individual destiny and of our individual relationship with God, not its *reality*. The distinction between the reality of death and its finality may be subtle, but it is crucial. It may even be argued that until we have fully accepted the fact that our death is real, there is no reason for us to even consider whether or not we have an afterlife.

Note that even scientists such as Dr. Sherwin Nuland (whose thinking we discussed in the first chapter) accept the reality of death, while rejecting its finality. They believe that, like plants and animals, all humans live on in the broader ecosystem:

> We die...so that others may live. The tragedy of a single individual becomes, in the balance of natural things, the triumph of ongoing life.[3]

I will never appreciate the full power of what Judaism says about my afterlife until I fully accept the fact of my death. Not simply death in the abstract, not my all-too-human mortality, not simply the acknowledgement that all living things must eventually die, but precisely *my* death in all its painful concreteness. If I never really die, why worry about an afterlife? It is precisely because I live daily with an impending awareness that I will soon live no more that the question of what will happen to me after I die presses upon me. And that it does so with increasing urgency the closer I come to the end of my days.

All living things eventually die, but only human beings live

246

with the awareness of their death. This is the terrifying paradox at the heart of human existence: We are animals who are yet conscious of our animal nature. We live an animal-like existence: We eat, drink and mate. Yet, we have self-consciousness. We are aware of our bodily functions and can control them. And we think, value and feel. We are capable of love and generosity, guilt and despair. We can search the mysteries of nature and create great art. We can even spin theories about our afterlife (as I am doing right now). Yet we die the death of animals.

William James calls death "the worm at the core of all our usual springs of delight."

> The fact that we *can* die, that we *can* be ill at all, is what perplexes us.... We need a life not correlated with death, a health not liable to illness, a kind of good that will not perish, a good that flies beyond the Goods of nature.[4]

To live with the constant awareness of that paradox is well nigh impossible, which is why most of us work desperately to deny it. But such denial is increasingly difficult to maintain, as we age or become mortally ill.

How I deal with my death is crucial to how I deal with my life. That is what lends the issue of my afterlife even greater urgency. Discussing the afterlife is not simply determining what will happen to me in some indefinite future; it affects how I live today. If my death is an integral part of the larger reality which constitutes my life, then to deal with my life demands that I deal with my death. Of course, I can also avoid the larger issue of my life's meaning; most of us do. But one who is not satisfied with simply living day by day without a broader purpose, without a sense of what it means to live as a human being, or of how a human life-experience coheres and acquires significance, will eventually have to confront his or her death and integrate that fact into the broader structure that constitutes the life that one is living.

No more than any other human being do I *know* what will happen to me after I die. But what I *believe* will happen to me after I die affects how I lead my life today. That is why the issue of my afterlife presses upon me *now*.

RELIGION AND THE AFTERLIFE

The impulse to create that broader structure, to knit together the discrete moments of a human life into a pattern of meaning is precisely the function of religion. Religion, the anthropologist Clifford Geertz reminds us, formulates "conceptions of a general order of existence."[5] The operative word here is "order." Religion orders our world, discerns patterns in what appears to be anarchy, wrests cosmos out of chaos, sense out of senselessness.

To claim that death is final is to subvert the order that religion imposes on our experience. And that, too, is our existential claim, one which cannot be supported by rational or empirical data, yet one that even a Sherwin Nuland would agree with. His entire book, *How We Die,* attempts to show that death is an indispensable part of the natural *order.* But in the light of what we referred to above as the paradox of human existence, to accept the finality of death is to revert to chaos. Death is the ultimate absurdity, the total annihilation of everything that a human life distinctively represents. That is the basis for John Hick's insistence that

> any religious understanding of human existence—not merely of one's own existence but of the life of humanity as a whole—positively requires some kind of immortality belief and would be radically incoherent without it.[6]

248

It is not only the fact of death that is incoherent. If death is an integral part of our broader life experience, then it also subverts that as well. To insist on the finality of death is to condemn the totality of human life to meaninglessness. Human life cannot be fulfilled here on earth. We are born and grow into adulthood with hopes and visions, goals and ideals, yet most of us prepare to die with a haunting sense of potentials unfulfilled, aspirations unrealized, relationships unresolved, accounts still not balanced. Our life-experience is inevitably fragmented. That pattern lends human life as a whole what Hick calls "a tragic character," and it leads him to recognize that

> if the human potential is to be fulfilled in the lives of individual men and women, those lives must be prolonged far beyond the limits of our present bodily existence.[7]

This is a singularly modern extension of the impulse which led the author of Daniel to insist that it is the need for retribution that demands a doctrine of resurrection. In Daniel, retribution was a moral issue: God had to reward the martyrs of that age for their loyalty and punish the evil-doers for their treachery, if not in their lifetime then in an afterlife. For us today, retribution is more than a moral issue. It represents the intuitive sense that since humans are born with an impulse to lead fulfilled lives, God must provide a setting for that fulfillment to be achieved, if not now, then in an afterlife.

THE LANGUAGE OF ESCHATOLOGY

The surest way to trivialize any eschatological doctrine is to understand it as literal truth, as a prediction of events that will take place just as they are described in some eventual future. That is the fatal flaw in the arguments, both of modern traditionalist and modern liberal Jews. The former accept it as literally true; the latter reject it because they understand it in the same way. But is there a middle ground?

I believe there is. I believe that the most fruitful way of making sense of these teachings is to understand them as part of Judaism's classic religious myth.

In the first chapter, I suggested several possible definitions of the term "myth." I will not recapitulate that discussion here. Suffice it to say that a myth is a way of connecting discrete experiences so that they form a coherent pattern and acquire meaning. Myths, then, are not objectively literal descriptions of some reality "out there" beyond the individual. But neither are they total fictions. Rather, they are subjective, somewhat imaginative portraits that make it possible for our experience of the world to hang together, to be ordered, and thus, to make sense.

Mythic thinking becomes progressively indispensable the more our experience eludes immediate sense-perception, the further we get from what we can directly perceive. That is why scientists who investigate the origins of the world, or the ultimate make-up of the material world, or the dynamics of the human psyche revert to myth. Each of these deals with events or realities that exist "beyond" the range of direct human perception. It is this elusive "beyondness" of some data that makes it inaccessible to our senses and that demands a different way of thinking and talking that can fulfill our need to understand our world.

Dealing with the "beyond" is intrinsic to religious language. All religions speak voluminously of God, a reality that, certainly in Judaism, is beyond direct human apprehension. The same can be said for doctrines of creation, or narratives that describe the founding events of that religion. That God descended upon a mountaintop and spoke to Moses and the children of Israel is classic myth. So is the doctrine that God revealed God's self in the person of Jesus of

Nazareth in the first century of the Common Era, that this man was crucified for the sins of humankind, was resurrected on the third day, and will return to judge all humanity.

These are mythic statements precisely because they speak of the "beyond." To understand them as literal truths is to trivialize them. To believe, for example, that God literally came down on Sinai and literally spoke to our ancestors is to commit the sin of idolatry, which, in its purest form, reduces God to a natural/human phenomenon. *People* descend and speak, *God* does not—except in a mythic way.

All eschatology deals with the "beyond," with events that will take place beyond the range of time, in some other "age" or "world." It is simply impossible for human beings to comprehend what this world will look like "after time." The very phrase is oxymoronic; there simply is no "after" to time. Every "after" remains within time.

Eschatology complements our thinking about creation. Together they deal with the beginnings and endings of all things, with the "beyond" before and after. Thus they provide a frame for the "in between," which, in classic Jewish religious thinking, is understood as the age of history, the age in which we are now located. They also provide the broad structure which Jews use to make sense of how everything came to be and how all things will eventually end. With this pattern in place, we know "where we are" within the broadest perspective of time. Creation and eschatology provide the frame which gives the portrait integrity. They are properly indispensable.

This book has focused on only one of the many themes that compose Jewish eschatology, the one that deals with the ultimate destiny of the individual human being. We have seen that during its richest phase, in the Talmudic era, Judaism proffered two doctrines on this theme. One taught that, at the end of time, our bodies will be resurrected; the other maintained that a part of us, our "soul," never dies, but continues in some other sphere under the loving protection of God. Eventually, these two doctrines were conflated

251

so that, at the end, God will restore our immortal souls to our resurrected bodies. From the age of the Talmud to the dawn of
modernity, most Jews accepted some form of this conflated version.

Both doctrines share the classic characteristics of myth. We
have no direct apprehension of what constitutes a "soul," nor can
anyone speak in literal terms of what will happen to our bodies after they become dust. Both doctrines take us "beyond" the
boundaries of human experience; both strain our normal conceptual faculties and our language. But the alternatives are not simply
uncritical literalism or silence. Our task is to understand how the
doctrines function as a way of completing the frame which lends
coherence to our life experience here on earth.

There are two core arguments for the indispensability of a
doctrine of the afterlife. One is theological, the other is anthropological. The theological argument stems from the Jewish
understanding of God; the anthropological, from its understanding of the nature of the human being.

THE THEOLOGICAL ARGUMENT:
GOD IS MORE POWERFUL THAN DEATH

Ask the typical Jew to describe the nature of God and he or she will
immediately tell you that God is omnipotent. No doctrine is more
central to popular Jewish religion. Of course, God can do whatever
God wants to do. That is what makes God, God! But even a brief
glance at the image of God as it emerges in our classic texts will
reveal that our ancestors understood God's omnipotence to be far
from absolute.

Read the Bible carefully and the overwhelming impression is
of God's dismal failure in accomplishing God's central purpose: The
creation of a sacred people who will be unquestionably loyal to God's
will. God's very first interaction with human beings, with Adam and

Eve in Eden, is a paradigmatic narrative since Adam and Eve are everybody. They disobey God's command with tragic results. The Bible recapitulates that pattern again and again with the role of Adam and Eve taken up by the people of Israel. Israel, too, rebels, with equally tragic results. God tries to re-establish a relationship with Israel, is challenged yet again, and the cycle continues. The whole is a poignant record of frustration suffused with hope and infinite yearning.[8]

In much of the Bible, the main impediment to the full manifestation of God's power is human freedom. That God created human beings free even to rebel against God is never questioned. Adam and Eve were free to eat the forbidden fruit; Cain to kill his brother; the Israelites to build a golden calf. God had to live with the fruits of that freedom. The only significant exception to that rule is Pharaoh. God hardened Pharaoh's heart, we are told, so that God's eventual redemption of Israel would be a striking manifestation of God's power:

> I will harden Pharaoh's heart, that I may multiply my signs and marvels in the land of Egypt. When Pharaoh does not heed you, I will lay My Hand upon Egypt and deliver My ranks, My people the Israelites, from the land of Egypt with extraordinary chastisements. And the Egyptians shall know that I am the Lord.... (Exodus 7:3-5)

The Bible goes out of its way to show that God deprived Pharaoh of his freedom to choose to release the Israelites. That is a clear signal that Pharaoh's inability to act freely is the exception that proves the rule.

Sometimes God's power is limited by God's own commitments. When God threatens to destroy the Israelites for having built the golden calf, Moses intercedes, pleading that God remember the covenant with Abraham, Isaac and Jacob:

"You swore to them by Your Self and said to them: I will make your offspring as numerous as the stars of heaven, and I will give to your offspring this holy land of which I spoke, to possess forever." And the Lord renounced the punishment He had planned to bring upon His people. (Exodus 32:13–14)

In this instance, the limitations on God's power are not intrinsic, but rather result from God's decisions about the destiny of Israel. There is no question that God has ultimate power. There is also no question that God chose not to exercise that power.

In other texts, the reasons for God's impotence are far more mysterious. The author of Psalm 44 has been told (by his ancestors) that in days of old, God had led Israel to victory over its enemies, but in his own day,

> ...You have rejected and disgraced us;
>   You do not go with our armies,
> You make us retreat before our foe;
>   our enemies plunder us at will.
> You let them devour us like sheep;
>   You disperse us among the nations....
> You make us a byword among the nations,
>   a laughingstock among the peoples....

The psalmist would understand God's abandonment of Israel if it had been disloyal to God. But this is not the case now:

> All this has come upon us,
>   yet we have not forgotten You,
>   or been false to Your covenant....

Indeed, the very opposite is the case:

254

It is for Your sake that we are slain all day long,
   that we are regarded as sheep to be slaughtered.

It is precisely for Israel's loyalty that it has been persecuted. Finally, the coda to the psalm:

Rouse Yourself, why do You sleep, O Lord?
Awaken, do not reject us forever!....
Arise and help us,
   redeem us, as befits Your faithfulness. (44:10ff)

Is Israel's vulnerability before its enemies a commentary on God's lack of power? Or is it a matter of God's will? There is no explicit answer to this question in the text. It may be the result of a deliberate decision by God. But it may also be the result of intrinsic divine impotence, some inherent limitation on God's power. That conclusion is certainly the implication of the psalmist's claim that Israel has not been unfaithful to God. Why then would God choose to abandon God's people? The psalmist is left to wonder, as is the author of Psalm 13:

How long, O Lord; will You ignore me forever?
How long will You hide Your face from me?
How long will I have cares on my mind,
   grief in my heart all day?
How long will my enemy have the upper hand?
   (Psalm 13:2–3)

The setting of this psalm is personal, not communal as in Psalm 44. But the experience of God's withdrawal is the same. In neither case is God's absence a form of punishment. Indeed, in the first of these, the author insists that Israel suffers not only despite, but paradoxically *because of* its loyalty to God.

255

However limited God's power may be in historical time, it is Judaism's overwhelming testimony that these limitations will vanish in the Age to Come. The central thrust of Jewish eschatology is that this Age will mark the ultimate manifestation of God's sovereignty over all creation. That promise forms the climax of one of the earliest Jewish eschatological visions on record:

> In all of My sacred mount
> Nothing evil or vile shall be done;
> For the land shall be filled with devotion to the Lord
> As water covers the sea. (Isaiah 11:9)

A far more elaborate statement of that vision is the concluding paragraph of the *Alenu* liturgy which dates from the second century of our era and now is the concluding prayer of every Jewish service of worship.

> We therefore hope, Lord our God, soon to behold Your majestic glory, when the abominations will be removed from the earth and the false gods exterminated; when the world will be perfected under the reign of the Almighty, and all mankind will call upon Your name, and all the wicked of the earth will be turned to You. May all the inhabitants of the world realize and know that to You every knee must bend, every tongue vow allegiance.... May they all accept the yoke of Your kingdom, and reign over them speedily forever and ever.

It is also expressed in the High Holiday *Amidah*.

> Now, Lord our God, put Your awe upon all that You have created.... Grant honor to your people, glory to those who revere You, hope to those who seek You....

May the righteous see this and rejoice, the upright exult, and the godly delight. Iniquity shall shut its mouth, wickedness will vanish like smoke, when You will abolish the rule of tyranny from the earth. You will reign over all whom You have made, You alone, O Lord, on Mount Zion the abode of Your majesty, in Jerusalem Your holy city, as it is written in Your Holy Scriptures, "The Lord will reign forever, Your God O Zion, for all generations." (Psalm 146:10)

This is the very same impulse that leads the tradition to forecast God's eschatological triumph over death as well.

The expectation that death itself will eventually die assumes that death was perceived to challenge God's power manifest in history. How we understand that expectation depends on how we deal with Judaism's differing accounts of the origins of death.

Earlier, we reviewed four biblical explanations for the presence of death in the world. Death may be part of God's original creation, it may be retribution for Adam and Eve's disobedience, it may be a trade-off for human self-awareness and our powers of discrimination; or it may represent a remnant of a pagan notion of death as a power that God did not or could not subdue at creation and that persists independently of God's will and power.

In reverse order, if death is a power that resisted God's ordering work of creation, it will vanish in an age when God's sovereignty will be complete. If death is understood as the fruit of the full flowering of our humanity, it becomes one of the many tensions that mark the nature of human life within this age of history, and which will be abolished when history has come to a close. If death is retribution for sin, it will disappear in an age when loyalty to God will be intuitive on the part of all humanity.

But if death is part of God's creation from the outset, we find ourselves in more difficulty. If from the outset, God created us to die, why then the eschatological promise to banish death?

The clue to understanding this paradox lies in the message of Psalm 44 and 13. Their authors despair at God's mysterious abandonment of Israel or of the psalmist. Where is God's power *now*? But history is replete with instances of God's apparent withdrawal, both in the communal sphere and also in the life of individuals. The psalmists make no attempt to account for God's withdrawal; they bemoan it and plead for God's renewed engagement. The psalms end with a plea that God's presence and protection be manifest once again, but also with no explicit assurance that this will, indeed, take place.

That God's presence is sometimes inexplicably eclipsed is the central paradox of the life of faith. This is what led Martin Buber to suggest the notion of "moment gods," and Rabbi Irving Greenberg to write of "moment faiths." The immediate context of Greenberg's discussion is our theological response to the Holocaust.

> After Auschwitz, faith means there are times when faith is overcome. Buber has spoken of "moment gods"; God is known only at the moment when presence and awareness are fused in vital life. This knowledge is interspersed with moments when only natural, self-contained, routine existence is present. We now have to speak of "moment faiths," moments when the Redeemer and vision of redemption are present, interspersed with times when the flames and smoke of burning children blot out faith—though it flickers again.

For Greenberg, in the light of the Holocaust, the dichotomy of theist and atheist is impossible to maintain. Instead, faith exists in a dialectic, it is

> a life response of the whole person to the Presence in

258

life and history. Like life, this response ebbs and flows. The difference between the skeptic and the believer is frequency of faith, and not certitude of position.[9]

It is not the Holocaust alone that challenges faith. History is replete with holocausts, communal and personal. They represent an enduring challenge to God's power. But the believer's response to that challenge is nourished by the assurance that the dialectic of faith is endemic to our historical situation alone, and that it will be resolved in an age when, in the words of the High Holiday liturgy:

> Iniquity shall shut its mouth, wickedness shall vanish like smoke, when You will abolish the rule of tyranny on earth. You shall reign over all whom You have made, You alone O Lord....

Death may well be an inexplicable part of God's created world, as inexplicable as the other manifestations of anarchy we see about us. But if Jewish eschatology views history as moving from chaos to cosmos, then God's victory over death is part of that broader mythic pattern.

On theological grounds, then, Judaism demands the death of death. If God is truly God, if God's will and power are absolute, then God must triumph over death as well. The death of death marks the final step in the triumph of the monotheistic God.[10]

THE ARGUMENT FROM ANTHROPOLOGY I:
MY BODY

The death of death is the ultimate eschatological promise. Judaism came to affirm that expectation because, certainly beginning with the middle of the second century BCE and possibly somewhat earlier, some Jews believed that in the foreseeable future, at least some of the dead would live again. Eventually, that promise was expanded to include all Jews who had ever lived. That doctrine soon achieved quasi-dogmatic status in the Jewish system of beliefs. Begin with that premise and the inevitable conclusion is that in such an age, death itself would be no more.

But what are we to make of that premise? What does it mean to say that God has the power to bring the dead to life?

We saw that this doctrine began as two separate doctrines that later merged. The first teaches that, at the end of time, bodies will be resurrected from their graves. The second, that there is a non-material "something" in every human called the "soul" which never dies, which departs the body at death and returns to God. The later conflation of the two doctrines led to the belief that, at the time of resurrection, the soul would be restored to the resurrected body, and that each individual human, with body and soul united as they were on earth, would come before God for judgement.

This scenario is profoundly true. Even more, it is indispensable for us if we are to make sense of our lives here on earth—as long as we accept it, not as crude biology, but as classic Jewish religious myth.

To characterize this phase of my argument as "anthropological" is to suggest that it stems from the Jewish view of the human person as a psycho-physical unity. The "psycho" part of that entity is what I call my "soul"; the "physical," my body.

To speak of "my body" is to capture a relationship that is totally unique, a relationship between something that is "me" and something else that is a "body." But what is that relationship? In what way is it unique?[11]

One possible way of construing that relationship is to suggest that my body is something that I "have" much as I "have" a watch. But surely the relationship with my body is far more intimate than my relationship with my watch. What I "have" I can dispose of. I can give you my watch and I remain myself, just as I was when I wore it on my wrist. But I cannot give you my body (except in some crude, sexual sense) without disposing of myself, of "me." When my body is born, I am born; when my body gets sick, I am sick; when my body dies, I die. I can dispose of my body by committing suicide, but I can only do that once. When I do that, I have also disposed of my "self," of me in my totality. To say that I simply "have" my body, then, is to miss that dimension of my relationship with my body which makes it a unique relationship.

A much more accurate way of capturing that relationship between me and my body is to claim that "I am my body." That formulation captures the felt relationship between whatever it is that "I" am and my body. It affirms the indissolubility of that bond, the fact that without my body, I am no longer me. I feel quite differently toward "my" body than I do toward "a" body. Were I a surgeon, the patient's body that lies before me on the operating table is simply "a" body; it could be "any" body, and after completing the surgery on this body, I will move on to another body.

In fact, medical ethics insists that the body on which a surgeon operates must be simply "a" body, certainly not his own body nor even the body of someone the surgeon feels particularly close to. Similarly, the mortician embalms "a" body. Even in the most intense of interpersonal, sexual relationships, what I feel toward the body that lies next to me is qualitatively different than what I feel toward my own body. The latter relationship is even infinitely more intimate than the former. I can divorce my wife and move on to a new, intimate relationship with someone else and with that person's body. But I cannot divorce my body.

That comparison is suggestive. We can posit a range of relationships between me and someone or something else which reveal a progressively diminishing sense of intimacy: Between me and my body, me and my wife, lover and children, me and my cat, me and the superintendent of my building, me and the people who share my bus trip, me and my watch, etc., etc., etc.... To use Buberian terminology, this range of relationships takes me progressively from the realm of the I-Thou to that of the I-It, from intimacy to detachment. My relationship with my body is the paradigmatic I-Thou relationship. I can enter into other I-Thou relationships because of the paradigmatic I-Thou relationship I have with my body.[12]

Even more, it is because of my body that I am inserted into time and space, into history and society. If I were not embodied, I would not be sitting at my word-processor on this very day. Nor would I be teaching my class or playing with my children. My body is the landmark which connects me with everything else that exists physically, specifically with all of history and society.[13]

The thrust of these reflections is to suggest, first, that my body is indispensable to my sense of self. Without my body, there is no "me." Whatever my ultimate destiny, then, whatever God has in store for me at the end, must include my body. That is why any doctrine of the afterlife must deal with my body as well. Belief in bodily resurrection is, then, indispensable to any doctrine of the afterlife.

It is indispensable for another reason. If my body inserts me into history and society, then the affirmation of bodily resurrection is also an affirmation of history and society. If my bodily existence is insignificant, then so are history and society. To affirm that God has the power to reconstitute me in my bodily existence is to affirm that God also cares deeply about history and society.

But we know that God does care deeply about history and society. Will Herberg is one of many thinkers who claim that it is Judaism that contributed "the sense of history" to Western culture. Every people and nation had their historians, but only in the Bible is history viewed, not as a series of random events, nor as an endless cycle without an ultimate goal, but rather as "a great and meaningful process." Herberg quotes the biblical scholar, J.P. Hyatt, as contending that the prophets conceived of God as a God of history, manifesting himself on the stage of time and controlling the destiny of men and nations.

History, in Judaism, has a beginning, an end, and a purpose. History is linear, and it understands the past as manifesting promises which would be fulfilled in the future.

Biblical historiography also takes time seriously. Herberg writes:

> God's ends are effected with time, in and through history; the salvation that is promised as the ultimate validation of life lies indeed beyond history but it lies beyond it as its fulfillment and consummation.... From this point of view, earthly history takes on a meaning and seriousness that are completely absent where the Hebraic influence has not been felt.

To take time seriously is to take the mundane events of everyday life seriously. Among the Greeks, Herberg notes, humanity

> had no destiny. The strivings and doings of men, their enterprises, conflicts and achievements, led nowhere. All, all would be swallowed up in the cycle of eternal recurrence that was the law of the cosmos.[14]

To shape "the strivings and doings of men" in minutest detail is the central purpose of biblical legislation, and in biblical prophecy, Israel's loyalty to God's moral law becomes the decisive factor in its national history. The purpose of the whole is to create a distinctive social structure, a unique community, an *"am kadosh,"* a "people" that is "holy" or "set apart."

Torah is suffused with this concern for Israel's social polity. It is implicit in every piece of legislation in the Torah affecting interpersonal relationships, but it is explicit in Leviticus 24, an entire chapter devoted to regulating the social life of the community. The legislative details pertain to the Sabbatical and Jubilee years, and to the redemption of land, of indentured servants and of slaves. In each case, the text begins with the phrase, "If your kinsman is in straits...." The whole chapter is permeated with such admonitions as "fear your God," or "I am the Lord your God who brought you out of the land of Egypt," or "for they [the indentured servants] are My servants...; they may not give themselves over into servitude."

The repeated emphasis on God's redemption of Israel from Egyptian servitude provides the equally explicit grounding for this legislation. Indeed, why were our ancestors enslaved in Egypt for 400 years if not to provide them with an object lesson about the evils of social oppression, if not to teach them how to create a social structure in which no one will be oppressed?

In the writings of the prophets, this emphasis on the primacy of morality reaches its apogee. Witness Amos' cry to

> ...let justice well up like water,
> Righteousness like an unfailing stream. (5:24)

or Isaiah's

> Learn to do good,
> Devote yourself to justice;
> Aid the wronged.
> Uphold the rights of the orphan;
> Defend the cause of the widow. (1:17)

Yehezkel Kaufmann, the noted Israeli biblical scholar, emphasizes that it is precisely

the commonplace 'venial' sins that offend the prophets:

264

bribe-taking, biased justice, false scales, extortion from the poor and defenseless, raising prices, and the like. For such sins they prophesy destruction and exile....God made Himself known to Israel, made with it a moral-religious Covenant, intended it to be a holy nation dedicated to do His will. But a people perverting justice, practicing violence, drunken and debauched, is no people of God! For the prophets, justice and righteousness are not a private affair. The entire nation is responsible for the moral state that prevails in it. Hence it will be judged as a whole both for idol worship and for moral sin on the day of reckoning.[15]

God's engagement both with human history and with Israel's social polity come together in prophetic eschatology. The prophets do more than rebuke and call for repentance. They also envision a future age when paganism will end and monotheism will become the heritage of all peoples, when war will be no more, and when all humankind will recognize God's moral law as absolute.[16]

To affirm that vision is effectively to affirm the value to God of human history and society as we participate in them during our lifetime. But that participation demands our embodied existence here on earth. That is why any Jewish doctrine of the afterlife must also affirm the significance of that dimension of my being.

THE ARGUMENT FROM ANTHROPOLOGY II: MY SOUL

But as clear as it is that "I am my body," it is also clear that "I am not only my body." The impulse behind all theories of the human soul is the sense that there are dimensions of my self that resist being reduced to mere bodily functions.

First, there is my self-consciousness. I am aware of my "self," of some overarching dimension of my being that unifies the various pieces of my life, that organizes my thoughts, feelings and experiences and identifies them as mine. Much of the work of this part of me operates within the range of my consciousness; I feel or am aware of this part of me doing its work. I am even aware of the fact that I am related to my body, and I ponder the nature of that relationship.

I am also aware of myself as a thinking being, and I can think about my thinking and wonder about my thoughts and about the nature of thought itself. I also have feelings, values, hopes, visions of what I can accomplish in my lifetime. I have, in short a personal myth, an overarching image of who I am and where I belong in the world. If asked, I can articulate what this larger image looks like and, thereby, tell you who I, distinctively, am.

It is this sense of an "inner" life that has led philosophers from antiquity onward to speak of human beings as possessing a "soul." Plato understood the human soul as a distinct ontological entity which pre-exists its insertion into the body and will continue to exist after the death of the body. We saw that this view of the soul leads to a sharply dualistic understanding of the human person as a composite of two distinct elements, body and soul. Ultimately it also leads to the doctrine of the immortality of the human soul which, as we have also seen, persists in philosophical and theological thinking to this day. Souls are immortal because they are non-material and, thus, indestructible. That's just the way souls are.

The problem with this sharp body/soul dualism is that it is counter-intuitive, that having created this sharp distinction between the body and the soul, we are at a loss to connect them again. Yet we feel that connection. We feel ourselves to be a single, indivisible psycho/physical individual. We feel an intimate relationship between our inner lives and our bodily functions. We are aware that each affects the other, that our feelings and thoughts influence our bodily functions; we feel tension and we perspire. We know that aspects of

266

our bodily faculties, such as our ability to see and hear, generate feelings and thoughts. We also feel, intuitively, that these two dimensions of our being form one concrete individuality. But once they are separated from each other, how can they be reunited?

The further implications of Platonic thinking are equally problematic. Plato identifies the soul as the "real" me, as that which makes me distinctly human and unique. The development of my soul is redemptive. It is my uniquely human mandate, my ultimate accomplishment. Plato understands my bodily existence to be an obstacle to that fulfillment, the "prison" in which my soul is incarcerated and from which I must try to liberate myself by philosophical reflection.

These implications of Platonic dualism pose insurmountable obstacles to any thinker who speaks out of the Jewish tradition. First, Judaism has never demeaned the body and its functions. Jewish liturgy speaks of the body as a miraculous piece of God's creation. Judaism has never affirmed the religious value of sexual abstinence. Indeed, the very first commandment to Adam and Eve is to procreate, and the value of sexual fulfillment has never been questioned by Jews. We celebrate all significant ritual moments with food and drink. Before burial, we wash and purify the body as we recite prayers that affirm the glory and the beauty of the human body.[17]

One of the most striking affirmations of the value of the human body is a liturgical passage recited daily, together with the passage that praises God for having created and preserved my soul, in the early morning worship service. This passage, also of Talmudic origin (Bab. Talmud, *B'rakhot* 60b), reads:

> Blessed are You, Lord our God, Sovereign of the universe, who has fashioned the human being with wisdom and created within him many openings and cavities. It is obvious to You...that should one of them be ruptured or one of them be blocked, it would be impossible to

267

survive and stand before You. Blessed are You, God, Who heals all flesh and acts wondrously.

The human body is of ultimate value and significance because it too is a manifestation of God's wondrous power. Would you discover God's presence? Look at the human body!

As we saw earlier, the Bible knows nothing of a Platonic entity called the soul. It understood the Hebrew terms *nefesh* or *neshamah* as a way of speaking of the living human person, or as the spark of life that vivifies the clod of earth out of which God formed the first human. Eventually, Greek thought did shape later Jewish thinking on the nature of the soul, but even then, Jewish tradition rejected its more extreme dualistic implications. For example, it saw the soul as created by God, and its immortality as a gift from God Who rules even over the world of human souls. At least until modernity, Judaism continued to insist that at the end of days, human bodies too would live again.

John Hick sharply rejects any sense of the soul as a distinct metaphysical entity and dualistic implications of that view. He understands the soul as "an indicator of value." In his view, the soul

> will express that sense of the sacredness of human personality and of the inalienable rights of the human individual which we have...seen to be the moral and political content of the western idea of the soul.... To speak of man as a soul is to speak mythologically, but in a way which is bound up with important practical attitudes and practices. The myth of the soul expresses a faith in the intrinsic value of the human individual as an end in itself.[18]

Hick, here, echoes one interpretation of the biblical claim that human beings were created "in the image of God" (Genesis 1:26–

268

27). The literal meaning of that claim is not at all clear, but to some later Jewish thinkers, preeminently Maimonides, it establishes the unique value of the human being among all of creation. It leads Maimonides to insist that true human perfection is intellectual.

> This is in reality the ultimate end; this is what gives the individual true perfection, a perfection belonging to him alone; and it gives him permanent perdurance; through it man is man.[19]

It also leads him to insist that ultimate human immortality is for the soul alone. But of all Jewish thinkers, Maimonides espouses the sharpest body/soul dualism.

Note that, for Hick, to speak of a human soul is to speak mythically. It refers to one more "beyond." This time, it is the various manifestations of what we call our "inner" life and which elude direct, overt apprehension. Another way of saying this is to view the soul as a construct, an imaginative unification of the dimensions of that inner life which pulls together all the dimensions of our awareness that do not explicitly reflect our bodily functioning. This, we identify as "soul."

In this view, the term "soul" is similar to the term "mind" with which it is often confused. But to speak of my mind is not to speak of a distinct entity buried deeply in my brain. I can hold a brain in my hand, but I cannot hold a mind. Though "mind" is a noun, it really functions as an adverb, a term which qualifies or describes modes of behavior. When I behave intelligently, when I deliberate what to do or not to do, when I think, I say that I am "using" my mind. But again, a mind is not something I "have" or "use." I cannot dispose of or surrender my mind, except in a metaphorical sense. "Mind," too, is a construct which unifies and identifies one dimension of my behavior.

The precise relationship between the mind and the body (or

the brain) is one of the perennial problems of philosophy.[20] It raises many of the same issues suggested by the relationship between body and soul. Is the distinction between the two a valid one? Are there existing entities to which we can apply each of these terms? If yes, what is the relationship between the two?

Philosophers' answers to these questions fall into two groups. One set of theories tends to reduce one reality to the other: Either there is only body, and references to mind are covert references to bodily functions. This view is called materialism. Its alternative, idealism, reduces all bodily references to mental events. In contrast, dualistic theories maintain not only that the distinction is a valid one, but that there are two distinct realities. All dualist theories are then forced to explain how body and mind are related to each other.

There has been no satisfactory resolution of that issue throughout the history of philosophy. But it remains clear that what precipitates the issue in the first place is the intuition that we function in these two distinctive ways, and that somehow or other, each affects the other.

When I affirm that "I am not only my body," I affirm that apart from my sense of my bodily existence, I am also aware of a dimension of my self which eludes identification with my bodily functions, but which remains as intrinsic to my identity as is my body.

In what sense is this soul immortal? For me, not in any Platonic sense, not as a distinct entity which survives my death and the burial of my body. If I am a psycho/physical entity, then when I die, *all* of me dies, my body together with my inner life.

The notion that the soul enjoys an intrinsic immortality denied to my body is also troubling because it takes God out of the eschatological picture. If the soul is intrinsically immortal, then God has nothing to do with my soul at the end of days, other than reuniting it with my body. But the whole point of Jewish thinking on the afterlife is that it affirms God's ultimate power, the final manifestation of God's unfettered sovereignty. The doctrine of bodily resurrection preserves that affirmation. The doctrine of the intrinsic immortality of the soul does not. When the *Gevurot* benediction affirms that God is *mehaye hametim,* that God "revives the dead," I believe it means the entire scenario: God gives new life to the dead, to the totality of me, to my body together with my soul.

This is the ultimate meaning of the Talmudic doctrine that at the end of days, God will bring my body and my soul together again and that I will be reconstituted as I was during my life on earth. The mythic thrust of this doctrine is that it is this totality in its concrete individuality, as manifest during my lifetime, that God treasures and that God will therefore preserve for all time.

I insist that my resurrection must affect all of me in my concrete individuality because I understand the central thrust of the doctrine of the afterlife as establishing the everlasting preciousness to God of the life I led here on earth. I lived that life as a concrete individual. A doctrine of the afterlife that has my soul merging into some cosmic soul after my death would defeat the entire purpose of the myth. The mishnah that records the court's admonition to witnesses in a case of capital punishment reminds me that God created but one single person from whom all of mankind descended.

> Therefore but a single person was created in the world, to teach that if anyone has caused a single soul to perish from Israel, Scripture imputes to him as though he had caused a whole world to perish; and if any person saves a single soul from Israel, Scripture imputes to him as though he had saved a whole world. (Mishnah *Sanhedrin* 4:5)[21]

Again, why did God create one single person?

> To proclaim the greatness of the Holy One, blessed be He; for a person stamps many coins with the one seal

271

and they are all like one another; but the King of Kings, the Holy One, blessed be He, has stamped every person with the seal of the first person, yet not one of them is like the other. Therefore every one must say, "For my sake was the world created."

There is no more powerful testimony to Judaism's insistence that it is precisely the single human being in all his or her individuality that is most precious to God. It is that individuality that God will preserve forever.

I insist, as well, that God's economy of salvation knows no religious distinctions. We are all descendants of "one single person," and it is precisely our individual "person-hood" that makes each of us worthy of God's ultimate concern. Judaism has always had its partisan nationalists and its generous universalists, but it is invariably the latter group, with its opinions on the place of the non-Jew in God's salvational plans, that has triumphed.[22] I am proud to appropriate that tradition.

The one distinction that Judaism does make in this regard pertains to that between the righteous and the evil-doer. The Jewish doctrine of the afterlife did originate, as we have seen, in the need for some notion of ultimate divine retribution beyond whatever transpires during human life on earth. Though in time, the emphasis passed from life after death as a manifestation of God's justice to one of God's power, the notion that we are all ultimately accountable for the lives we live on earth never totally disappeared from Jewish teachings on the afterlife. That dimension of Jewish eschatology remains important for me. It teaches me that the moral quality of the life I lead here on earth is of importance to God, and that God will hold me responsible for that life. But moral issues are complex, and human motivations are obscure. I then forego my right to pass judgement on my fellow human beings. That judgement I am prepared to leave in God's hands, convinced as I am that, in the words of the liturgical formula I recite upon hearing of a death, God's judgement is always true.

That is my hope. That is my expectation.

RECLAIMING THE MYTH

But I am also a product of modernity, a child of the enlightenment. I pride myself on being a rational being, on using my critical faculties, and on appreciating the value of scientific method. That part of me makes it difficult to ignore the raised eyebrows, the charges of denial, of wishful or "mushy" thinking, of lacking the courage to confront my death with equanimity, that confront me whenever I speak of my hope for the hereafter. I acknowledge my vulnerability to those criticisms because I can identify with them, because I see them within myself. I understand where they come from.

But at those moments, I cling by my very fingernails to the realization that my rational self is not the whole of me, that there are dimensions of my experience that elude the critical temper, that the world remains for me a realm of enchantment. I do science but I also appreciate poetry; I work but I also play. I then seize that tiny window of opportunity, that sliver of openness that takes me beyond criticism to a new level of understanding. I "re-enchant" the world. Or, to use the term to which I referred earlier, I enter the stage of "second" or "willed naiveté."

Second naiveté is not the naiveté of the child, not the primordial state of innocence that we enjoy when we first confront the world into which we are born. It is, rather, a naiveté that fully acknowledges the indispensability of critical thinking but resists its imperialism. It is permeated with self-awareness, with a rueful mix of nostalgia and sophistication. It is both regressive (in that it takes me back to a prior stage of awareness), and aggressive (in that it impels me beyond science and rationality). "Something has been lost, irremediably lost," you recall, Paul Ricoeur concedes: "Immediacy of belief. But if we can no longer live the great symbolisms of the sacred in accordance with the original belief, we can, we modern men, aim at a second naiveté in and through criticism." And then, "we can *hear* again."[23]

My second naiveté takes me "in and through criticism." It does not ignore, deny, or side-step my critical faculties. It acknowledges their legitimacy, even their power. And it takes me beyond their reach. It is what makes it possible for me to hope that my life here on earth is not my entire destiny. That kind of hope takes me beyond the conclusions of my rational self. It refuses to surrender to the charges of denial and wishful thinking. It comes from some other dimension of my being, from that intuitive sense that I form a part of a broader order of existence that lends my life coherence.[24]

Or to use another terminology, I then reclaim my myth, precisely as myth, broken perhaps, but still very much alive—and I revel in its power. At that moment, I recite the *Gevurot* benediction of the *Amidah* and praise the goodness and the majesty of God Who gives life to the dead.

NOTES

CHAPTER I

1. Leo Tolstoy, *The Death of Ivan Ilyich* (New York: Bantam Books, 1981), pp. 133–134.

2. Sherwin B. Nuland, *How We Die: Reflections on Life's Final Chapter* (New York: Alfred A. Knopf, 1994), p. 267.

3. For a more extensive statement of Nuland's position, see Hans Jonas, "The Burden and Blessing of Mortality," Hastings Center Report (January–February 1992), pp. 34–40.

4. Clifford Geertz, "Religion as a Cultural System" in *The Interpretation of Cultures* (New York: Basic Books, Inc., 1973), p. 90.

5. Geertz, p. 90. Emphasis Langer's.

6. The parallel is suggested by Will Herberg, *Judaism and Modern Man* (New York: Farrar Straus and Young, 1951), pp. 230–231.

7. A more thoroughgoing summary of the major themes in classical Jewish eschatology can be found in my *Sacred Fragments: Recovering Theology for the Modern Jew* (Philadelphia: The Jewish Publication Society of America, 1990), ch. 10.

8. Rollo May, *The Cry for Myth* (New York: A Delta Book, Dell Publishing), 1991, p. 15.

9. Ian Barbour, *Myths, Models and Paradigms: A Comparative Study in Science and Religion* (New York: Harper and Row, 1974), pp. 19-20.

10. John Hick, *Death and Eternal Life* (Louisville, Kentucky: Westminster/ John Knox Press, 1994), p. 353. For additional attempts to define myth, see Will Herberg's "Some Variant Meanings of the Word 'Myth'" in his *Faith Enacted as History: Essays in Biblical Theology*, edited with an introduction by Bernhard W. Anderson (Philadelphia: The Westminster Press, 1976), ch. 10.

11. On the truth and falsity of myths, see Paul Tillich, *Dynamics of Faith* (New York: Harper Torchbooks, Harper and Row, 1957), ch. 5. On the existential criterion for truth, see *Franz Rosenzweig: His Life and*

Thought, presented by Nahum N. Glatzer (New York: A Shocken Book, Published with Farrar, Straus and Young, 1953), pp. 205–206.

12. On the varying responses to the breaking of a myth, see Tillich's *Dynamics of Faith,* pp. 48–54. An illuminating expansion of Tillich's thinking can be found in James Fowler, *Stages of Faith: The Psychology of Human Development and the Quest for Meaning* (San Francisco: Harper and Row, 1981), chs. 19–20. The phrase "second (or "willed") naiveté" is in Paul Ricoeur, *The Symbolism of Evil,* trans. Emerson Buchanan (Boston: Beacon Press, 1967), pp. 351–352.

13. Ricoeur, p. 351. Emphasis Ricoeur's.

14. Abraham Joshua Heschel, *God in Search of Man* (Philadelphia: The Jewish Publication Society of America, 1965), p. 185. Part 2 of this book deals with Heschel's theology of revelation.

15. For an expanded version of my theological assumptions, see *Sacred Fragments,* chs. 1–4.

16. Nuland, p. 58.

CHAPTER II

1. "Death," in *Man, Myth and Magic: The Illustrated Encyclopedia of the Supernatural,* ed. Richard Cavendish (North Bellmore, N.Y.: Marshall Cavendish Ltd., 1970), vol. 5, pp. 612–616.

2. JPS *Tanakh* translates "good and bad" instead of the more familiar "good and evil," doubtless to accentuate the polarization of the two. "Bad" is more clearly the opposite of "good" than "evil." We will retain the JPS translation except when quoting directly from another author.

3. For a comprehensive review of the varied interpretations of the phrase, see Claus Westerman, *Genesis 1–11,* trans. John J. Scullion (Minneapolis: Augsburg Publishing House, 1984), pp. 242–245. For a briefer review of the main interpretations, see Martin Buber, *Images of Good and Evil,* trans. Michael Bullock (London: Routledge and Kegan Paul, 1952), pp. 17–19, and James Barr, *The Garden of Eden and the Hope of Immortality* (Minneapolis: Fortress Press, 1992), pp. 61–63.

4. Barr, p. 62. For Barr's interpretation of this passage, see pp. 62–73.

5. Barr, p. 65.

6. Buber, p. 25.

7. Barr pursues this argument in chapter 2 of his book.

8. For my refutation of Barr's argument that human beings were destined to die from the outset, see the following chapter of this book.

9. On the composition of our biblical text out of varying traditions, see Richard Elliot Friedman, *Who Wrote the Bible?* (New York: Summit Books, 1987), and E.A. Speiser's "Introduction" to *Genesis*, The Anchor Bible (Garden City, N.Y.: Doubleday and Co., Inc., 1962).

10. The doctrine of *creatio ex nihilo* ("creation out of nothing") was considered indispensable by medieval philosophers because of the fear that its alternative, the notion that God created the world out of a pre-existing "something," would lead to theological dualism, namely, to the doctrine that two realities pre-existed the world, God and that other "something." See, e.g., Saadia Gaon, *Book of Doctrines and Beliefs*, abridged edition translated from the Arabic with an introduction and notes by Alexander Altman, in *Three Jewish Philosophers* (Atheneum, New York, 1982, Reprinted by arrangement with The Jewish Publication Society of America) ch. 1, pp. 49–73

11. Jon D. Levenson, *Creation and the Persistence of Evil: The Jewish Drama of Divine Omnipotence* (San Francisco: Harper and Row, 1988), p. 19. I am indebted to Levenson's work for this entire discussion.

12. Ras Shamra, in Northern Syria, is the modern site of the ancient city of Ugarit from the second millennium BCE. The excavations at this site uncovered an archive of clay tablets which are a rich source of information about the culture of the Ancient Near East and which illuminate countless biblical passages. See "Ugarit," in *Encyclopedia Judaica* (Jerusalem: Keter Publishing House, 1972), vol. 15, pp. 1501–1508.

13. On the battle between Baal and Mwt, see "Baal Worship" and "Death" in *Encyclopedia Judaica*, vol. 4, pp. 10–12, and vol. 5, p. 1420 respectively.

14. On this ancient god of death, see the references in Lloyd R. Bailey, Sr., *Biblical Perspectives on Death* (Philadelphia: Fortress Press, 1979), pp. 15, 41.

15. *Sifre, A Tannaitic Commentary on the Book of Deuteronomy*, translated from the Hebrew with introduction and notes by Reuven Hammer

(New Haven and London: Yale University Press, 1986), *Piska* 323, p. 335.

16. *Genesis Rabbah* in *Midrash Rabbah*, trans. Rabbi Dr. H. Friedman and Maurice Simon (London: The Soncino Press, 1939), 9:5, p. 66. Rabbi Meir plays on the similarity of the Hebrew word for "very," *meod*, and the Hebrew word for "death," *mavet*.

17. English translation for the United States of America (Liguori, Mo.: Liguori Publications, United States Conference of Bishops, 1994), 402, p. 101. On Christian interpretations of the afterlife, see the anthology *Immortality and Resurrection*, edited with an introduction by Krister Stendahl (New York: The Macmillan Company, 1965), in particular, Oscar Cullman's "Immortality of the Soul or Resurrection of the Dead?" pp. 9–53.

CHAPTER III

1. On the precise nature of Moses' sin at Meribah, see Excursus 50, *The JPS Torah Commentary, Numbers,* commentary by Jacob Milgrom (Philadelphia, New York: The Jewish Publication Society, 1990). This is a comprehensive review of all regnant interpretations of this enigmatic story. Milgrom's conclusion is that, contrary to the usual interpretation, Moses' sin had nothing to do with striking the rock instead of addressing it. His alternative explanation is compelling.

2. I am indebted to Barr, *The Garden of Eden,* pp. 30–34, for this qualification to my broader thesis on the condition of the inhabitants of *Sheol.*

3. On the story of Saul and the woman from En-dor and more generally on varying explanations for the Bible's prohibition of necromancy, see Lloyd R. Bailey, Sr., *Biblical Perspectives on Death,* pp. 32–36. Though I disagree with Bailey on the issue of necromancy, his book is a comprehensive and eminently accessible overview of many of the issues covered in this chapter.

4. On Orphism, see *The Encyclopedia of Religion,* ed. Mircea Eliade (New York: Macmillan Publishing Company, 1987), vol. 11, pp. 111–114. Orphism celebrated the figure and the writings of a mythical figure, Orpheus, who was believed to have triumphed over death.

5. *Phaedo,* in *The Dialogues of Plato,* 2 vols., trans. B. Jowett (New York: Random House, 1937), vol. 1, p. 447.

6. On Plato's notion of the soul, see "Immortality," "Plato," and "Psyche," in *Encyclopedia of Philosophy,* ed. Paul Edwards (New York: The Free Press, 1967), vol. IV, pp. 139–150, vol. VI, pp. 314-333, and vol. VI, p. 512 respectively.

7. On biblical anthropology and the biblical understanding of the terms for "soul," see Bailey, pp. 41–47.

8. On the cult of Moloch, see "Moloch," *Encyclopedia Judaica,* vol. 12, pp. 230–233.

9. *Phaedo,* p. 450.

10. This use of passages from the notably erotic poems in Song of Songs may simply reflect the fact this is the only book in the Bible which glorifies the human body, lovingly and in some detail. On the other hand, it also reflects the honor with which Judaism views the human body. In a similar vein, the fact that the names for the shrouds with which we clothe the body before burial are identical with those used to describe the garments of the High Priest (in Exodus 28) may simply be a reflection that only here does the Bible give names to specific articles of clothing. But the terminology also suggests that every human being, at death, becomes a High Priest. Both are to encounter God. The most comprehensive and popular compilation of the liturgies and rituals dealing with sickness, death, and burial is the *Ma'avar Yabok,* written in the seventeenth century by Rabbi Aaron Berechiah ben Moses of Modena, but never translated into English.

11. For a comprehensive review of the Jewish rituals around death, burial and mourning, see Isaac Klein, *A Guide to Jewish Religious Practice* (New York: The Jewish Theological Seminary of America, 1979), chs. 19–20.

12. For the complete text of this version of this *kaddish,* see *The Complete ArtScroll Siddur,* a new translation and anthologized commentary by Rabbi Nosson Scherman (Brooklyn, N.Y.: Mesorah Publications, Ltd., 1984), p. 800. The translation is my own.

13. This same version of the *kaddish* is also recited when we complete the study of a tractate of Talmud. The study of Torah, for the Jew, is the gateway to eternal life.

14. *Midrash,* from the Hebrew root *drsh,* literally "to search out," hence to interpret, or to do exegesis of a biblical letter, word, verse, law or narrative. The term denotes a process, a way of reading the biblical text in order to discover in it new layers of meaning. The result of the process is called "a" *midrash.* The body of literature produced through this process is called "the" *midrash.*

CHAPTER IV

1. On the detailed historical background for the events described in Daniel 11, see The Book of Daniel, A New Translation with notes and commentary on chs. 1–9 by Louis F. Hartman, C.SS.R, introduction, and commentary on chs. 10–12 by Alexander A. Di Lella, O.F.M., The Anchor Bible (Garden City, N.Y.: Doubleday and Company, Inc., 1978), pp. 286–305. The discrepancy between Daniel's version of the death of Antiochus IV and other historical accounts of that death is discussed on p. 305.

2. A detailed chronology of the period under consideration is in Elias Bickerman, *From Ezra to the Last of the Maccabees* (New York: Schocken Books, 1947), pp. 183–184. For Bickerman's brief discussion of the historical setting of Daniel 10–12, see pp. 93–95.

3. On "the persecutions of Epiphanes," see Bickerman, pp. 98–99.

4. Bickerman's understanding of the impetus behind the persecutions is discussed on pp. 93–111.

5. Victor Tcherikover, *Hellenistic Civilization and the Jews,* trans. S. Applebaum (Philadelphia: The Jewish Publication Society of America, 1959), ch. 5.

6. On the theology of The Book of Job, see Moshe Greenberg, "Reflections on Job's Theology," *in The Book of Job: A New Translation According to the Traditional Hebrew Text* (Philadelphia: The Jewish Publication Society of America, 1980), pp. xvii-xxiii.

7. For this interpretation of Daniel 12:2, see George W.E. Nickelsburg, Jr., *Resurrection, Immortality, and Eternal Life in Intertestamental Judaism,* Harvard Theological Studies XXVI (Cambridge: Harvard University Press, 1972), pp. 11–27. This volume is almost impossible to obtain now, but for an essentially parallel interpretation, see John

J. Collins, *Daniel: A Commentary on the Book of Daniel* (Minneapolis: Fortress Press, 1983), pp. 390–398. Nickelsburg's and Collins' understanding of this passage, specifically of the reference to the "some" and the "others" in 12:2, is more convincing than that of the Anchor *Daniel,* pp. 307–311.

8. The term "theodicy" comes from the Greek *theos,* God, and *dike,* right, or just. Hence, theodicy is the attempt to "make God just," to vindicate God's judgement. For an overview of classical Jewish theodicy, see my *Sacred Fragments,* ch. 8.

9. H.L. Ginsberg argues for a post-400 BCE date, but also suggests that it might be as late as the second century. See his introduction to The Book of Isaiah (Philadelphia: The Jewish Publication Society of America, 1973), p. 12.

10. On the author of Daniel 12's use of Isaiah 24–27, see Nickelsburg, pp. 17–20.

11. On the dating of First and Second Isaiah and the issues surrounding Third Isaiah, see introduction to Second Isaiah, introduction, translation, and notes by John L. McKenzie, The Anchor Bible (Garden City, N.Y.: Doubleday and Company, Inc., 1968), pp. xv–xx.

12. On the author of Daniel 12's use of Isaiah 66, see Nickelsburg, pp. 19–23.

13. See, for example, the footnote to the Jewish Publication Society translation of Isaiah 25:8, in *Tanakh,* p. 667.

14. On the interpretation of the servant songs and the identity of the servant, see Ginsberg, pp. 20–21, McKenzie, pp. xxxviii–lv, and *Encyclopedia Judaica,* "Isaiah," vol. 9, pp. 65–66. If the servant is an individual, he may be a figure from the past, a contemporary of the prophet, possibly the prophet himself, or some figure to appear in the future, possibly a king of the House of David, or the Messiah. The Christian Church reads these texts as prophesying the career of Jesus of Nazareth. If the reference is to some collective body, it might be to an elite group within Israel (as here in Daniel 12), or to an ideal Israel that will arise sometime in the future. McKenzie combines the two approaches by suggesting that the servant is an individual who "recapitulates in himself all the religious gifts and the religious mission of Israel" (p. liii). For a review of Jewish interpretations of these pas-

sages, see *The Fifty-Third Chapter of Isaiah According to the Jewish Interpreters*, vol. 1, Texts, ed. Ad. Neubauer; vol. 2, Translations by S.R. Driver and Ad. Neubauer (Oxford and London: James Parker and Co., 1877; New York: Ktav Publishing House, Inc., 1969). On Daniel's use of these texts, see Nickelsburg, pp. 24–26 and Collins, pp. 393–394. For further reading, see McKenzie's "Selected Bibliography," pp. lxxiii-lxiv.

15. Collins, pp. 393–394 and Anchor Daniel, pp. 309–310.

16. ArtScroll *Siddur,* p. 144. The recitation of this prayer dates from the time of the Crusades. See Ismar Elbogen, *Jewish Liturgy: A Comprehensive History,* trans. Raymond P. Scheindlin (Philadelphia: The Jewish Publication Society; New York: The Jewish Theological Seminary of America, 1993), p. 162.

17. On the case for and against foreign borrowing, and the possible source of that borrowing, see Collins, pp. 396–397. On Egyptian and Zoroastrian references to the afterlife, see *Encyclopedia of Religion,* vol. 5, pp. 37–54 and vol. 15, pp. 579–591 respectively.

18. I am indebted to my friend and colleague Professor Tikva Frymer-Kensky for suggesting this line of thinking.

19. I depart here from the JPS translation which reads "...forgiving iniquity, transgression, and sin," because the continuation of the passage claims explicitly that God does *not* totally forgive sins. I read the passage as indicating that God will not punish immediately, that God will tolerate, or live with the people's sin, or even mitigate their punishment, but never, at least in this context, completely forgive. That doctrine is later explicitly repudiated in prophetic literature (as in Jonah 4:2) because by that time, the notion of repentance as pre-empting punishment has become a hallmark of biblical religion. The later liturgical use of Exodus 34:6–7 in our *Selihot* (Confessional) prayers on Yom Kippur is based on Jonah's re-reading of Exodus, and represents a stark subversion of the Exodus doctrine through a deliberate violation of the most elementary rules of Hebrew syntax. Again we admire the power of midrash! On the liturgical use of the Exodus passage, see Abraham Millgram, *Jewish Worship* (Philadelphia: The Jewish Publication Society of America, 1971) pp. 228–230. On the liturgical "recycling" of Exodus, see Yochanan Muffs, *Love and Joy:*

Law, Language and Religion in Ancient Israel (New York: The Jewish Theological Seminary of America, 1992), pp. 16–24.

20. "Apocrypha," from the Greek for "hidden away," or "spurious," hence books that were kept out of the Jewish canon. "Pseudepigrapha," also from the Greek for "falsely ascribed," hence books that were falsely ascribed to biblical personalities or times. The authoritative collection of the pseudepigraphal material *is The Old Testament Pseudepigrapha*, 2 vols., ed. James H. Charlesworth, New York: Doubleday, 1983). Unless otherwise specified, all further references to these texts will be from this edition. On the relationship of this material to Judaism, see Samuel Sandmel's "Foreword for Jews," pp. xi-xiii. On its general background, see Charlesworth's "Introduction for the General Reader," pp. xxi–xxxiv.

21. Though Collins dates Enoch earlier than Daniel, pp. 396–397.

22. For a masterful and exhaustive study of this book as a whole, see II Maccabees, A New Translation with Introduction and Commentary, by Jonathan A. Goldstein, The Anchor Bible (New York: Doubleday, 1983). On the dating of the book and its historical context, see Goldstein's introduction. On the story of the mother and her seven sons, see pp. 291–317. My translations are Goldstein's. For a more concise treatment, see Nickelsburg, pp. 93–109. For a fascinating study of the impact of this story on the later Jewish consciousness, see Gerson D. Cohen's "Hannah and Her Seven Sons in Hebrew Literature," in *Gerson D. Cohen: Studies in the Variety of Rabbinic Cultures* (Philadelphia: The Jewish Publication Society, 1991).

23. For an overview of references to an afterlife in these texts, see Nickelsburg, pp. 112–143.

24. Collins, pp. 397–398.

25. See the treatment of this passage in Lawrence H. Schiffman, *Reclaiming the Dead Sea Scrolls: The History of Judaism, the Background of Christianity, the Lost Library of Qumran* (Philadelphia: The Jewish Publication Society, 1994), pp. 347–350. Schiffman agrees with Collins that the notion of the resurrection of the dead is "rare in the Qumran corpus" (p. 347).

26. For an overview of Plato's thought as a whole, see "Plato," *Encyclopedia of Philosophy*, vol. 6, pp. 314ff.

27. Trans. B. Jowett, vol. 1, p. 450.

28. The Wisdom of Solomon, A New Translation with Introduction and Commentary, by David Winston, The Anchor Bible (New York: Doubleday, 1979). On issues of the book's historical background, authorship, dating, contents and influence, etc., see Winston's introduction. The translations are Winston's.

29. On the interpretation of these passages, see Winston, pp. 121–123 and 125–129.

30. On parallels in Philo, see Winston, pp. 125–128.

31. See the references in Winston, pp. 125–128.

32. On the Essenes, see the next chapter.

CHAPTER V

1. In Hebrew, *olam haba*. The word *olam* is ambiguous: It could have a spatial or a temporal reference. For the latter, see Psalm 146:10, "The Lord shall reign forever [*leolam*]...." The common translation, "world to come," assumes the former; "age to come," the latter. The Jewish eschatological scenario certainly does speak of a spatial transformation, of a new "world" setting, but it speaks pre-eminently of a new temporal setting. I will translate it as "age to come" except when quoting directly from an English source that uses the common translation.

2. The midrash plays on the word "land" (Hebrew, *aretz*). To "inherit the land" is to earn a share in the world or the age to come.

3. The Epicurean is one who denies divine supervision of human affairs. See Shaye J.D. Cohen, *From the Maccabees to the Mishnah* (Philadelphia: The Westminster Press, 1987), p. 220.

4. On theological themes in the Mishnah, see Cohen pp. 219–220.

5. On the two readings in the mishnah, see Ephraim A. Urbach, *The Sages, Their Concepts and Beliefs*, trans. Israel Abrahams, 2 vols. (Jerusalem: The Magnes Press, The Hebrew University, 1975), vol. 1, p. 652 and vol. 2, p. 991, n. 11.

6. My discussion of the Pharisees follows the interpretation of Professor Shaye Cohen. Cohen's repeated references to the controversies permeating recent scholarly discussions of these issues amply document

the paucity and the ambiguity of our sources. Cohen's work has the advantage, first, of reflecting the most recent scholarly consensus, and second, of exhibiting proper scholarly caution. As an example of the latter, locating of the origins of the Pharisees in the late second century BCE has led some scholars to view them as an outgrowth of the Hasidean body who opposed hellenization and produced the author of Daniel. This would account neatly for the Pharisaic appropriation of the doctrine of resurrection. Cohen (p. 161) dismisses this reconstruction as lacking any supporting evidence.

7. On the evidence from Josephus, see Cohen, pp. 144–147.

8. My translations of Josephus throughout are adapted from that of William Whiston in *The Works of Flavius Josephus* (New York: Leavitt and Company, 1851).

9. Cohen agrees that the Qumran community that produced the Dead Sea Scrolls was a community of Essenes, pp. 150-153. For another opinion, see Schiffman, *Reclaiming the Dead Sea Scrolls*, pp. 78–80, 156–157.

10. Bickerman, *From Ezra to the Last of the Maccabees*, pp. 164–165.

11. For Bickerman's broader thesis, see his chapter, "Genesis and Character of Maccabean Hellenism," pp. 153–165.

12. Cohen, p. 226.

13. On the evidence from the Gospels, see Cohen, pp. 147–150.

14. Translations from The Holy Bible, New Revised Standard Version (New York, Oxford: Oxford University Press, 1989).

15. On the evidence from rabbinic literature, see Cohen pp. 154–160. On "the emergence of rabbinic Judaism," see pp. 214ff. On the eventual triumph of the rabbis in the seventh century CE, see p. 221.

16. The text is in *The Fathers According to Rabbi Nathan*, trans. Judah Goldin (New Haven and London: Yale University Press, 1955), ch. 5, p. 39. See the brief discussion in Cohen, pp. 155–156.

17. Though in its current form, it contains nineteen benedictions. Yet the name "Eighteen" survives. For an exhaustive and admittedly somewhat confusing discussion of the *Amidah*, its dating, composition, history and contents, see the discussion in Elbogen, *Jewish Liturgy, A Comprehensive History*, pp. 24–54. For a more superficial overview,

see Millgram, *Jewish Worship*, pp. 101–108; Israel Abrahams, *A Companion to the Authorised Daily Prayerbook*, New Revised Edition (New York: Hermon Press, 1966), pp. 55–60; and Reuven Hammer, *Entering Jewish Prayer* (New York: Schocken Books, 1994), ch. 9.

18. The parentheses are added between Sukkot and Passover, the season of rain in the Holy Land.

19. My translation adapted from the ArtScroll *Siddur.*

20. On the "Great Assembly," see George Foot Moore, *Judaism in the First Centuries of the Christian Era: The Age of the Tannaim*, 3 vols. (Cambridge: Harvard University Press, 1950), vol. 1, ch. 2. For a survey of scholarly opinions on this body, see vol. 3, p. 7, n. 4. The central issue involved in dating the body requires an understanding of rabbinic chronology. On this, see vol. 3, p. 12, n. 4.

21. *The Pharisees: The Sociological Background of Their Faith*, 2 vols., Third Edition With Supplement (Philadelphia: The Jewish Publication Society of America, 1962), vol. 1, p. 158. Finkelstein's "Supplement," ch. 21 in vol. 2 of this third edition (pp. 570–798), significantly revises the conclusions he reaches in the earlier editions. Finkelstein wrote extensively on the Pharisees. See the collection *Pharisaism in the Making: Selected Essays* (New York: Ktav Publishing House, Inc., 1972), specifically ch. 11, "The Development of the Amidah," on our issue.

22. *Sifre*, trans. R. Hammer, *piska* 306, pp. 307–308. See also the reference in Moore, vol. 2, p. 383 and n. 5.

23. The point is completely lost in translation. It revolves around the grammatical subject of the Hebrew verb *vekam* ("and... will rise") in the original Hebrew. Who will rise? Moses or this people? In its literal meaning, it can only be the people; Hebrew syntax places some forms of the verb before the subject. But Rabban Gamaliel interprets it homiletically by applying the verb to what immediately precedes it, namely to Moses. JPS *Tanakh* translates: "You are soon to lie with your fathers. This people will thereupon go astray...." My translation of the verse here suggests its midrashic implications.

24. A number of similar homiletical exercises can be found in Bab. Talmud, *Sanhedrin* 90b–92a.

25. The point is made by Judah Goldin, "The Three Pillars of Simeon the Righteous," in *Judah Goldin: Studies in Midrash and Related Literature,* ed. Barry L. Eichler and Jeffrey H. Tigay (Philadelphia: The Jewish Publication Society, 1988) pp. 27 ff.

26. Translated and annotated with introduction and notes by Gerald Friedlander (New York: Hermon Press, 1965), p. 228. For a fascinating discussion of the enduring tradition that Isaac did in fact die on the altar and was then resurrected, see Shalom Spiegel, *The Last Trial,* trans. Judah Goldin (Philadelphia: The Jewish Publication Society of America, 1967); Reprinted with a new preface by Judah Goldin (Woodstock, Vt.: Jewish Lights Publishing, 1993).

27. For a fascinating study of Christian interpretations of the "mechanics" of resurrection, see Caroline Walker Bynum, *The Resurrection of the Body in Western Christianity, 200–1336* (New York: Columbia University Press, 1995).

28. Trans. John T. Townsend (Hoboken, N.J.: Ktav Publishing House, Inc., 1989), p. 165.

29. All translations from *Midrash Rabba* are from the Soncino edition, ed. Rabbi Dr. H. Freedman and Maurice Simon (London: The Soncino Press, 1939).

30. See the brief discussion of some of these views in Bynum, p. 25, n. 9.

31. For a comprehensive overview of the doctrine of resurrection in talmudic sources, see G.F. Moore, vol. 2, pp. 295–322, 379–395.

32. *Tosefta Sanhedrin,* 13:2. See the discussion of this and other passages on this issue in Moore, vol. 2, pp. 385f.

33. Laws of Repentance, 3:5.

34. On the righteous gentile and the seven Noahide laws, see Moore, vol. 1, pp. 274–280, and vol. 2, pp. 385f. The seven Noahide laws are so-named because they were derived from God's admonitions to Noah after the flood as recorded in Genesis 9:7. Since they were addressed to Noah, they are considered by the rabbis to be binding on all human beings. For an exhaustive, scholarly discussion of the doctrine, see David Novak, *Jewish-Christian Dialogue: A Jewish Justification* (New York: Oxford University Press, 1989), ch. 1.

35. Translation adapted from ArtScroll *Siddur,* p. 18.

36. ArtScroll, p. 2.

37. For the complete text of the bedtime *Sh'ma,* see ArtScroll *Siddur,* pp. 288–294. On references to sleep as death, see the paragraph immediately preceding the *Sh'ma* itself, p. 288.

38. See the extended midrashic version of Moses' death in Urbach, vol. 1, pp. 173–177.

39. Abrahams, *Companion,* p. 15.

40. On the distinctions between the Days of the Messiah and the Age to Come, see Moore, vol. 2, pp. 375–376.

41. The reference is to the Patriarch, Rabbi Judah the Prince, commonly known simply as "Rabbi," and credited with having composed the Mishnah (ca. 200 CE). Antoninus was a proselyte. See note in Moore, vol. 1, p. 347.

42. Aquila was a first-century CE proselyte who is reported to have translated the Bible into Greek. See Moore, vol. 1, p. 352.

43. On the *Had Gadya* song, see *Encyclopedia Judaica,* vol. 7, pp. 1048–1050. On the Angel of Death, see vol. 2, pp. 952-956.

44. ArtScroll *Siddur,* p. 195.

45. In the reference to "the day that will be entirely Sabbath, and contentment for the eternal life." ArtScroll *Siddur,* p. 479. One of the rabbinic characterizations of the age to come is "a day which will be entirely Sabbath."

46. ArtScroll *Siddur,* p. 409.

CHAPTER VI

1. Included in *Crisis and Leadership: Epistles of Maimonides,* texts translated and notes by Abraham Halkin, discussions by David Hartman (Philadelphia: The Jewish Publication Society of America, 1985), p. 211. All further references to the *Essay* will be from this edition.

2. Translated with an introduction and notes by Shlomo Pines with an introductory essay by Leo Strauss (Chicago: The University of Chicago Press, 1963), Part III, ch. 54, p. 635.

3. *Guide,* I:36, Pines, p. 84.

4. The Mishnah was compiled ca. 200 CE; the Jerusalem (or Palestinian) Talmud, ca. 400 CE; and the Babylonian, ca. 500 CE. The generic term "Talmud," typically refers to a text which includes the Mishnah and the *"Gemara"* (Aramaic for "study" or "instruction"), the discussions, elaborations and extensions of the Mishnah which emerged from the academies of either Palestine or Babylonia. Thus there is a single Mishnah text (though with some variants in the two talmudic traditions), and two versions of the Gemara. A reference to "the Talmud" usually refers to its Babylonian version which was accepted as more authoritative and was studied much more extensively than its Jerusalem counterpart.

5. On the goals and achievements of Maimonides' Commentary on the *Mishnah,* see Isadore Twersky's Introduction to *A Maimonides Reader,* edited with introductions and notes by Isadore Twersky (New York: Behrman House, Inc. Publishers, 1972), pp. 11–15.

6. Twersky, pp. 16–19. The claim that the *Mishneh Torah* changed the landscape of rabbinic literature is on p. 33.

7. I owe this observation regarding the absence of references to resurrection in the *Guide* to Arthur Hyman, "Maimonides' Thirteen Principles," *Jewish Medieval and Renaissance Studies,* ed. Alexander Altmann (Cambridge: Harvard University Press, 1967), p. 136.

8. All references to *Introduction to Helek* will be from Twersky's edition, *A Maimonides Reader,* pp. 401–423.

9. Twersky, p. 409.

10. p. 411.

11. p. 412.

12. I have not located this passage in *B'reshit Rabbah.* It can be found in Bab. Talmud, *Taanit,* 7a.

13. Twersky, p. 417.

14. p. 415.

15. p. 417.

16. See the version in ArtScroll *Siddur,* pp. 178–181

17. Twersky, p. 422.

18. p. 403.

19. Chapter 8, "The Laws of Repentance," *Mishneh Torah*, Translation and Commentaries by Rabbi Eliyahu Touger, 18 vols. (New York, Jerusalem: Moznaim Publishing Corp., 1986), 8:1, vol. 3, pp. 29f. All further translations from the *Mishneh Torah* are from this edition.

20. 8:3, 8:8.

21. The entire comment can be found in the sidebar to 8:2 in the Hebrew text. For an English version of part of the statement and an attempt to reconcile the two views, see the commentary to 8:2 in the Moznaim edition, pp. 31–32.

22. Isadore Twersky, *Introduction to the Code of Maimonides (Mishneh Torah)* (New Haven and London: Yale University Press, 1980), p. 502.

23. Hartman, p. 219.

24. pp. 217–218.

25. p. 212.

26. p. 219.

27. pp. 219–220.

28. p. 221.

29. p. 225.

30. The point is David Hartman's in his discussion of the *Essay*, p. 260. Hartman's discussion is a superb analysis of this work.

31. *Helek*, Twersky, pp. 414–415; *Essay*, p. 222.

32. p. 222.

33. The Hebrew Scriptures are commonly understood to be divided into three large portions: *Torah* (the Pentateuch), *Nevi'im* (the Prophets), and *Ketubim* (the Writings). Hence the acronym *TaNaKh* formed by the first letters of the three and used to refer to the whole.

34. *Essay*, pp. 229–230.

35. p. 233.

36. For an extended exposition of this thesis and on the meaning of the *Essay* as a whole, see Joshua Finkel, "Maimonides' Treatise on Resurrection: A Comparative Study," *Proceedings of the American Academy of Jewish Research*, vol. 9, 1939, ch. 4.

37. Leo Strauss, *Persecution and the Art of Writing* (Glencoe, Ill.: The Free Press, 1952). On Strauss' main thesis and on Maimonides' *Guide,* see ch. 2. The reference to reading between the lines is on p. 36.

38. Twersky, p. 233.

39. *Essay,* p. 402.

40. There is no book-length study of Jewish medieval philosophical speculation on the afterlife. See however the discussion of Maimonides' thirteenth principle in Louis Jacobs, *Principles of the Jewish Faith: An Analytical Study* (Northvale, N.J.: Jason Aronson, 1988), pp. 398–454, and Jacobs' further bibliographical references. For an excellent survey of medieval Jewish philosophy, see Colette Sirat, *A History of Jewish Philosophy in the Middle Ages* (Cambridge: Cambridge University Press, and Paris: Editions De La Maison Des Sciences de l'Homme, 1985). See also the index references in Menachem Kellner, *Dogma in Medieval Jewish Thought* (Oxford: Oxford University Press, 1986). In what follows, I use the anthologized selections from medieval thinkers, also arranged according to Maimonides' Thirteen Principles, in *With Perfect Faith: The Foundations of Jewish Belief,* edited with an introduction by J. David Bleich (New York: Ktav Publishing House, Inc., 1983), pp. 619ff.

41. Bleich, pp. 619–637.

42. Bleich, p. 620. See also Louis Jacobs, p. 406-408, and Joshua Finkel, p. 98 f.

43. Bleich, pp. 620, 657–662. Jacobs, pp. 408f.

44. Bleich, pp. 620, 663–680; also 620. Jacobs, p. 409f.

45. Bleich, pp. 681–687; Jacobs, pp. 410f.

CHAPTER VII

1. The development of this ritual is described in Gershom Scholem, *On the Kabbalah and its Symbolism,* trans. Ralph Manheim (New York: Schocken Books, 1965), pp. 139–145.

2. *On the Kabbalah,* pp. 138–139.

3. The phrase, *mishum tikkun olam,* is in mishnah *Gittin* 5:3, where it refers to certain rabbinic ordinances enacted, as Danby translates, "as

a precaution for the general good." The translation does not capture the precise sense of the Hebrew which suggests an act of "repairing" or "perfecting" the world or society. But here, the emphasis is on the social order alone. The phrase acquires a far more cosmic significance in Lurianic mysticism, as I shall discuss below. See also the phrase *letaken olam bemalchut Shaddai,* "to perfect the world under the sovereignty of God," which appears in the paragraph following the *Alenu* passage in our liturgy (ArtScroll *Siddur,* pp. 160–161). This is closer to the talmudic meaning of the term than to its later Lurianic meaning.

4. The point is made by Gershom G. Scholem, *Major Trends in Jewish Mysticism* (New York: Schocken Books, 1946), pp. 22ff. Scholem created the field of Jewish mysticism as an academic discipline. He was the first modern scholar to take this form of Jewish religious expression seriously, to unearth and study its texts, trace the development of their ideas, locate them within the broader field of the history of religions, and delineate their impact on future generations of Jews. This volume was Scholem's first attempt to present the results of his studies to the English-speaking scholarly audience. It remains a classic.

5. The definition is quoted in Scholem, *Trends,* p. 4. See Rufus Jones, *Studies in Mystical Religion* (London: Macmillan and Company, Ltd., 1909), p. xv.

6. On this early stage in the history of Jewish mysticism, see Gershom Scholem, *Jewish Gnosticism, Merkabah Mysticism, and Talmudic Tradition,* Second Improved Edition (New York: The Jewish Theological Seminary of America, 1965).

7. Gershom Scholem, *Kabbalah* (Jerusalem: Keter Publishing House Jerusalem Ltd., 1974; Published in the Western Hemisphere by Quadrangle/The New York Times Book Co.), pp. 312–316. This book contains the various articles written by Scholem on Jewish mysticism for the *Encyclopedia Judaica.* Though *Sefer haBahir* may have "appeared" in the twelfth century, its origins and composition are far more elusive. See Scholem's extended study of this book in *Origins of the Kabbalah,* ed. R.J. Werblowsky, trans. Allan Arkush (Philadelphia: The Jewish Publication Society and Princeton University Press, 1987). For an English version (though not a critical edition), see *The Bahir,*

translation, introduction and commentary by Aryeh Kaplan (Northvale, N.J.: Jason Aronson Inc., 1995). For Scholem's most detailed exposition of the doctrine of *gilgul*, see *On the Mystical Shape of the Godhead: Basic Concepts in the* Kabbalah (New York: Schocken Books, 1991), ch. 5.

8. Reincarnation has also become a very popular topic in recent writings on the spiritual life in general. To take but one example, witness the popularity of Brian L. Weiss, M.D., *Many Lives, Many Masters* (New York: Simon and Schuster, 1988).

9. *Godhead*, pp. 198–199.

10. *Kabbalah*, p. 156f. On the fate of these three parts of the soul after death, see p. 333.

11. *Kabbalah*, pp. 345–346; *Trends*, p. 281.

12. *Sefer haBahir*, Section 195.

13. Reincarnation is also used to explain the biblical institution of levirate marriage (Deuteronomy 25:5–10), whereby the brother of a man who dies childless is commanded to marry the widow in order that his brother may procreate through him. In effect, the dead brother's soul is reincarnated in order to fulfill the command of procreation.

14. On the evolution of the doctrine, see *Kabbalah*, pp. 344ff, and Scholem, *Godhead*, ch. 5. The *Zohar* was attributed to the second century CE Rabbi Simeon ben Yohai, but all scholars agree with Scholem that the author was the thirteenth-century Spanish kabbalist, Moses de Leon. See *Trends*, ch. 5. For an English translation of the complete work, see *The Zohar*, trans. Harry Sperling and Maurice Simon, 5 vols. (London: The Soncino Press, 1931). For a more useful, thematic anthology, see *The Wisdom of the Zohar: An Anthology of Texts*, 3 vols., arranged by Fischel Lachower and Isaiah Tishby, with extensive introductions and explanations by Isaiah Tishby, trans. David Goldstein (Oxford: Oxford University Press, 1989).

15. On the doctrine of soul sparks, see *Godhead*, pp. 215–217.

16. For a detailed elaboration of the teachings of Lurianic *kabbalah*, see *Trends*, ch. 7. In what follows on Lurianic mysticism, its origins, development and eventual impact, I am clearly echoing Scholem's thesis. I am also aware that the thesis is highly controversial and has been questioned by the current generation of scholars of Jewish mysticism.

For a critique of Scholem's broad thesis, see Moshe Idel, *Kabbalah: New Perspectives* (New Haven, Conn.: Yale University Press, 1988). For a defense of Scholem, see Joseph Dan's Foreword to *Godhead*. Both Idel and Dan were Scholem's students at the Hebrew University in Jerusalem.

17. The Hebrew text can be found in ArtScroll *Siddur*, p. 4. I have adapted the translation.

18. *Godhead*, pp. 239–240.

19. On reincarnation in Lurianic teaching, see Scholem, *Trends*, pp. 280–284, *Godhead*, ch. 5, and *Kabbalah*, pp. 347–348.

20. *Godhead*, p. 241.

21. *Trends*, p.284.

22. ArtScroll *Siddur*, p. 288.

23. On *ibbur* and *dybbuk*, see *Kabbalah*, pp. 348–350. For a comprehensive review of hasidic literature on all of these issues, see Scholem, *Godhead*, ch. 5; Gedalyah Nigal, *Magic, Mysticism and Hasidism*, trans. Edward Levin (Northvale, N.J.: Jason Aronson Inc., 1994), ch. 4; and Simcha Paull Raphael, *Jewish Views of the Afterlife* (Northvale, N.J.: Jason Aronson, Inc., 1994), chs. 8–9.

24. Raphael's concluding chapter is an intriguing exploration of the convergences of mystical/hasidic thought and contemporary New Age, Jungian and oriental religions.

25. For a particularly striking study of the controversies fueled by the Sabbatian movement, see Elisheva Carlebach, *The Pursuit of Heresy: Rabbi Moses Hagiz and the Sabbatian Controversies* (New York: Columbia University Press, 1990).

26. See Scholem's "The Neutralization of the Messianic Element in Early Hasidism," in *The Messianic Idea in Judaism* (New York: Schocken Books, 1971).

27. On Scholem's thesis regarding the impact of Lurianic mysticism, see *Major Trends*, pp. 287–344. For a much more comprehensive elaboration of his thesis, see his magisterial *Sabbatai Sevi: The Mystical Messiah* (Princeton, N.J.: Princeton University Press, 1973). For a critique of Scholem's thesis, see Moshe Idel, *Kabbalah: New Perspectives*.

28. Heinrich Graetz, *Popular History of the Jews,* trans. Rabbi A.B. Rhine, ed. Alexander Harkavy, vol. IV (New York: Hebrew Publishing Company, 1923), p. 442.

29. See Scholem's own evaluation of the treatment of Jewish mysticism in the work of these scholars in "The Science of Judaism–Then and Now," *The Messianic Idea in Judaism,* pp. 304ff.

CHAPTER VIII

1. For a masterful review of intellectual currents in Jewish modernity, see Salo Baron, "The Modern Age," *Great Ages and Ideas of the Jewish People,* ed. Leo W. Schwarz (New York: Random House, 1956).

2. An English translation of *Phaedon* was published in 1789. I have no record of any later version. A copy of the 1789 text can be found in the rare book room of The Jewish Theological Seminary library. Its title page reads, *"Phaedon; or, The Death of Socrates,* by Moses Mendelssohn, a Jew, Late of Berlin." See, however, the comprehensive study of the work in Alexander Altmann, *Moses Mendelssohn: A Biographical Study* (University, Alabama: The University of Alabama Press, 1973), pp. 140–158. See also Allan Arkush, *Moses Mendelssohn and the Enlightenment* (Albany, N.Y.: State University of New York Press, 1994) pp. 54–66. For Mendelssohn's most widely read statement on the nature of Judaism, see *Jerusalem or on Religious Power and Judaism,* trans. Allan Arkush, introduction and commentary by Alexander Altmann (Hanover and London: University Press of New England, 1983). In the discussion that follows, I have drawn on the discussions of *Phaedon* in Altmann and Arkush.

3. Altmann, p. 149.

4. The halakhic stipulations regarding the use of this formula stem from its incorporation of the Tetragrammaton, or "four-letter" name of God (usually transcribed into English as YHWH). The source of these stipulations is Exodus 20:7, "You shall not take the name of the Lord Your God in vain." Accordingly, Jewish law insists that the formula be used exclusively with the specific wording and on the specific occasions prescribed by talmudic law. To change the wording of the benediction, to create new benedictions, or to use ancient ones on unstipulated occasions constitute a violation of Jewish law.

5. For a scholarly and comprehensive history of Reform Judaism, see Michael A. Meyer, *Response to Modernity: A History of the Reform Movement in Judaism* (New York, Oxford: Oxford University Press, 1988).

6. Jakob J. Petuchowski, *Prayerbook Reform in Europe: The Liturgy of European Liberal and Reform Judaism* (New York: The World Union for Progressive Judaism, Ltd., 1968), p. 215. This book is indispensable for the study of Jewish liturgy in modern times.

7. Petuchowski, p. 66.

8. On the controversy surrounding the Hamburg Temple Prayerbook, see Petuchowski, pp. 49ff.

9. Quoted in W. Gunther Plaut, *The Rise of Reform Judaism: A Sourcebook of its European Origins* (New York: World Union for Progressive Judaism, Ltd., 1963), pp. 157–158. Both this volume and its companion, *The Growth of Reform Judaism: American and European Sources until 1948* (New York: World Union for Progressive Judaism, Ltd., 1965), provide a rich anthology of original documents dealing with the history of Reform Judaism in Europe and America.

10. Petuchowski, p. 166. A rich anthology of Geiger's writings on the range of issues confronting the early Reformers is *Abraham Geiger and Liberal Judaism: The Challenge of the Nineteenth Century*, compiled with a biographical introduction by Max Wiener, trans. of texts, Ernst J. Schlochauer (Cincinnati: Hebrew Union College Press, 1981).

11. On the history of the Charleston congregation, its creed and its liturgical reforms, see David Philipson, *The Reform Movement in Judaism*, New and Revised Edition (New York: The Macmillan Company, 1931), pp. 329–334, and Meyer, *Response*, pp. 228–235. See also Barnett A. Elzas, *The Jews of South Carolina from the Earliest Times to the Present Day* (Philadelphia: Press of J.B. Lipincott Company, 1905), ch. 9.

12. Meyer, pp. 231–232, and Philipson, pp. 332-333. A facsimile of the Society's prayer book can be found in the rare book room of the Jewish Theological Seminary library. Its title page reads "*The Isaac Harby Prayerbook*, Manuscript form prepared by Isaac Harby for the Reformed Society of Israelites founded November 21, 1824." The prayer book exists only in this manuscript form; it was never published. Meyer identifies Harby as "the outstanding intellectual of the

Society...., a native-born Charlestonian of Sephardi ancestry who had achieved some prominence as a playwright, literary and political essayist, educator, and editor."

13. Philipson, p. 366.

14. The phrase is taken from the traditional second benediction recited by one who is called to the reading of the Torah.

15. *Gates of Understanding, a Companion volume to* Shaarei Tefillah: *Gates of Prayer,* ed. Lawrence A. Hoffman (New York: Published for the Central Conference of American Rabbis by the Union of American Hebrew Congregations, 1977), p. 189. The note adds that other Reform prayer books retained the traditional text but interpreted it in terms of spiritual immortality. As we have seen, this was a common practice in early Reform and other liberal prayer books.

16. Philipson, p. 355.

17. On the story of the Conference that produced the Pittsburgh Platform, the Platform itself and its impact, see *The Changing World of Reform Judaism: The Pittsburgh Platform in Retrospect* (Pittsburgh: Rodef Shalom Congregation, 1985). The Platform itself is on pp. 107–109. See also Plaut, *Growth,* pp. 31–36, and Meyer, ch. 7 and pp. 387–388 (for the text of the platform).

18. See the "Authentic Report of the Proceedings," *Retrospect,* pp. 109–111.

19. Republished (New York: Ktav Publishing House, Inc., 1968).

20. On the Columbus Platform, see Plaut, *Growth,* pp. 96–100; Meyer, *Response,* pp. 318–320 and pp. 388–391 (for the text of the Platform).

21. On the origins of the Conservative movement, its break with Reform and its early history, see Moshe Davis, *The Emergence of Conservative Judaism: The Historical School in 19th Century America* (Philadelphia: The Jewish Publication Society of America, 1963), and my *Conservative Judaism: The New Century* (West Orange, N.J.: Behrman House, Inc., 1993).

22. The Preface (p. iii) justifies the choice of a Festival (*Sukkot,* Passover and *Shavuot*) prayer book (presumably, as opposed to a daily or Sabbath prayer book) as "the first of a series planned by the United Synagogue of America [the original name of the congregational arm

of the Movement, recently changed to The United Synagogue of Conservative Judaism] to meet the needs of the Congregations affiliated with it, and of American Congregations in general," on the grounds that at that time, the only available prayer books with adequate translations for the three Festivals had been issued in three separate volumes, which made the set unwieldy and expensive.

23. A limited edition, apparently designed for the use of more "liberal" Conservative congregations, makes one significant change in the *Musaf* service (p. 226); it transposes, both in the Hebrew and in the translation, the prayer for the future restoration of the sacrificial cult into a recollection of the service that existed in the past. But not a single word in the preface of this limited edition announces or explains that change. Subsequently, this "liberal" version of the prayer for sacrifices was adopted by all Conservative prayer books.

24. *Sabbath and Festival Prayer Book* (The Rabbinical Assembly of America and The United Synagogue of America, 1946), pp. viii–ix.

25. *Siddur Hadash: Worship, Study, and Song for Sabbath and Festival Mornings,* compiled and edited by Rabbi Sidney Greenberg and Rabbi Jonathan D. Levine (New York and Bridgeport, Conn.: The Prayer Book Press of Media Judaica, 1991), pp. 122–123. The Prayer Book Press was originally founded by Rabbi Morris Silverman, the compiler of the *Sabbath and Festival Prayer Book* that was later adopted by the Conservative movement.

26. Revised and Augmented Edition (New York: Bloch Publishing Company, 1971), p. 250. Emphasis in the original.

27. pp. 251–252.

28. For the further evolution of Reform and Conservative thinking on the afterlife in recent decades, see the following chapter.

29. Though this statement is frequently quoted in Kaplan's name, I have not found it in print in this precise form. See however its approximation in Kaplan's *Questions Jews Ask: Reconstructionist Answers* (New York: Reconstructionist Press, 1956), p. 5. Kaplan's original and most comprehensive statement of his thinking is his *Judaism as a Civilization: Toward a Reconstruction of American-Jewish Life,* Enlarged Edition (New York: The Reconstructionist Press, 1934; 1957). More accessible is his *The Future of the American Jew* (New York, The Macmillan

Company, 1958). For a useful thematic anthology, see *Dynamic Judaism: The Essential Writings of Mordecai M. Kaplan,* edited and with introductions by Emanuel S. Goldsmith and Mel Scult (New York: Schocken Books, The Reconstructionist Press, 1985). Two of the many studies of Kaplan's thinking and contributions are Eugene B. Borowitz, *Choices in Modern Jewish Thought: A Partisan Guide* (West Orange, N.J.: Behrman House, Inc., 1983; Revised Edition, 1995), pp. 99–121; and William E. Kaufman, *Contemporary Jewish Philosophies* (Lanham, New York, London: University Press of America, 1985), pp. 175–216. See also the fascinating biography by Mel Scult, *Judaism Faces the Twentieth Century: A Biography of Mordecai M. Kaplan* (Detroit: Wayne State University Press, 1993).

30. *Sabbath Prayer Book* (New York: The Jewish Reconstructionist Foundation, Inc., 1945), p. xviii. This introduction, a significant statement of the principles of Reconstructionism, is, unfortunately, not to be found in more recent issues of this prayer book.

31. pp. xxvii–xxviii. The publication of Kaplan's prayer book raised a storm of controversy. Kaplan was attacked by three senior colleagues on the Jewish Theological Seminary faculty, and he was excommunicated and his prayer book burned in a public ceremony by a group of Orthodox rabbis. This is the clearest example, in recent times, of the controversial nature of liturgical changes. Kaplan's writings and teachings had been radically offensive to traditionalists for decades, but only when he applied his thinking to the liturgy, was he excommunicated. On the controversies inspired by Kaplan's teaching, see Scult, chs. 6–7.

32. *Questions Jews Ask: Reconstructionist Answers* (New York: Reconstructionist Press, 1956), p. 180f. This book, composed of Kaplan's answers to questions submitted to him by his readers, is a useful thematic introduction to his thought on a wide range of issues.

33. *Kol Haneshamah: Shabbat Vehagim* (Wyncote, Pa.: The Reconstructionist Press, 1994), pp. 94–95.

34. Steinberg served congregations in Indianapolis and New York City, and wrote on a wide range of theological and communal issues. His tragic death at the age of 47 robbed American Jewry of one of its most articulate thinkers. For a book-length study of his life and work,

see Simon Noveck, *Milton Steinberg: Portrait of a Rabbi* (New York: Ktav Publishing House, Inc., 1978).

35. (New York: Harcourt, Brace and Company, 1947), p. 160.

36. pp. 162–164.

37. ArtScroll *Siddur* p. 101.

CHAPTER IX

1. For a fascinating study of the impact of the last millennial, see Norman Cohn, *The Pursuit of the Millennium: Revolutionary Millenarians and Mystical Anarchists of the Middle Ages*, Revised and expanded edition (New York: Oxford University Press, 1970).

2. Eugene B. Borowitz, *Renewing the Covenant: A Theology for the Postmodern Jew* (Philadelphia: The Jewish Publication Society, 1991), p. 23. This is a thorough and rigorous reworking of the major issues in Jewish theology from a postmodern perspective. See also the anthology, *Interpreting Judaism in a Postmodern Age*, ed. Steven Kepnes (New York: New York University Press, 1996). Kepnes' Introduction is a helpful outline of the main tenets of postmodernism and their application to Jewish issues.

3. On the ambiguities of modernity, see Borowitz, pp. 9–52.

4. For a critique of *Wissenschaft*, see Kepnes, pp. 2ff. On its impact on the training of American rabbis, see my "On the Religious Education of American Rabbis," in *Caring for the Commonweal: Education for Religious and Public Life*, eds. Parker J. Palmer, Barbara G. Wheeler, and James W. Fowler (Macon, Ga.: Mercer University Press, 1990), pp. 111ff.

5. On the impact of feminism on the creation of new Jewish rituals and liturgies, see *Lifecycles, V.1: Jewish Women on Life Passages and Personal Milestones,* ed. and with introductions by Rabbi Debra Orenstein (Woodstock, Vt.: Jewish Lights Publishing, 1994).

6. An excellent introduction to Levinas' writings is the anthology *The Levinas Reader,* ed. Sean Hand (Oxford: Basil Blackwell, 1986). For an appreciation of his thought, see the issue of *Sh'ma,* 22/429, March 6, 1992.

7. Zygmunt Bauman, *Intimations of Postmodernity* (London: Routledge, 1992), p. x. Emphasis Bauman's.

8. Abraham Joshua Heschel, *God in Search of Man*, p. 57. On the faculty of "radical amazement," see pp. 45–48.

9. New York: Farrar Straus and Young, 1951.

10. Herberg's chapter on the end of days is titled "History: Meaning and Fulfillment," pp. 211ff. On the structural parallels between Marxist and biblical eschatology, see pp. 230ff.

11. pp. 229–230.

12. pp. 203–206.

13. p. 229.

14. The classic exposition of the doctrine of religious symbolism is in Tillich's *Dynamics of Faith* (New York: Harper and Row, Publishers, 1957), pp. 51–54.

15. (New York: Charles Scribner's Sons, 1987), pp. 807–813.

16. p. 811.

17. pp. 811–812.

18. p. 812.

19. p. 808.

20. First published in 1986 and later anthologized *in The Pursuit of the Ideal: Jewish Writings of Steven Schwarzchild,* ed. Menachem Kellner (Albany: State University of New York Press, 1990), pp. 209–228.

21. *Pursuit,* p. 217.

22. "Resurrection," *Pro Ecclesia,* vol. 1, no. 1 (Fall 1992), pp. 104–112.

23. p. 109. For Wyschogrod, the outstanding difference between Judaism and Christianity is that for Judaism, resurrection has not as yet occurred, while for Christianity, it has, in the case of Jesus of Nazareth. But Wyschogrod insists that this is not "a great difference."

24. (New York: Behrman House, Inc. Publishers, 1973), pp. 318–322. See also Jacobs' discussion of the issue in *Principles of the Jewish Faith: An Analytical Study* (London: Vallentine-Mitchell, 1964), pp. 398–454. The latter volume is structured around Maimonides' Thirteen Principles. Particularly helpful in both of these books is Jacobs' practice of inserting extended bibliographical notes on the issue at hand

in the body of his discussion. These insertions (in the latter volume, called "Excursus") are a rich treasure-trove of suggestions for further study for the interested reader.

25. The statement as a whole (together with the earlier Pittsburgh and Columbus Platforms) can be found in the Appendix to Michael A. Meyer, *Response to Modernity: A History of the Reform Movement in Judaism*, pp. 391–394.

26. Meyer, p. 392.

27. Meyer, p. 389.

28. (New York: Behrman House, Inc., 1983); Book Two, *What We Believe*, pp. 42-49.

29. pp. 45–46.

30. pp. 47–48.

31. pp. 48–49.

32. (New York: Union of American Hebrew Congregations, 1984).

33. p. 222.

34. p. 14.

35. pp. 16–17.

36. pp. 18–20.

37. (New York: UAHC Press, 1990).

38. Supplementing this published material, I can testify to numerous conversations with individual Reform rabbis who have expressed a good deal of unhappiness with the classical Reform position on the afterlife as reflected in Reform liturgy, and have indicated that the revision of Reform prayerbooks, currently in process, may see the movement return to the traditional formula. These revisions may also affirm a commitment to bodily resurrection along the lines suggested in my concluding chapter which follows.

39. (New York: The Jewish Theological Seminary of America, The Rabbinical Assembly, The United Synagogue of America, 1988).

40. pp. 28–29. The procedures adopted by the Commission had one member assume responsibility for drafting each plank of the platform and then shepherding it through its revisions until it was adopted by the entire group. I was responsible for the statement on eschatology.

Though it represents my personal views at the time of writing, it was adopted by the Commission as a whole and thus represents the consensus, at least of the Commission itself.

41. *Judaism,* Spring 1968 (vol. 17, no. 2), pp. 186–196.

42. pp. 189–190.

43. p. 191.

44. (Northvale, N.J.: Jason Aronson, Inc., 1994).

CHAPTER X

1. For recent philosophical analyses of our issues, see, for example, *Body, Mind, and Death: A Reader,* edited with an introduction by Antony Flew (London: The Crowell-Collier Publishing Company, 1964); *Death and Immortality in the Religions of the World,* eds. Paul and Linda Badham (New York: Paragon House, 1987); Ernest Becker, *The Denial of Death* (New York: The Free Press, 1973); and Norman Brown, *Life Against Death* (Middletown, Conn.: Wesleyan University Press, 1959).

2. Simcha Paull Raphael, *Jewish Views of the Afterlife,* contains a wealth of material reflecting this approach. For more published material, see Raphael's bibliography, pp. 443–456.

3. *How We Die,* p. 267.

4. William James, *The Varieties of Religious Experience* (New York: Random House, The Modern Library, 1936), pp. 137–138. Emphasis James'.

5. *The Interpretation of Cultures,* p. 90.

6. John Hick, *Death and Eternal Life* (Louisville, Ky.: Westminster/John Knox Press, 1994), p. 15.

7. p. 156.

8. On this view of the biblical image of God, I have been influenced by Abraham Joshua Heschel's notion of "divine pathos" as developed in *The Prophets* (Philadelphia: The Jewish Publication Society of America, 1962), chs. 12–14.

9. "Clouds of Smoke, Pillar of Fire: Judaism, Christianity, and Modernity after the Holocaust," in *Auschwitz: Beginning of a New Era? Reflections*

on the Holocaust, ed. Eva Fleischner (New York: Ktav Publishing House, Inc., The Cathedral Church of St. John the Divine, Anti-Defamation League of B'nai B'rith, 1977), p. 27.

10. This final claim is a *verbatim* quote from a lecture by my teacher, the late Professor Shalom Spiegel, in a class on Jewish liturgy, during the academic year 1956–57. I have never forgotten it.

11. In what follows on my relationship with "my body," I borrow liberally from the thought of the twentieth-century French philosopher, Gabriel Marcel. The theme is omnipresent in Marcel's many writings, but see, in particular, *Metaphysical Journal,* trans. Bernard Wall (Chicago: The Henry Regnery Company, 1952), pp. 243–244, 269, 315, and the summary essay "Existence and Objectivity," appended to that volume, particularly pp. 332–339; *The Mystery of Being, vol. 1: Reflection and Mystery,* trans. G.S. Fraser (South Bend, Ind.: Gateway Editions, Ltd.), pp. 99–102; *Being and Having,* trans. Katharine Farrer (Boston: Beacon Press, 1951), pp. 10–12, 82, 137. See also my doctoral dissertation, *Gabriel Marcel and the Problem of Religious Knowledge* (Washington, D.C.: University Press of America, 1980), pp. 85–89, 107–109, 135ff. The claim, "I am my body," is Marcel's, *Metaphysical Journal,* p. 243 and *Being and Having,* p. 12; that "I am not only my body" is implied in his critique of materialism, *Mystery of Being,* pp. 100–101.

12. The distinction between I-It and I-Thou, commonly identified with the thought of Martin Buber, is also used by Gabriel Marcel, *Metaphysical Journal,* pp. 157–160.

13. On Marcel's notion that the sense of "my body" extends my relationship to the rest of the existing universe, see *Metaphysical Journal,* p. 269. What we here call "society," Marcel identifies as the experience of "intersubjectivity." See *Religious Knowledge,* p. 92ff.

14. Herberg's discussion of Judaism's view of history is in *Judaism and Modern Man,* ch. 15. Quotations are from pp. 193–195.

15. Yehezkel Kaufmann, "The Biblical Age," in *Great Ages and Ideas of the Jewish People,* ed. Leo W. Schwarz (New York: Random House, 1956), p. 64.

16. Kaufmann in *Great Ages,* pp. 64–71.

17. I refer here to the ritual "purification" (or *tohorah*) of the body before burial.

18. *Death and Eternal Life,* p. 45.

19. *The Guide of the Perplexed,* part III, ch. 54. Pines edition, p. 635.

20. For the range of philosophical attempts to deal with the mind/body relationship, see the anthology *Body, Mind, and Death,* and Antony Flew's introduction to the volume.

21. The Danby translation notes that "some texts omit 'from Israel,'" p. 388.

22. See our discussion of the destiny of the non-Jew in the age to come in chapter 5 above.

23. *Symbolism of Evil,* p. 331. Emphasis Ricoeur's.

24. On the religious significance of hope, see Gabriel Marcel, *Homo Viator: Introduction to a Metaphysic of Hope,* trans. Emma Craufurd (New York: Harper and Brothers, 1962), pp. 29–67.

FOR FURTHER STUDY

Bailey, Lloyd R., Sr. *Biblical Perspectives on Death* (Philadelphia: Fortress Press, 1979).

Barr, James. *The Garden of Eden and the Hope of Immortality* (Minneapolis: Fortress Press, 1992).

Borowitz, Eugene B. *Liberal Judaism* (New York: Union of American Hebrew Congregations, 1984).

Bynum, Carolyn Walker. *The Resurrection of the Body in Western Civilization, 200–1336* (New York: Columbia University Press, 1995).

Collins, John J. *Daniel: A Commentary on the Book of Daniel* (Minneapolis: Fortress Press, 1993).

Herberg, Will. *Judaism and Modern Man: An Interpretation of Jewish Religion* (New York: Farrar Straus and Young, 1951).

Hick, John. *Death and Eternal Life* (Louisville, Ky.: Westminster/John Knox Press, 1994).

Moore, George Foot. *Judaism in the First Centuries of the Christian Era, The Age of the Tannaim*, 3 vols. (Cambridge: Harvard University Press, 1950).

Nickelsburg, George W.E., Jr. *Resurrection, Immortality, and Eternal Life in Intertestamental Judaism* (Cambridge: Harvard University Press, 1972).

Nuland, Sherwin B. *How We Die: Reflections on Life's Final Chapter* (New York: Alfred A. Knopf, 1994).

Petuchowski, Jakob J. *Prayerbook Reform in Europe: The Liturgy of European Liberal and Reform Judaism* (New York: The World Union for Progressive Judaism, Ltd., 1968).

Raphael, Simcha Paull. *Jewish Views of the Afterlife* (Northvale, N.J.: Jason Aronson, 1994).

Scholem, Gershom. *On the Mystical Shape of the Godhead: Basic Concepts in the Kabbalah* (New York: Schocken Books, 1991).

Soncino, Rifat, and Daniel B. Syme, *What Happens After I Die? Jewish Views of Life After Death* (New York: UAHC Press, 1990).

Twersky, I., ed. *A Maimonides Reader* (New York: Behrman House, Inc., 1972).

INDEX

311

Jacob, death of, 64
Jacobs, Rabbi Louis, *A Jewish Theology,* 229–230
James, William, 247
Jastrow, Rabbi Marcus, 200
Jeremiah, 49–50
Jesus of Nazareth, 120–121
"Jewish Eschatology, On" (Schwarzschild), 227
Jewish Theological Seminary, The, 205, 208
Jewish Theology, A (Jacobs), 229–230
Jewish Theology: Systematically and Historically Considered (Kohler), 203
Jewish Views of the Afterlife (Paull), 239–240
Job, Book of
  on boundaries for human life, 62–63
  on creation, 47
  on finality of death, 63
  on *Sheol,* 67
Jonah, 70
Jones, Dr. Rufus, 174
Joseph, death of, 64, 67
Josephus
  Antiquities of the Jews, 115, 116
  on beliefs of Essenes, 111
  on Pharisees, 115–120
  on Sadducees, 116–119
  Wars of the Jews, 115, 117
Joshua ben Hananiah, Rabbi, 133
Journal of Reform Judaism, 234
Journey, soul's, 108, 173–182, 204
Judah, Rabbi, The Prince, 53
Judaism
  and anthropological dualism, 108
  Conservative (*see* Conservative movement)
  death as tragic, 81
  importance of history in, 263
  Kaplan's view of, 209
  myth, classic religious, 260
  Orthodox, 212–213
  Reconstructionist movement (*see* Reconstructionist movement)
  Reform (*see* Reform movement)
  Renewal movement, 239–240
  on sexual fulfillment, 267

Judaism and Modern Man (Herberg), 220

Kabbalah, 173–186
  influence of, 173
  Lurianic, 179–185, 293*n*16
Kabbalat Shabbat, 174
Kaddish, 80–81
Kaddish d'itchadeta, 81
Kaplan, Mordecai, 194, 208–211
  and controversy over liturgical changes, 299*n*31
Kaufmann, Yehezkel, 264–265
Kiss of death, 137
Knowledge, death and, 41
Kohler, Rabbi Kaufman, 202
  Jewish Theology: Systematically and Historically Considered, 203
Kol Haneshamah (Reconstructionist prayer book), 210
K'riat Sh'ma al Hamitah, 136
Kübler-Ross, Dr. Elisabeth, 239–240

Langer, Susanne K., 19–20
Language
  of eschatology, 249–252
  of mystical experience, 176
  theological, 25–31, 213
Laws of Repentance, The (Maimonides), 148, 155
Lebensanschauung, 20
Lekha Dodi, 173–174
Levenson, Jonathan, 49
Leviathan, 47
Levinas, Emanuel, 219
Levy, Richard N., 234–235
Liberal Judaism (Borowitz), 232
Life-blood, 76
Lifebreath (*see* Breath of life)
Liturgy, strategies for translating, 193–196
Luria, Rabbi Isaac, 179

Ma'avar Yabok, 279*n*10
Maccabees II, resurrection in, 101–103
Mahzor for Rosh Hashanah and Yom Kippur, 207
Maimonides, 143–168
  on Age to Come, 156–157
  agenda of, 144–146
  audiences of, 165

315

Reason
  faith and, 172
  humanity and, 217
  as Maimonides' image of God, 144
Reconstructionist movement, 208–211
  prayer books, 193, 208–210
Redemption
  Christian, 54
  Herberg on, 223
  of Israel, 185
  Luria's view, 181
Reformed Society of Israelites, The,
  199–200, 296–297n12
Reform Judaism Today (Borowitz), 231
Reform movement, 193–204
  American, 194
  American classical, 204
  defining itself in postmodernity,
    234
  early changes, 197
  European, 194
  German, 196–199
  Israeli congregation, 201
  liturgical changes, 198
  prayer books, 193–204, 297n15
  on resurrection, 196–199
  on spiritual immortality, 198, 204
  worship service, 197
Reforms, modern liturgical, 193–207,
  208–211
Regeneration, national, 74–75, 97
Reincarnation, 176–188
  as expression of judgement and
    mercy, 178
  influence after 1550, 183
  and marriage, Levirate, 293n13
  origins, 177
  personal redemption and, 185
  today, 187
Religion
  afterlife and, 248–249
  anthropological, 19
  as community product, 31
  defined, 19–21
  minimalist, 19
  Orphic, 75
  purpose, 18
Renewal movement, Jewish, 239–240
*Renewing the Covenant: A Theology for
  the Postmodern Jew* (Borowitz),
  233–234

Resurrection, 34, 71 (*see also* Afterlife)
  affirmation of embodied existence,
    228
  in apocryphal and pseudepigraphal
    literature, 101–104
  in biblical references, 59, 90, 159
  canonical status of, 125–127
  characterized, 220–230
  conflation of doctrines, 134–140
  Conservative view, 237
  controversy, 127
  and death, 94–95, 176–177
  in Daniel and Isaiah, 92
  doctrines, 91, 96, 134–140, 195,
    226
  of evildoers, 89, 94
  extended to everyone, 104–105
  in Ezekiel, 74
  intermediate stage, 138
  in Isaiah, 72
  Jewish consciousness of, 88
  in Judaism vs. Christianity, 301n23
  Maimonides on, 151–152, 157–
    159, 161
  mechanics of, 131
  models for, 90, 127, 132–133, 136
  monotheism and, 57
  of non-Jews, 133–134
  in postmodern writings, 241
  Reform views, 196–204, 230–236
  of righteous, 92
  Saadia on, 169
  as symbol, 224, 225
  themes of, 22
  in Torah, 127–131, 161–163
  as twofold event, 119, 134–140
  universal, 103–108
Retribution
  divine, 272
  for sin, 88
  justice and, 89
  manifestation of God's power, 102
  Pittsburgh Conference on, 203
Revelation, 31–34, 276n14
Reversals,
  Garden of Eden, 42–43
  wrongs righted, 126
Rewards
  attainment of, 63
  after death of, 64

316

Spirituality

MEDITATION FROM THE HEART OF JUDAISM
Today's Teachers Share Their Practices, Techniques, and Faith
Ed. by *Avram Davis*

A "how to" guide for both beginning and experienced meditators, *Meditation from the Heart of Judaism* will help you start meditating or help you enhance your practice.

Here, in their own individual voices, 22 masters of meditation—rabbis, scholars, psychologists, teachers—explain why and how they meditate. *A detailed compendium of the experts' "Best Practices"* offers practical advice, starting points, and—most of all—direction for making meditation a source of spiritual energy in our own lives.

> "A treasury of meditative insights and techniques....Each page is a meditative experience that brings you closer to God."
> —*Rabbi Shoni Labowitz, author of* Miraculous Living: A Guided Journey in Kabbalah

6" x 9", 256 pp. Hardcover, ISBN 1-879045-77-X **$21.95**

SELF, STRUGGLE & CHANGE
Family Conflict Stories in Genesis and Their Healing Insights for Our Lives
by *Norman J. Cohen*

How do I find greater wholeness in my life and in my family's life?

The stress of late-20th-century living only brings new variations to timeless p⟨e⟩sonal struggles. The people described by the biblical writers of Genesis were⟨in⟩ situations and relationships very much like our own. We identify with the⟨m⟩ Their stories still speak to us because they are about the same problems we d⟨eal⟩ with every day.

A modern master of biblical interpretation brings us greater understanding of the ancient text and ourselves in this intriguing re-telling of conflict between husband and wife, father and s⟨on⟩ brothers, and sisters.

> "Delightfully written ... rare erudition, sensitivity and insight."
> — *Elie Wiesel*

6" x 9", 224 pp. Quality Paperback, ISBN 1-879045-66-4 **$16.95**; Hardcover, ISBN -19-2 **$21.95**

ECOLOGY & THE JEWISH SPIRIT
Where Nature and the Sacred Meet
Ed. and with Introductions by *Ellen Bernstein*

What is nature's place in our spiritual lives?

A focus on nature is part of the fabric of Jewish thought. Here, experts bring us a richer understanding of the long-neglected themes of nature that are woven through the biblical creation story, ancient texts, traditional law, the holiday cycles, prayer, *mitzvot* (good deeds), and community.

For people of all faiths, all backgrounds, this book helps us to make nature a sacred, spiritual part of our own lives.

> "A great resource for anyone seeking to explore the connection between their faith and caring for God's good creation, our environment."
> —*Paul Gorman, Executive Director, National Religious Partnership for the Environment*

6" x 9", 288 pp, Hardcover, ISBN 1-879045-88-5 **$23.95**

Spirituality

MY PEOPLE'S PRAYER BOOK
Traditional Prayers, Modern Commentaries
Vol. 1—The Sh'ma and Its Blessings
Edited by Rabbi Lawrence A. Hoffman

y People's Prayer Book provides a diverse and exciting commentary to the tra-
tional liturgy, written by 10 of today's most respected scholars and teachers
om all perspectives of the Jewish world.

ne groundbreaking first volume examines the oldest and best-known of Jewish
ayers. Often the first prayer memorized by children and the last prayer recited
a deathbed, the *Sh'ma* frames a Jewish life.

7" x 10", 168 pp. Hardcover, ISBN 1-879045-79-6 **$19.95**

FINDING JOY
A Practical Spiritual Guide to Happiness
by *Dannel I. Schwartz* with *Mark Hass*

Searching for happiness in our modern world of stress and struggle is common;
finding it is more unusual. This guide explores and explains how to find joy
through a time-honored, creative—and surprisingly practical—approach based
on the teachings of Jewish mysticism and Kabbalah.

"This lovely, simple introduction to Kabbalah....is a singular contribution to
tikkun olam, repairing the world."

AWARD WINNER●
—*American Library Association's* Booklist

6" x 9", 192 pp. Hardcover, ISBN 1-879045-53-2 **$19.95**

THE DEATH OF DEATH
Resurrection and Immortality in Jewish Thought
by *Neil Gillman*

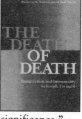

oted theologian Neil Gillman explores the original and compelling argument
at Judaism, a religion often thought to pay little attention to the afterlife, not
ly offers us rich ideas on the subject—but delivers a deathblow to death itself.
exploring Jewish thought about death and the afterlife, this fascinating work
esents us with challenging new ideas about our lives.

nables us to recover our tradition's understanding of the afterlife and breaks
rough the silence of modern Jewish thought on immortality.... A work of major significance."
—*Rabbi Sheldon Zimmerman, President, Hebrew Union College–Jewish Institute of Religion*

6" x 9", 336 pp, Hardcover, ISBN 1-879045-61-3 **$23.95**

THE EMPTY CHAIR: FINDING HOPE & JOY
Timeless Wisdom from a Hasidic Master,
Rebbe Nachman of Breslov
Adapted by Moshe Mykoff and the Breslov Research Institute

A "little treasure" of aphorisms and advice for living joyously and spiritually
today, written 200 years ago, but startlingly fresh in meaning and use. Challenges
and helps us to move from stress and sadness to hope and joy.

Teacher, guide and spiritual master—Rebbe Nachman provides vital words of
WARD WINNER inspiration and wisdom for life today for people of any faith, or of no faith.

"For anyone of any faith, this is a book of healing and wholeness, of being alive!"
— *Bookviews*

4" x 6", 128 pp., 2-color text, Deluxe Paperback, ISBN 1-879045-67-2 **$9.95**

Spirituality—The Kushner Series

INVISIBLE LINES OF CONNECTION
Sacred Stories of the Ordinary
by *Lawrence Kushner*

Through his everyday encounters with family, friends, colleagues and stranger Kushner takes us deeply into our lives, finding flashes of spiritual insight in tl process. This is a book where literature meets spirituality, where the sacred mee the ordinary, and, above all, where people of all faiths, all backgrounds can me one another and themselves.

•AWARD WINNER•

"Does something both more and different than instruct—it inspirits. Wonderfu stories, from the best storyteller I know."
— *David Mamet*

5 1/2" x 8 1/2", 160 pp. Hardcover, ISBN 1-879045-52-4 **$21.95**

HONEY FROM THE ROCK
An Easy Introduction to Jewish Mysticism
by *Lawrence Kushner*

"Quite simply the easiest introduction to Jewish mysticism you can read."

An introduction to the ten gates of Jewish mysticism and how it applies to daily life.

"Captures the flavor and spark of Jewish mysticism. . . . Read it and be rewarded." —*Elie Wiesel*

6" x 9", 168 pp. Quality Paperback, ISBN 1-879045-02-8 **$14.95**

THE BOOK OF WORDS
Talking Spiritual Life, Living Spiritual Talk
by *Lawrence Kushner*

In the incomparable manner of his extraordinary *The Book of Letters*, Kush now lifts up and shakes the dust off primary religious words we use to describe spiritual dimension of life. For each word Kushner offers us a startling, mov and insightful explication, and pointed readings from classical Jewish sources t further illuminate the concept. He concludes with a short exercise that helps u the spirit of the word with our actions in the world.

"This is a powerful and holy book."
—*M. Scott Peck, M.D., author of* The Road Less Traveled *and other books*

"What a delightful wholeness of intellectual vigor and meditative playfulness, and all in a tone of gentleness that speaks to this gentile."
—*Rt. Rev. Krister Stendahl, formerly Dean, Harvard Divinity School/Bishop of Stockholm*

6" x 9", 152 pp. Hardcover, beautiful two-color text ISBN 1-879045-35-4 **$21.95**

THE BOOK OF LETTERS
A Mystical Hebrew Alphabet
by *Rabbi Lawrence Kushner*

In calligraphy by the author. Folktales about and exploration of the mystical meanings of the Hebrew Alphabet. Open the old prayerbook-like pages of *The Book of Letters* and you will enter a special world of sacred tradition and religious feeling. Rabbi Kushner draws from ancient Judaic sources, weaving Talmudic commentary, Hasidic folktales, and Kabbalistic mysteries around the letters.

"A book which is in love with Jewish letters."
— *Isaac Bashevis Singer* (לז)

•AWARD WINNE

• **Popular Hardcover Edition** 6"x 9", 80 pp. Hardcover, two colors, inspiring new Foreword. ISBN 1-879045-00-1 **$24.95**

• **Deluxe Gift Edition** 9"x 12", 80 pp. Hardcover, four-color text, ornamentation, in a beautiful slipcase. ISBN 1-879045-01-X **$79.95**

• **Collector's Limited Edition** 9"x 12", 80 pp. Hardcover, gold embossed pages, hand assembled slipcase. Wit silkscreened print. **Limited to 500 signed and numbered copies.** ISBN 1-879045-04-4 **$349.00**

To see a sample page at no obligation, call us

Spirituality

GOD WAS IN THIS PLACE & I, i DID NOT KNOW
Finding Self, Spirituality & Ultimate Meaning
by Lawrence Kushner

Who am I? Who is God? Kushner creates inspiring interpretations of Jacob's dream in Genesis, opening a window into Jewish spirituality for people of all faiths and backgrounds.

In this fascinating blend of scholarship, imagination, psychology and history, seven Jewish spiritual masters ask and answer fundamental questions of human experience.

"Rich and intriguing."
—*M. Scott Peck, M.D., author of* The Road Less Traveled *and other books*

6" x 9", 192 pp. Quality Paperback, ISBN 1-879045-33-8 **$16.95**

THE RIVER OF LIGHT
Spirituality, Judaism, Consciousness
by Lawrence Kushner

manual" for all spiritual travelers who would attempt a spiritual journey in times. Taking us step by step, Kushner allows us to discover the meaning of own quest: "to allow the river of light—the deepest currents of conscious-—to rise to the surface and animate our lives."

ilosophy and mystical fantasy....Anybody—Jewish, Christian, or other-...will find this book an intriguing experience."
—*The Kirkus Reviews*

6" x 9", 180 pp. Quality Paperback, ISBN 1-879045-03-6 **$14.95**

GODWRESTLING—ROUND 2
Ancient Wisdom, Future Paths
by *Arthur Waskow*

BEST RELIGION BOOK OF THE YEAR

This 20th anniversary sequel to a seminal book of the Jewish renewal movement deals with spirituality in relation to personal growth, marriage, ecology, feminism, politics, and more. Including new chapters on recent issues and concerns, Waskow outlines original ways to merge "religious" life and "personal" life in our society today.

"A delicious read and a soaring meditation."
—*Rabbi Zalman M. Schachter-Shalomi*

"Vivid as a novel, sharp, eccentric, loud....An important book for anyone who wants to bring Judaism alive."
—*Marge Piercy*

6 x 9, 352 pp. Hardcover, ISBN 1-879045-45-1 **$23.95**

BEING GOD'S PARTNER
How to Find the Hidden Link Between Spirituality and Your Work
by *Jeffrey K. Salkin* Introduction by *Norman Lear*

ook that will challenge people of every denomination to reconcile the cares of k and soul. A groundbreaking book about spirituality and the work world, a Jewish perspective. Helps the reader find God in the ethical striving and ch for meaning in the professions and in business and offers practical sugges-s for balancing your professional life and spiritual self.

is engaging meditation on the spirituality of work is grounded in Judaism is relevant well beyond the boundaries of that tradition."
—Booklist *(American Library Association)*

6" x 9", 192 pp. Quality Paperback, ISBN 1-879045-65-6 **$16.95** HC, ISBN -37-0 **$19.95**

Spirituality

HOW TO BE A PERFECT STRANGER, In 2 Volumes
A Guide to Etiquette in Other People's Religious Ceremonies
Edited by Stuart M. Matlins & Arthur J. Magida

"A book that belongs in every living room, library and office!"

Explains the rituals and celebrations of America's major religions/denominations, helping an interested guest to feel comfortable, participa to the fullest extent possible, and avoid violating anyone's religious principl Answers practical questions from the perspective of *any* other faith.

VOL. 1: America's Largest Faiths

VOL. 1 COVERS: Assemblies of God • Baptist • Buddhist • Christian Science • Churches of Christ Disciples of Christ • Episcopalian • Greek Orthodox • Hindu • Islam • Jehovah's Witnesses • Jewi • Lutheran • Methodist • Mormon • Presbyterian • Quaker • Roman Catholic • Seventh-d Adventist • United Church of Christ

6" x 9", 432 pp. Hardcover, ISBN 1-879045-39-7 **$24.95**

VOL. 2: Other Faiths in America

VOL. 2 COVERS: African American Methodist Churches • Baha'i • Christian and Missionary Alliance • Christian Congregation • Church of the Brethren • Church of the Nazarene • Evangelical Free Church of America • International Church of the Foursquare Gospel • International Pentecostal Holiness Church • Mennonite/Amish • Native American • Orthodox Churches • Pentecostal Church of God • Reformed Church of America • Sikh • Unitarian Universalist • Wesleyan

6" x 9", 416 pp. Hardcover, ISBN 1-879045-63-X **$24.95**

GOD & THE BIG BANG
Discovering Harmony Between Science & Spirituality
by *Daniel C. Matt*

Mysticism and science: What do they have in common? How can one enligh the other? By drawing on modern cosmology and ancient Kabbalah, Matt sh how science and religion can together enrich our spiritual awareness and help recover a sense of wonder and find our place in the universe.

"This poetic new book...helps us to understand the human meaning of creation.
—*Joel Primack, leading cosmologist, Professor of Physics, University of California, Santa Cruz*

6" x 9", 216 pp. Hardcover, ISBN 1-879045-48-6 **$21.95**

MINDING THE TEMPLE OF THE SOUL
Balancing Body, Mind & Spirit through Traditional Jewish Prayer, Movement & Meditation
by *Tamar Frankiel* and *Judy Greenfeld*

This new spiritual approach to physical health introduces readers to a spiritual tradition that affirms the body and enables them to reconceive their bodies in a more positive light. Relying on Kabbalistic teachings and other Jewish traditions, it shows us how to be more responsible for our own psychological and physical health. Focuses on the discipline of prayer, simple Tai Chi-like exercises and body positions, and guides the reader throughout, step by step, with diagrams, sketc and meditations.

7" x 10", 184 pp, Quality Paperback Original, illus., ISBN 1-879045-64-8 **$16.95**

Audiotape of the Prayers, Movements & Meditations (60-min. cassette) **$9.95**
Videotape of the Blessings & Meditations (46-min. VHS) **$20.00**

Theology/Philosophy

ISRAEL
An Echo of Eternity
by *Abraham Joshua Heschel* with New Introduction by *Susannah Heschel*

In this classic reprint originally published by Farrar, Straus & Giroux, one of the foremost religious figures of our century gives us a powerful and eloquent statement on the meaning of Israel in our time. Heschel looks at the past, present and future home of the Jewish people. He tells us how and why the presence of Israel has tremendous historical and religious significance for the whole world.

5 1/2" x 8", 272 pp. Quality Paperback Original, ISBN 1-879045-70-2 **$18.95**

THE SPIRIT OF RENEWAL
Finding Faith After the Holocaust
by *Edward Feld*

oldly redefines the landscape of Jewish religious thought after the Holocaust."
—*Rabbi Lawrence Kushner*

ying to understand the Holocaust and addressing the question of faith after the
olocaust, Rabbi Feld explores three key cycles of destruction and recovery in
vish history, each of which radically reshaped Jewish understanding of God,
ople, and the world.

• AWARD WINNER •

profound meditation on Jewish history [and the Holocaust]....Christians, as
ll as many others, need to share in this story."
—*The Rt. Rev. Frederick H. Borsch, Ph.D., Episcopal Bishop of L.A.*

6" x 9", 224 pp. Quality Paperback, ISBN 1-879045-40-0 **$16.95** HC, ISBN-06-0 **$22.95**

SEEKING THE PATH TO LIFE
Theological Meditations On God
and the Nature of People, Love, Life and Death
by *Rabbi Ira F. Stone*

For people who never thought they would read a book of theology—let alone understand it, enjoy it, savor it and have it affect the way they think about their lives. In 45 intense meditations, each a page or two in length, Stone takes us on explorations of the most basic human struggles: Life and death, love and anger, peace and war, covenant and exile.

AWARD WINNER • "A bold book....The reader of any faith will be inspired...."
— *The Rev. Carla V. Berkedal, Episcopal Priest*

6" x 9", 132 pp. Quality Paperback, ISBN 1-879045-47-8 **$14.95** HC, ISBN-17-6 **$19.95**

THEOLOGY & PHILOSOPHY...Other books—Classic Reprints

pects of Rabbinic Theology by Solomon Schechter, with a new introduction by Neil
lman 6" x 9", 440 pp, Quality Paperback, ISBN 1-879045-24-9 **$18.95**

e Earth Is the Lord's: The Inner World of the Jew in Eastern Europe
Abraham Joshua Heschel with woodcut illustrations by Ilya Schor
5 1/2" x 8", 112 pp, Quality Paperback, ISBN 1-879045-42-7 **$13.95**

daism & Modern Man: An Interpretation of Jewish Religion by Will Herberg; new
roduction by Neil Gillman 5.5" x 8.5", 336 pp, Quality Paperback, ISBN 1-879045-87-7 **$18.95**

*e Last Trial: On the Legends and Lore of the Command to Abraham to Offer
ac as a Sacrifice* by Shalom Spiegel, with a new introduction by Judah Goldin
6" x 9", 208 pp, Quality Paperback, ISBN 1-879045-29-X **$17.95**

Passion for Truth: Despair and Hope in Hasidism by Abraham Joshua Heschel
5 1/2" x 8", 352 pp, Quality Paperback, ISBN 1-879045-41-9 **$18.95**

rmented Master: The Life and Spiritual Quest of Rabbi Nahman of Bratslav
Arthur Green 6" x 9", 408 pp, Quality Paperback, ISBN 1-879045-11-7 **$18.95**

ur Word Is Fire Edited and translated with a new introduction by Arthur Green and
rry W. Holtz 6" x 9", 152 pp, Quality Paperback, ISBN 1-879045-25-7 **$14.95**

Healing/Recovery/Wellness

Experts Praise *Twelve Jewish Steps to Recovery*

"Recommended reading for people of all denominations."
—*Rabbi Abraham J. Twerski, M.D.*

TWELVE JEWISH STEPS TO RECOVERY
A Personal Guide to Turning from Alcoholism & Other Addictions...Drugs, Food, Gambling, Sex...
by *Rabbi Kerry M. Olitzky & Stuart A. Copans, M.D.*
Preface by *Abraham J. Twerski, M.D.*; Intro. by *Rabbi Sheldon Zimmerman* "Getting Help" by *JACS Foundation*

A Jewish perspective on the Twelve Steps of addiction recovery programs with consolation, inspiration and motivation for recovery. It draws from traditional sources and quotes from what recovering Jewish people say about their experiences with addictions of all kinds. Inspiring illustrations of the twelve gates of the Old City of Jerusalem.

6" x 9", 136 pp. Quality Paperback, ISBN 1-879045-09-5 **$13.95**

Recovery from Codependence: A Jewish Twelve Steps Guide to Healing Your Soul
by Dr. Kerry M. Olitzky

6" x 9", 160 pp. Quality Paperback Original, ISBN 1-879045-32-X **$13.95**   HC, ISBN -27-3 **$21.9**

Renewed Each Day: Daily Twelve Step Recovery Meditations Based on the Bible
by Dr. Kerry M. Olitzky & Aaron Z.

6" x 9", Quality Paperback Original, **V. I**, 224 pp. **$12.95**   **V. II**, 280 pp. **$14.95**
Two-Volume Set ISBN 1-879045-21-4   **$27.90**

One Hundred Blessings Every Day: Daily Twelve Step Recovery Affirmations, Exercises for Personal Growth & Renewal Reflecting Seasons of the Jewish Year
by Dr. Kerry M. Olitzky

4 1/2" x 6 1/2", 432 pp. Quality Paperback Original, ISBN 1-879045-30-3 **$14.95**

HEALING OF SOUL, HEALING OF BODY
Spiritual Leaders Unfold the Strength and Solace in Psalms
Edited by *Rabbi Simkha Y. Weintraub, CSW, for The Jewish Healing Cente*

A source of solace for those who are facing illness, as well as those who care for them. The ten Psalms which form the core of this healing resource were originally select 200 years ago by Rabbi Nachman of Breslov as a "complete remedy." Today, for an one coping with illness, they continue to provide a wellspring of strength. Each Psal is newly translated, making it clear and accessible, and each one is introduced by eminent rabbi, men and women reflecting different movements and backgrounds. all who are living with the pain and uncertainty of illness, this spiritual resource offe an anchor of spiritual comfort.

"Will bring comfort to anyone fortunate enough to read it. This gentle book is a luminous gem of wisdom."
—*Larry Dossey, M.D., author of* Healing Words: The Power of Prayer & the Practice of Medicine

6" x 9", 128 pp. Quality Paperback Original, illus., 2-color text, ISBN 1-879045-31-1 **$14.95**

Life Cycle

MOURNING & MITZVAH
• With over 60 guided exercises •
A Guided Journal for Walking the Mourner's Path Through Grief to Healing
by *Anne Brener, L.C.S.W.;* Foreword by *Rabbi Jack Riemer;* Introduction by *Rabbi William Cutter*

"Fully engaging in mourning means you will be a different person than before you began." For those who mourn a death, for those who would help them, for those who face a loss of any kind, Brener teaches us the power and strength available to us in the fully experienced mourning process. Guided writing exercises help stimulate the processes of both conscious and unconscious healing.

stunning book! It offers an exploration in depth of the place where psychology and religious al intersect, and the name of that place is Truth."
—*Rabbi Harold Kushner, author of* When Bad Things Happen to Good People

7 1/2" x 9", 288 pp. Quality Paperback Original, ISBN 1-879045-23-0 **$19.95**

A TIME TO MOURN, A TIME TO COMFORT
A Guide to Jewish Bereavement and Comfort
by *Dr. Ron Wolfson*

guide to meeting the needs of those who mourn and those who seek to pro-
e comfort in times of sadness. While this book is written from a layperson's
nt of view, it also includes the specifics for funeral preparations and practi-
guidance for preparing the home and family to sit *shiva.*

sensitive and perceptive guide to Jewish tradition. Both those who mourn
those who comfort will find it a map to accompany them through the whirlwind."
—*Deborah E. Lipstadt, Emory University*

7" x 9", 320 pp. Quality Paperback, ISBN 1-879045-96-6 **$16.95**

WHEN A GRANDPARENT DIES
A Kid's Own Remembering Workbook for Dealing with Shiva and the Year Beyond
by *Nechama Liss-Levinson, Ph.D.*

Drawing insights from both psychology and Jewish tradition, this workbook helps children participate in the process of mourning, offering guided exercises, rituals, and places to write, draw, list, create and express their feelings.

"Will bring support, guidance, and understanding for countless children, teachers, and health professionals."
—*Rabbi Earl A. Grollman, D.D., author of* Talking about Death

8" x 10", 48 pp. Hardcover, illus., 2-color text, ISBN 1-879045-44-3 **$15.95**

LIFE CYCLE...Other books

New Jewish Baby Book: Names, Ceremonies, Customs—A Guide for Today's
nilies by Anita Diamant 6" x 9", 328 pp, Quality Paperback, ISBN 1-879045-28-1 **$16.95**

/Bat Mitzvah Basics: A Practical Family Guide to Coming of Age Together
by Cantor Helen Leneman 6" x 9", 240 pp, Quality Paperback, ISBN 1-879045-54-0 **$16.95**

ting God on the Guest List, 2nd Ed.: How to Reclaim the Spiritual Meaning of
r Child's Bar or Bat Mitzvah by Rabbi Jeffrey K. Salkin 6" x 9", 224 pp, Quality
rback, ISBN 1-897045-59-1 **$16.95**; HC, ISBN -58-3 **$24.95**

That Your Values Live On: Ethical Wills & How to Prepare Them
by Rabbi Jack Riemer & Professor Nathaniel Stampfer 6" x 9", 272 pp. Quality Paperback,
1-879045-34-6 **$17.95**

ef in Our Seasons: A Mourner's Kaddish Companion
Rabbi Kerry Olitzky 4" x 6", 390 pp (est.), Deluxe PB, ISBN 1-879045-55-9 **$18.95**

Art of Jewish Living Series for Holiday Observan‹

THE SHABBAT SEDER
by *Dr. Ron Wolfson*

The Shabbat Seder is a concise step-by-step guide designed to teach people meaning and importance of this weekly celebration, as well as its practice

Each chapter corresponds to one of ten steps which together comprise Shabbat dinner ritual, and looks at the *concepts, objects,* and *meani* behind the specific activity or ritual act. The blessings that accompany meal are written in both Hebrew and English, and accompanied by Eng transliteration. Also included are craft projects, recipes, discussion ideas other creative suggestions for enriching the Shabbat experience.

"A how-to book in the best sense...."
—*Dr. David Lieber, President, University of Judaism, Los Angeles*

7 x 9, 272 pp. Quality Paperback, ISBN 1-879045-90-7 **$16.95**

Also available are these helpful companions to *The Shabbat Seder*:
- •Booklet of the Blessings and Songs   ISBN 1-879045-91-5 $5.00
- •Audiocassette of the Blessings   DNO3 $6.00
- •Teacher's Guide   ISBN 1-879045-92-3 $4.95

HANUKKAH
by *Dr. Ron Wolfson*
Edited by *Joel Lurie Grishaver*

Designed to help celebrate and enrich the holiday season, *Hanukkah* discusses the holiday's origins, explores the reasons for the Hanukkah candles and customs, and provides everything from recipes to family activities.

There are songs, recipes, useful information on the arts and crafts of Hanukkah, the calendar and its relationship to Christmas time, and games played at Hanukkah. Putting the holiday in a larger, timely context, "December Dilemmas" deals with ways in which a Jewish family can cope with Christmas.

"This book is helpful for the family that strives to induct its members into the spirituality and of Jewishness and Judaism...a significant text in the neglected art of Jewish family education."
—*Rabbi Harold M. Schulweis, Cong. Valley Beth Shalom, Encino, C*

7 x 9, 192 pp. Quality Paperback, ISBN 1-879045-97-4 **$16.95**

THE PASSOVER SEDER
by *Dr. Ron Wolfson*

Explains the concepts behind Passover ritual and ceremony in clear, ea to-understand language, and offers step-by-step procedures for Passo observance and preparing the home for the holiday.

Easy-to-Follow Format: Using an innovative photo-documentary technic real families describe in vivid images their own experiences with the Passo holiday. **Easy-to-Read Hebrew Texts:** The Haggadah texts in Hebr English, and transliteration are presented in a three-column format desig to help celebrants learn the meaning of the prayers and how to read them.

Abundance of Useful Information: A detailed description of how to perform the rituals is inclue along with practical questions and answers, and imaginative ideas for Seder celebration.

"A creative 'how-to' for making the Seder a more meaningful experience."
—*Michael Strassfeld, co-author of* The Jewish Catalog

7 x 9, 336 pp. Quality Paperback, ISBN 1-879045-93-1 **$16.95**

Also available are these helpful companions to *The Passover Seder*:
- •Passover Workbook   ISBN 1-879045-94-X $6.95
- •Audiocassette of the Blessings   DNO4 $6.00
- •Teacher's Guide   ISBN 1-879045-95-8 $4.95

Life Cycle

A HEART OF WISDOM
Making the Jewish Journey from Midlife Through the Elder Years
Edited by *Susan Berrin*

We are all growing older. *A Heart of Wisdom* shows us how to understand our own process of aging—and the aging of those we care about—from a Jewish perspective, from midlife through the elder years.

How does Jewish tradition influence our own aging? How does living, thinking and worshipping as a Jew affect us as we age? How can Jewish tradition help us retain our dignity as we age? Offers insights and enlightenment from Jewish tradition.

thoughtfully orchestrated collection of pieces that deal candidly and compassionately with a od of growing concern to us all: midlife through old age."
—*Chaim Potok*

6" x 9", 384 pp. HC, ISBN 1-879045-73-7 **$24.95**

EMBRACING THE COVENANT
Converts to Judaism Talk About Why & How
Edited & with Intros. by *Rabbi Allan L. Berkowitz* and *Patti Moskovitz*

ractical and inspirational companion to the conversion process for Jews-by-ice and their families. It provides highly personal insights from over 50 peo-who have made this life-changing decision.

ssionate, thoughtful and deeply felt personal stories....A wonderful resource, to light the way for many who choose to follow the same path."
—*Dru Greenwood, MSW, Director, UAHC-CCAR Commission on Reform Jewish Outreach*

6" x 9", 192 pp. Quality Paperback, ISBN 1-879045-50-8 **$15.95**

LIFECYCLES
V. 1: Jewish Women on Life Passages & Personal Milestones
Ed. and with introductions by *Rabbi Debra Orenstein*
V. 2: Jewish Women on Biblical Themes in Contemporary Life
Ed. and with introductions by
Rabbi Debra Orenstein and *Rabbi Jane Rachel Litman*

This unique three-volume collaboration brings together over one hundred women writers, rabbis, and scholars to create the first comprehensive work on Jewish life cycle that fully includes women's perspectives.

"Nothing is missing from this marvelous collection. You will turn to it for rituals and inspiration, prayer and poetry, comfort and community. *Lifecycles* is a gift to the Jewish woman in America."
—*Letty Cottin Pogrebin, author of* Deborah, Golda, and Me: Being Female and Jewish in America

6 x 9, 480 pp. HC, ISBN 1-879045-14-1, **$24.95**; V. 2: 6 x 9, 464 pp. HC, ISBN 1-879045-15-X, **$24.95**

LIFE CYCLE...Other books— The Art of Jewish Living Series for Holiday Observance
by Dr. Ron Wolfson

ukkah—7" x 9", 192 pp. Quality Paperback, ISBN 1-879045-97-4 **$16.95**

Shabbat Seder—7" x 9", 272 pp, Quality Paperback, ISBN 1-879045-90-7 **$16.95**; Booklet of ings **$5.00**; Audiocassette of Blessings **$6.00**; Teacher's Guide **$4.95**

Passover Seder—7" x 9", 272 pp, Quality Paperback, ISBN 1-879045-90-7 **$16.95**; Passover book, **$6.95**; Audiocassette of Blessings, **$6.00**; Teacher's Guide, **$4.95**

Children's Spirituality

A PRAYER FOR THE EARTH
The Story of Naamah, Noah's Wife

A PRAYER for the EARTH
The Story of Naamah,
Noah's Wife

For ages 4-8

by *Sandy Eisenberg Sasso*
Full color illustrations by *Bethanne Andersen*

NONSECTARIAN, NONDENOMINATIONAL.

This new story, based on an ancient text, opens readers' religious imaginations to new ideas about the well-known story of the Flood. When God tells Noah to bring the animals of the world onto the ark, God *also* calls on Naamah, Noah's wife, to save each plant on Earth.

•AWARD WINNER•

"A lovely tale....Children of all ages should be drawn to this parable for our times."
　　　　　　　　　—Tomie dePaola, artist/author of books for children

9" x 12", 32 pp. Hardcover, Full color illus., ISBN 1-879045-60-5 **$16.95**

THE 11TH COMMANDMENT
Wisdom from Our Children

For all ages

by The Children of America

MULTICULTURAL, NONSECTARIAN, NONDENOMINATIONAL.

"If there were an Eleventh Commandment, what would it be?"

Children of many religious denominations across America answer this question in their own drawings and words—in *The 11th Commandment.*

"Wonderful....This unusual book provides both food for thought and insight into the hopes and fears of today's young."
　　　　　　　　　—American Library Association's Booklist

8" x 10", 48 pp. Hardcover, Full color illus., ISBN 1-879045-46-X **$16.95**

SHARING BLESSINGS
Children's Stories for Exploring the Spirit of the Jewish Holidays

For ages 6-10

by *Rahel Musleah* and *Rabbi Michael Klayman*
Full color illustrations by *Mary O'Keefe Young*

**What is the spiritual message of each of the Jewish holidays?
How do we teach it to our children?**

Many books tell children about the historical significance and customs of the holidays. Now, through engaging, creative stories about one family's spiritual preparation, *Shar Blessings* explores ways to get into the *spirit* of 13 different holidays.

"A beguiling introduction to important Jewish values by way of the holidays."
　　　　—Rabbi Harold Kushner, author of When Bad Things Happen
　　　　to Good People *and* How Good Do We Have to Be?

7" x 10", 64 pp. Hardcover, Full color illus., ISBN 1-879045-71-0 **$18.95**

THE BOOK OF MIRACLES
A Young Person's Guide to Jewish Spiritual Awareness

For ages 9-13

by *Lawrence Kushner*

With a Special 10th Anniversary Introduction and all new illustrations the author.

From the miracle at the Red Sea to the miracle of waking up this morning, intriguing book introduces kids to a way of everyday spiritual thinking to la lifetime. Kushner, whose award-winning books have brought spirituality to for countless adults, now shows young people how to use Judaism as a foun tion on which to build their lives.

6" x 9", 96 pp. Hardcover, 2-color illus., ISBN 1-879045-78-8 **$16.95**

Children's Spirituality

For ages 8 and up

BUT GOD REMEMBERED
tories of Women from Creation to the Promised Land
by *Sandy Eisenberg Sasso*
Full color illustrations by *Bethanne Andersen*

ONSECTARIAN, NONDENOMINATIONAL.

fascinating collection of four different stories of women only briefly men-
ned in biblical tradition and religious texts, but never before explored.
ward-winning author Sasso brings to life the intriguing stories of Lilith,
ach, Bityah, and the Daughters of Z, courageous and strong women from
cient tradition. All teach important values through their faith and actions.

•AWARD WINNER•

"Exquisite....a book of beauty, strength and spirituality."
—*Association of Bible Teachers*

9" x 12", 32 pp. Hardcover, Full color illus., ISBN 1-879045-43-5 **$16.95**

IN GOD'S NAME
For ages 4-8

by *Sandy Eisenberg Sasso*
Full color illustrations by *Phoebe Stone*

MULTICULTURAL, NONSECTARIAN, NONDENOMINATIONAL.

Like an ancient myth in its poetic text and vibrant illustrations, this modern
fable about the search for God's name celebrates the diversity and, at the same
time, the unity of all the people of the world. Each seeker claims he or she
alone knows the answer. Finally, they come together and learn what God's
name really is, sharing the ultimate harmony of belief in one God by people
of all faiths, all backgrounds.

AWARD WINNER•   "I got goose bumps when I read *In God's Name*, its language and illustrations are that
moving. This is a book children will love and the whole family will cherish for its beauty
and power."
—*Francine Klagsbrun, author of* Mixed Feelings: Love, Hate, Rivalry,
and Reconciliation among Brothers and Sisters

"What a lovely, healing book!"
—*Madeleine L'Engle*

Selected by
Parent Council Ltd.™

9" x 12", 32 pp. Hardcover, Full color illus., ISBN 1-879045-26-5 **$16.95**

---

ages 4-8

GOD'S PAINTBRUSH
by *Sandy Eisenberg Sasso*
Full color illustrations by *Annette Compton*

LTICULTURAL, NONSECTARIAN, NONDENOMINATIONAL.

tes children of all faiths and backgrounds to encounter God open-
n their own lives. Wonderfully interactive, provides questions
t and child can explore together at the end of each episode.

•AWARD WINNER•

excellent way to honor the imaginative breadth and depth of the
tual life of the young."
—*Dr. Robert Coles, Harvard University*

11" x 8 1/2", 32 pp. Hardcover, Full color illus., ISBN 1-879045-22-2 **$16.95**

Also Available!
Teacher's Guide: A Guide for Jewish & Christian Educators and Parents

8 1/2" x 11", 32 pp. Paperback, ISBN 1-879045-57-5 **$6.95**

AVAILABLE FROM BETTER BOOKSTORES.
TRY YOUR BOOKSTORE FIRST.

Order Information

# of Copies	Book Title / ISBN (Last 3 digits)	$ Amount
_____	_____	_____
_____	_____	_____
_____	_____	_____
_____	_____	_____
_____	_____	_____
_____	_____	_____
_____	_____	_____
_____	_____	_____
_____	_____	_____
_____	_____	_____
_____	_____	_____
_____	_____	_____
_____	_____	_____
_____	_____	_____

For shipping/handling, add $3.50 for the first book, $2.00 each
add'l book (to a max of $15.00) $ S/H _____

TOTAL _____

Check enclosed for $_____ *payable to:* JEWISH LIGHTS Publishing

Charge my credit card: ❏ MasterCard   ❏ Visa

Credit Card #_____Expires _____

Signature _____Phone (_____)_____

Your Name _____

Street_____

City / State / Zip _____

Ship To:

Name _____

Street_____

City / State / Zip _____

Phone, fax or mail to: JEWISH LIGHTS Publishing

P.O. Box 237 • Sunset Farm Offices, Route 4 • Woodstock, Vermont 05091
Tel (802) 457-4000   Fax (802) 457-4004   www.jewishlights.com

Credit card orders **(800) 962-4544** (9AM–5PM ET Monday–Friday)

Generous discounts on quantity orders. SATISFACTION GUARANTEED. Prices subject to change.